THE LETTERS OF MADAME DE SÉVIGNÉ

Carnavalet Edition

NEWLY RE-EDITED, REVISED AND CORRECTED,
INCLUDING OVER THREE HUNDRED
LETTERS NOT PREVIOUSLY
TRANSLATED INTO
ENGLISH

IN SEVEN VOLUMES

VOLUME I

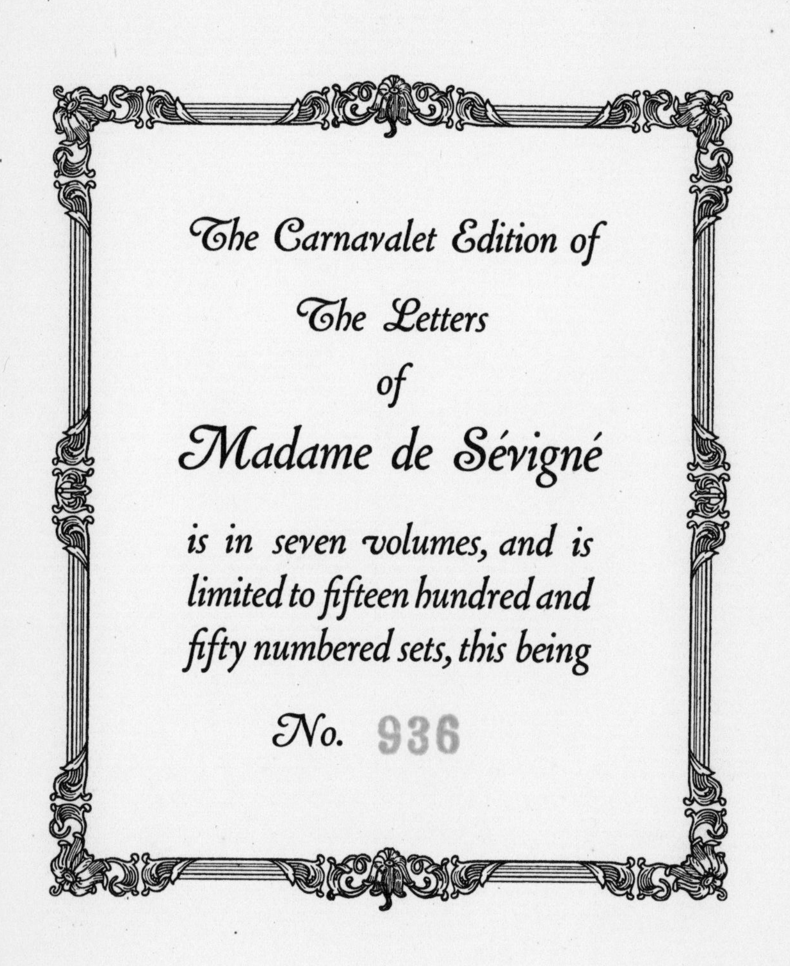

The Carnavalet Edition of

The Letters

of

Madame de Sévigné

is in seven volumes, and is limited to fifteen hundred and fifty numbered sets, this being

No. 936

REPRODUCED FROM AN OLD ENGRAVING AFTER NANTEUIL IN THE COLLECTION OF ELLIS AMES BALLARD, ESQ., OF PHILADELPHIA.

THE LETTERS OF MADAME DE SÉVIGNÉ

WITH AN INTRODUCTION

BY

A. EDWARD NEWTON

PHILADELPHIA

J. P. HORN & COMPANY

1927

Printed in the United States of America.

CONTENTS

OF THE FIRST VOLUME

THE LETTERS IN THIS VOLUME

Number 1 *to Number* 168

PERIOD

March 15th, 1647 to January 13th, 1672.

ILLUSTRATIONS

IN THE FIRST VOLUME

INTRODUCTION

QUITE unconsciously a year ago, I qualified for writing this little paper, when, spending a few weeks in Paris, I haunted for several days the purlieu of the Place des Vosges, that famous open Square or Place which now occupies the site of the former Palais des Tournelles, so called from its many turrets. It was in the great court-yard of this palace that Henry II., tilting with the Count de Montgomerie accidentally received the wound which caused his death. In consequence of this event, his wife, Catherine de Medici, caused the palace to be demolished and the present buildings were erected forty years later, during the reign of Henry IV. This was formerly the Court end of the city, and everywhere, even to-day, there are evidences of former pomp and luxury. The fact that Victor Hugo lived in the Place des Vosges many years, and that other great moderns are identified with this quarter, does not over-shadow the fact that Marie de Chantal, who afterwards became Madame de Sévigné, once resided there, and, during and after a somewhat chequered married career,—which was not then, nor is it now, unusual,—wrote some of the famous letters on which her fame so securely rests, from the Carnavalet Mansion, only a stone's throw away.

Visitors to Paris, overcome,—tired it may be of the regular symmetrical beauty of that section of Paris of which the M. Garnier's magnificent Opera House is the centre,—may find much to delight and interest them in the distant Place des Vosges, and will be well repaid for a visit to the Musée de Carnavalet, which now houses one of the most delightful of the many collections of the relics of Paris of centuries long past.

The life of Madame de Sévigné was what it was. As a girl she received the most elaborate education which could then be given to a young maiden, and, in an age when to mention virtue was to cause a smile, she retained until her death an unsullied reputation. Men of letters assisted in the development of her talents, which were early discovered, and her lessons were continued after her marriage, and even during her widow-hood.

Marie de Chantal was born on February 5, 1626. Her parents died while she was an infant, and she was brought up under the care of her uncle. An orphan and an heiress at an early age, her hand was sought in marriage by several of the most distinguished men in France, and it was France of the grand epoch,—if one epoch more than another can be so described in a country with such a magnificent history. Well may a Frenchman be proud, as he certainly is, of Paris and of France. Well may English kings have sought to add the name of *la belle France* to their title! "King of England and of France," etc.

Into what a world was the little Marie ushered! Of statesmen there were Mazarin and Colbert: Condé and Turenne had learned and had put into practice the art of war. Corneille, Racine, and Molière, were the dramatists of the time; while La Fontaine, La Rochefoucauld, and Bossuet, were otherwise making themselves immortal. Madame de Rambouillet and a host of other great ladies were giving the *salon* a distinction it never had before, and which it perhaps has not enjoyed since. And acquaintance with all these and many more, were Madame de Sévigné's by right of birth and of intelligence, and of fortune.

How comes it that at two o'clock in the morning of the first day of August, in the year 1644, the young girl was married to Henri de Sévigné, a handsome, rich, dashing young Marquis, who traced his ancestors back for at least three centuries? Is such a usual hour for a wedding? I do not know. That the marriage was "arranged," we may be sure: not otherwise do they marry in France. Marie was pretty, if not beautiful, and there was love, it is said, on her side at least. But the husband had faults: "he is quarrelsome" says one; "he loves everywhere" says another. Nevertheless, they led a gay life with their establishments in Paris and their château *Les Rochers* in Brittany. But in seven years it was all over: the Marquis was killed by the thrust of a sword in a duel, and the young Marquise was left a widow with two young children: a son and a daughter. Although she had many offers, the young widow never married again. She devoted herself to the bringing up of her children; and it is to her daughter, who subsequently became the Comtesse de Grignan, that most of her letters were written. Between the mother and daughter there was great affection: during the early part of their lives they resided together, and the letters which have given immortality to both writer and recipient were written during more than twenty years of separation.

What is the fascination of these famous letters? It is more easily felt than understood: who would attempt to analyse the perfume that they exhale? Other letters we have that deal with greater events, that have greater historic value, but the letters of Madame de Sévigné are unique in their indefinable charm. They tingle with personality, and are as wise and witty and sprightly as the Marquise herself; they recreate for us a gay and naughty world in which we would fain be alive. Did the fair lady know that she was courting immortality? that she was making herself a classic?

Horace Walpole, who wrote letters,—it was said that he lived his life merely to write about it,—declared that such letters as flowed so gaily from the pen of the widowed Marquise could never be written again. And his prophecy was correct, unless his own letters disprove it. The Sévigné letters are a monument to the lady's skill in using a logical and magnificent instrument—the French language—in so simple and direct a manner that even in translation their charm and naturalness are not extinguished.

And the most famous letter—perhaps the best known letter in any literature—is that "guessing" letter, addressed to M. de Coulanges, in which he is invited to guess something: ". . . . . the most astonishing, the most surprising, the most marvellous, the most miraculous, the most magnificent, the most confounding, the most unheard of, the most singular, the most extraordinary, the most incredible, the most unforeseen, the greatest, the least, the rarest, the most common, the most public, the most private till to-day, ... I cannot bring myself to tell it you: guess what it is. I give you three times to do it in. What, not a word to throw at a dog? Well then, I find I must tell you. Monsieur de Lauzun is to be married next Sunday at the Louvre, to . . . . ., pray guess to whom! I give you four times to do it in, I give you six, I give you a hundred. . . . . . He is to be married next Sunday, at the Louvre, with the King's leave, to Mademoiselle, Mademoiselle de . . . . ., Mademoiselle . . . . . guess, pray guess her name: he is to be married to . . . . ." But, you, reader, must find out to whom for yourself.

How many years ago is it that I, as a lad, first struggled with these letters in their original French, and became so fascinated with them that I threw the volume aside and finished them in English?—of what interest is this to anyone? It does prove, however, my early devotion to this delightful writer, and my visit a year ago to the room in the Carnavalet Mansion from whence some of them were written, shows that their charm, for me, has not evaporated: nor can it. Some knowledge of the Letters of Madame de Sévigné is part of an education, which can certainly not be called liberal without it.

A. Edward Newton.

"Oak Knoll"
Daylesford, Pennsylvania.
May 31st, 1927.

EDITOR'S PREFACE

AS the present English translation of Madame de Sévigné's correspondence with her daughter, with members of her family, as well as with her friends, contains every letter included in the best Paris edition, from the date of the first, in 1647, to the very last, which was written in the year 1696, a more accurate account of them cannot be given, than that of the French editor, Philippe A. Grouvelle, who appears, from the many historical and other notes with which he embellished the collection, to have been a man of considerable talents, and extensive reading.

What Monsieur Grouvelle, long an assiduous reader of Madame de Sévigné's letters, often wished to see executed by another, he finally executed himself. The undertaking was a pleasure of choice, and he endeavoured to render it complete in every detail.

The letters, as models of style, form an admirable book. They are interesting also as a collection of anecdotes, and they exhibit the picture of an age, and a Court, that greatly influenced the manners, not of France only, but of all Europe. They will accordingly be sought after by every mind, whether little or much cultivated: and it is not easy to regard with indifference any attempt that is made to render their perusal more pleasing.

Almost all of the French editions of Madame de Sévigné's letters which have hitherto appeared, are reprints of that of 1754, with the several letters added that have been discovered since. But numerous as these editions are, there is only one that is complete, or even arranged as it should be.

Monsieur Grouvelle formed out of the different collections a monument worthy of Madame de Sévigné, by the careful correction of the text, interesting additions, a methodical arrangement, and the insertion of instructive notes, enabling us to appreciate better, the authoress and her letters.

As Madame de Sévigné acted in other capacities than an affectionate mother, her letters to her daughter are not the only ones we are desirous of reading. Being without a rival in the epistolary art, whatever she wrote of interest finds its place here. Although all the letters are not Madame de Sévigné's, they bear such a close relationship to hers and are so intimately connected with her life that they do not admit of being separated; in effect most of them were written during the same period and by the same persons with whom Madame de Sévigné lived in the most intimate friendship.

Some letters of this kind were inserted in preceding editions, and well received, so it was decided to add many more to the present edition. It is hoped that these, which are now for the first time added, will not be less acceptable. If we are pleased with the sprightly Coulanges, why should not Bussy-Rabutin, who knew so well how to clothe his just and ingenious thoughts in an elegant, pure, and concise diction, equally delight us? It is a new figure, which renders the group more complete.

The intermixture, besides, of the letters of men of understanding, with those of a woman, will furnish the reader with occasional opportunities of exercising discrimination. It is said, that women possess the epistolary talent in a greater degree than men. Whether we dispute or allow this privilege, it is pleasing to see the energy or urbanity belonging to the one, placed in the balance with the vivacity, delicacy, playfulness, and easy fascinating manners peculiar to the other. In preceding editions, such letters have generally been added as a supplement to the work, but in the present, we have followed another and a better order, by which every letter is arranged according to its date.

It is said, that there are still many undiscovered letters of Madame de Sévigné, but the pains that have been taken to discover where these treasures are, have not been attended with any success.

There will be found in the present collection many letters written by her that will appear new, inasmuch as they have never been collected before, but have been scattered in books, that are little read, or that have become scarce. Such, in particular, are those with which we begin our collection, and which are the more curious from their being of a much earlier date, than the letters with which everybody is acquainted. The first was written by her in 1647, when Madame de Sévigné had scarcely entered into the twenty-first year of her age; others exhibit her to us in the subsequent years; the last was written in 1696, so the correspondence thus extends over forty-nine years, instead of twenty-seven only, to which it was previously confined. The last letter in the collection we consider as particularly valuable, not so much from its being scarcely known, as from the time when it was written, which was a little more than two weeks before her death. These pathetic lines are most probably the very last that were written by her already languishing hand.

The publishers of this, the "Carnavalet" edition of The Letters wish it to be known, that though the old translation has been made use of, the present may be considered as a practically new one, for the errors, which were almost innumerable in earlier editions, have been corrected, as far as it has been practicable to correct them; the omissions and suppressions, which were equally numerous and remarkable, have been faithfully restored; almost all the "starred" and hidden names have been supplied and filled in, and most important of all, the collection has been enlarged by the inclusion of no less than three hundred and eight letters which have never previously been translated into English.

As Madame de Sévigné's letters are immortal, and as they will be handed down to posterity, the publishers considered it absolutely necessary and essential that this, the most complete edition in the English language, should be one of rare typographical excellence, so that it will always be recognized as the best library edition extant.

BIOGRAPHICAL SKETCH

OF

MADAME DE SÉVIGNÉ

THERE have always been those who believed and those who disbelieved in the talents and accomplishments of women.

It is pleasing to observe, in the present instance, that Madame de Sévigné, by a singular advantage, must unite the partisans of these contrary opinions in her favour. We may praise her with impunity, both before those who proscribe the talents of women, and those who admire their minds as much as their persons: before the first, because they cannot reproach her with being an authoress; that is, with having written to be read by the public; and because, if she became celebrated, we may strictly say, that it was not her fault: before the second, because, whether voluntarily or unknown to her, she has left us a book, which is a model of its kind; and thus is her triumph at once that of her sex.

Who then can blame us for accumulating here all that appeared calculated to set forth the worth of a woman, whom every literary nation envies?

This biographical sketch that we are about to consecrate to her, will be neither a panegyric nor a history. Her panegyric has already been pronounced by numerous persons; and history belongs to those who have influenced great public events, or, at least, the progress of the Arts and Sciences: in which case, biographical details derive, from general utility, an interest, which makes the pains we take to satisfy the public curiosity acceptable, however minute. But this does not belong to Madame de Sévigné. Though the chance of birth placed her in the superior ranks of society, as she had no desire to govern those who governed the rest, it would be difficult for us to make any excursion into the political events of her time, or even into the secret adventures of Courts: and, in like manner, though an original writer, we cannot see how her studies, her success in that respect, or her failure, could furnish any digressions on rhetoric, criticism, or grammar. We may therefore apply to her what has been said of nations: "happy are they who lend little to history!" And, certainly, the sterility of the subject, from this point of view, is no disadvantage to her.

In reality, the union between the talents and character of Madame de Sévigné is so close, that her person interests us as much even as her writings. We want to know more of her fate, and of all that relates to her, than her letters convey; we should like to see every particular, which is scattered in them, collected into a focus. What has been published does not, in this respect, satisfy the desires of the reader [1]; and the art of writing exacts, that we should leave him nothing to be wished. Let us see how far this can be done.

Marie de Rabutin-Chantal was born on the fifth of February, 1626, of Celse-Bénigne de Rabutin, Baron de Chantal and Marie de Coulanges. She was only a year and a half old, when the English made a descent upon the island of Rhé, in aid of Rochelle, and the Protestants of France. M. de Chantal opposed them at the head of a corps of gentlemen, who volunteered upon the occasion. The artillery of the enemy's fleet, which protected the disembarkation, poured shot upon the French.

[1] Bayle wrote in his *Letters*: "I very much wish I could know something of this lady; I would put it into my Dictionary." Chauffepied endeavoured to supply it in his; but, notwithstanding the numerous quotations with which it is loaded, his account is as imperfect, as it is dry and uninteresting.

Their chief was killed upon the spot, with almost the whole of his company. It has even been said, that he fell by the hand of Cromwell. Historians have praised the valour of Chantal; but his exploits gained him more renown than favour. What we read of him in his daughter's letters [1], sufficiently shows, that he was less a courtier than a warrior, and that his proud and caustic language could not descend to the tone which the great French lords began to assume before the terrible and artful Richelieu.

It appears, that Mademoiselle de Rabutin lost her mother shortly after; for, in the year 1636, her maternal grandfather, M. de Coulanges, took the care of her education: he died, however, before the end of that year: and her uncle, Christophe de Coulanges, Abbé de Livry, then supplied to her the place of a father; and there is little doubt that this was a happy event for her, since, on her widowhood, we see her place herself again under the protection of this good uncle, and, fifty years after, we hear her deplore his death, with expressions of the most filial regard.

If we may judge of the manner in which women of her rank were brought up, by the influence they held in affairs of State, and in society, we must suppose that, to use the language of the times, nothing was wanting to their *goodly nurture*. Mademoiselle de Rabutin seldom left her relations, who were well-informed persons. She tells us, that she was the associate of her cousin de Coulanges, whose education was a very excellent one. She tells us also, that she was brought up at Court: this Court was less the Court of Louis XIII., than of Richelieu, who, tyrant though he was, had understanding himself, and loved to discover it even in women. We will not say, that the knowledge that displays itself in her letters, gives the measure of her education; for we perceive that she knew how to improve it herself, as it often happens with well-organized minds. Ségrais informs us, that

[1] See Letter 329, of — August, 1675, in the second volume; also Letter 713, of 13th December, 1684, in the fifth volume.

it was not till late in life, that Madame de La Fayette thought of applying herself to the study of the Latin tongue; and apparently her friend did not begin it much earlier. What she says of Italian, indicates that she taught it to herself, assisted by Ménage or Chapelain, who were both assiduous in their attentions to her. It was late, no doubt, before she acquired many sorts of information; for if there ever was a time when the enthusiasm of learning took possession of women, it certainly was not at the period of Madame de Sévigné's entrance into the world. Be this as it may, it is evident from her letters, that her education was particularly attended to; there prevails in all she wrote an excellence of style, that cannot be attained without great exercise and cultivation.

An exact portrait of her person, would savour of romance, and would be out of place; we may, however, represent the young Rabutin to our imagination, as a truly handsome woman, with more character of countenance than beauty; with features more expressive than commanding; an easy figure, a stature rather tall than short; a redundancy of fine light hair; excellent health; a fine colour; a brilliant complexion; eyes, the vivacity of which gave additional animation to her language; a pleasing voice; as much knowledge of music and singing as existed in those days, and of dancing, in which she excelled. This is the idea that her portraits, her friends, or herself give of her. And certainly her nose, tending a little towards the square, which she herself ridicules, and her party-coloured eyelids, of which Bussy says too much, could not spoil her whole appearance as much as the age of eighteen embellished it, when, in 1644, she married Henri, Marquis de Sévigné, of an ancient family of Brittany. To this appendage of merit and charms, she added a dower of a hundred thousand crowns, which, at that period, were not of less value than seven hundred thousand francs [1]. M. de Sévigné, who

[1] The silver mark was at that time worth twenty-six livres, ten sous; and we know that, besides this difference, that in the price of provisions ought likewise to be added to it.

was also rich, was besides related to the family of de Retz. The Archbishop and the Coadjutor of Paris were his near relations, while his wife was the niece of the Grand-Prior of the Temple, the Commander de Rabutin enjoying moreover a revenue of a hundred thousand livres a year, of which he bestowed more upon the world than the church. M. de Sévigné, or Sévigny [1], for it appears that at that time the name was thus pronounced, was addicted to pleasure and expense. He possessed, if not the taste and understanding which distinguished his son, at least all the gaiety, levity, and imprudence, which marked the youth of the latter. Bussy is not the only one who has thus described him. A curious pamphlet of the poet Charleval's represents him to us as a great jeerer and punster. [2] It is evident, that the lovely Burgundian heiress was not obliged to conceal her high spirits, before this lively Breton, and that it depended only on her to have a very pleasant house.

To say, that the first years of this marriage were happy, is not to abuse conjecture; it is only to catch the tone of the first letters of this collection. The fruits of the marriage were slow. The first was a son, Charles de Sévigné, born in March, 1647 [3]. His sister followed him shortly after.

The relationship of the Sévignés to the famous Coadjutor de Retz, attached them to the Fronde [4]. The

[1] It is found thus written in the *Mémoires de Joly,* the *Amours des Gaules,* the *Ménagiana,* the *Ségraisiana,* etc. It was not an error, as the last editor supposed, but an ancient custom, or provincial mode of pronunciation. It was thus Madame de Maintenon often signed *d'Aubigny,* and yet she well knew her name.

[2] The title of this pamphlet is, *Retraite du Duc de Longueville,* (Retreat of the Duc de Longueville). It is a satire of the Frondeurs, through which runs the best vein of humour.

[3] See the first Letter in this volume.

[4] The Civil Wars of the Fronde were between the Court party headed by Cardinal Mazarin and the Parliamentary party (called *Frondeurs*) headed by Turenne and Cardinal de Retz. They occurred in 1648-1654 during the minority of Louis XIV., and had their origin in the despotic policy of Cardinal Mazarin to whom the Queen-Mother had entrusted the entire management of affairs.

The name *Frondeurs* translated into English means *slingers,* and was given the Parliamentary party on account of an incident in a street quarrel.

Marquis, however, does not appear to have taken so active a part in it as his uncle, Renaud, Chevalier de Sévigné. Though the latter died in the arms of piety, at Port-Royal, we see him in 1649, during the siege of Paris, negotiating with the Court, in the name of the Coadjutor, and, what is more, fighting at the head of a regiment raised at the expense of the prelate, under the name of the *Regiment de Corinthe*; an unlucky adventure, which was called, as is well known, *the First of Corinthians* [1].

Madame de Sévigné was a zealous Frondeur, and diverted herself at the expense of Mazarin as heartily as anyone. We infer this from a letter of Bussy's [2], which makes it less doubtful, because it is addressed to herself. The spirit of party easily springs up in an imagination like hers; and the spirit of family willingly drags along with it all those of its order. Besides, she lived in great intimacy with the Duchess de Châtillon [3], who at that time was mourning for her husband, killed in fighting for the Fronde [4]. She called her sister; and, as women often weep from imitation, it is not singular that they should love and hate in fellowship.

But at that time she wanted no personal motives for ill humour. If it be true, as is maintained in the love theses brought into vogue by the pedantic gallantry of Cardinal de Richelieu, that a beauty had rather see the man she loves, dead, than unfaithful, M. de Sévigné took every step to place his wife in a similar situation to that of Madame de Châtillon. It was about this time, after many private and transient infidelities, he at last abandoned

[1] *Le Courier burlesque de la Guerre de Paris* (The burlesque Courier of the Parisian War), a sort of journal in verse, speaks of this retreat as having been well managed, and well understood before a troop superior in numbers.

[2] See the sixth Letter in this volume.

[3] See Letter 1030, of the 3rd of February, 1695, in the seventh volume.

[4] The battle of Charenton. The great Condé shed tears at the news of his death, which did not prevent him from showing great cruelty upon the occasion. In a sonnet composed on this event, the grief of Madame de Châtillon is compared to that of *Artemisia*.

her more openly [1] for a woman too worthy of this rivalship by her charms; the celebrated Ninon de Lenclos, who, born for the happiness of all that was amiable at that period, seemed destined to be the torment of Madame de Sévigné alone, during almost her whole life.

Bussy, her cousin, handsome, brave, replete with talents, and the confidant of her husband, became her confidant also; and it was he who, proclaiming the injury, offered the revenge. He was refused with a calm firmness, and without the ostentatious noise of prudery. With whatever malignant charm he clothes his recital, his epigrams do less harm to his cousin, than his boastings do good to himself. It is in vain for him to make a jest of his double breach of confidence, of the indiscretion which crowned his stratagem, and of the sequel of this adventure; his malice savours too strongly of the spite of wounded vanity; the part of his cousin is too noble, his too indelicate. A wicked proceeding can only make a good story with persons of the same character.

Madame de Sévigné was at that time only twenty-four years of age, for this passed (the date is certain) in the early part of the year 1650. A few months afterwards she experienced a still more painful trial. She lost her husband by a sanguinary death. He was killed in a duel over a woman [2]. But of what avail is it to concern ourselves respecting the motives of a duel in those times? Frequently the combatants themselves were at a loss to know the why or the wherefore.

Whoever has read Madame de Sévigné, will readily believe what is related of her extreme grief. But, as she says herself, speaking of the Abbé de Coulanges, "he extricated me from the abyss in which I was plunged by the

[1] When Madame de Sévigné, in Letter 74, of 13th March, 1671, (which is in this volume), says that Ninon had corrupted the morals of her husband, she sufficiently confirms the long account given in the *Amours des Gaules,* a work that contains more scandal than falsities.

[2] We know not where M. de Vauxelles could have taken this idea, which every fact disproves. It is much more probable that Madame de Sévigné herself was jealous. See Letter 654, of 6th August, 1680, in the fifth volume.

death of M. de Sévigné," we conclude, that she was soon obliged to deprive herself of the relief of tears, to fulfill her new duties, that of attending to the education of her two young children, and of repairing the frightful ruin of their fortune. The success with which this widow of twenty-five discharged this double duty, appears in her letters by a thousand interesting details.

Her good sense, natural rectitude, and laudable pride, gave her a taste for economy; and the advice of her uncle taught her to understand it. Her mind, notwithstanding the habit of sacrificing to the Graces, had no repugnance to business. She well knew how to sell or let estates, receive her rents, direct her workmen, etc. She did not trust to her beauty alone for gaining law-suits. Ménage relates, that one day, arguing an action with great ease and simplicity before the President de Bellièvre, she felt herself at last a little embarrassed with the terms to be used, when she said, "At least, Sir, I know the tune perfectly, but I forget the words."

With regard to education, not only do the merit of her son and daughter, as well as their virtues, show the extent of her capacity in this respect, but it would be easy to extract from her letters a series of maxims upon the subject; by which it would be seen, that, far from adhering to the false methods in vogue in her days [1], she had foretold many of the improvements, of which we are justly vain in ours.

We see few other traces of what became of Madame de Sévigné during the first three years of her widowhood. But in the winter of 1654, we find her again in the most brilliant society of Paris and the Court, with all the success of wit and beauty attending her. We see her assiduously frequenting the circles of Madame de Montausier. From the period of her marriage, the latter attracted to her house all the men of talents and connoisseurs, or, at

[1] In Letter 411, of 6th May, 1676, in the third volume, she regrets having placed her daughter in a convent, according to the custom of the times.

least, all who pretended to this name; which made the Rambouillet Mansion, with the exception of a few follies, very agreeable and even useful, since we are indebted to it for having taught men of the world to estimate letters, while men of letters learned there a knowledge of the world, and that part of good taste which neither nature nor even reading can bestow.

It was there, that, among those who aspired to please her who pleased every one, the Prince de Conti, brother of the great Condé, was particularly distinguished[1]. He possessed the insinuating graces of mind, which were wanting in his elder brother; and he announced a premeditated design to attack the heart of Madame de Sévigné: but the marriage of this Prince, which took place in the following winter, precluded him, no doubt, from pursuing his gallant intentions.

At the same period, a similar enterprise was also attempted, and in a much more serious manner, by a personage who was scarcely less formidable, the celebrated and unfortunate Fouquet. He had hardly been Chief-Controller of the Finances for a year; and his gallantries, less notorious and less numerous than they afterwards became, had as yet nothing very alarming to a woman of delicacy, jealous of her reputation. We know, too, that he had the requisites of understanding, credit, and magnificence, that were calculated to make him succeed. He failed, however, to his extreme regret, and at the same time not for want of perseverance, for it was more than a year before he would give up the hope, and resign himself to innocent friendship, which alone was pleasing to our prudent and exemplary widow. It is seldom that a refusal ends thus, with a man spoiled by all sorts of favours; and we have to lament, that the ascendant of virtue has not given us a sufficient account of this triumph. We wish to know the expedients to which Madame de Sévigné had recourse, to comfort the pride she had disheartened. Her great art seems to have been her cheerfulness and her candour. The

[1] See Letter 8, of 16th June, 1654, in this volume.

little importance she attached to her severity, led him who suffered from it to treat it more lightly. Not appearing to see his pretensions, she caused him to forget them.

In the number of her adorers, we remark further, a man of letters, a courtier and author, and a third who was neither the one nor the other.

Now the Abbé Ménage is the first of these. And his was not mere poetical gallantry, as might be supposed from the Italian madrigal he composed on her. His reply to her reproaches for not having written to her, shows a serious attachment. "I did write a letter," said he, "but I thought it too impassioned to send to you." He paid her a visit in Brittany. He relates himself, that, during this journey with Madame de Lavardin, he said tender things to her, and took her hands to kiss them; upon which this lady said to him, "I see you are rehearsing for Madame de Sévigné." Ménage could ill brook Madame de Sévigné's jests upon this curious passion. One day that he made an attempt to accompany her in her carriage, she playfully threatened to escort him back to his apartment. He betrayed great ill humour at seeing himself treated so lightly; and when Bussy published this anecdote, he shot a Latin epigram at him. For, agreeably to the taste of the times, the good Ménage loved to bite in a learned language, as well as to sigh in a foreign one.

The courtier and author who was his rival, is less known by his writings than by his long intimacy with Madame de Maintenon, whose education he had in some degree finished, and whom he wished at two very different periods to marry; at the time of her greatest distress, and that of her highest fortune; when she became the widow of an indigent and palsied poet, and when a handsome and powerful monarch offered her his hand. This was the Chevalier de Méré. Ménage, in dedicating a book to him, speaks of their former competition for Madame de Sévigné. "I willingly bore her greater love for you, because I also loved you better than I loved myself." Some allowance must be made here for the style of a dedication.

Meanwhile, the mixture of chivalrous gallantry with the taste for wit, had established in society the usage of certain avowed attachments, of which the only expense were a few attentions, and a great many writings: it was a commerce purely of wit, and preferable to the Italian system of cicisbeï, though somewhat similar to it. This is all we can see in the connection between Madame de Sévigné, and the Chevalier de Méré. His mind was besides more opposite to hers than any that could be found even in the society of the *Précieuses* [1]. This Méré has written a great deal upon eloquence: the invention of the phrase *de bonne compagnie,* in the perverted sense which is often given to it, is ascribed to him. But his attempts at elegant turns and phrases have converted his language into bombast, and the most tasteless affectation. Madame de Sévigné never mentions him in her letters, without a sort of rancour against his *chien de style* (villainous style); which renders the success of the homage he had consecrated to her more than doubtful [2].

Lastly, the Comte du Lude passed also for having made love to her. But even Bussy, with all his desire to place his cousin in the list of women of gallantry, has not a word to say upon this connection. The letters of Madame de Sévigné exhibit only an agreeable and true friend in this pretended lover. M. du Lude was a man of sense, quoted for his witticisms, and he eagerly sought after the conversation of a person who suffered not the smallest

[1] This is the name which was given to the ladies of the highest rank who frequented the Rambouillet Mansion, which was the rendezvous of the most famous wits and celebrities of the day during the 17th century. They were termed *"Les Précieuses,"* which signified persons who were finical, fastidious, fussy and affected, sticklers for elegance of manners, and purity of speech.

[2] He was named Georges Brossin, was of an ancient family of Poitou, and had served well in the Marine Department. He died in 1690. He was born in the beginning of the century, and was twenty years older than Madame de Sévigné. The following is a singular instance of his pedantic turn for taste and delicacy. He asserts in one of his Treatises, that Alexander, in calling his captive, the Queen of Persia, *mother,* was deficient in politeness, because it was reminding her that she was no longer young; a thing highly offensive to ladies.

spark to escape her notice. She is described to us, and she represents herself, as delighting in sallies of wit, ready to seize and embellish the first text that presented itself, taking fire at the first prime, and returning a thousand shots for one, to whoever roused her imagination. She even carried this charming disposition to the extreme. But apparently M. du Lude preferred this extreme (and who is not of the same taste?) to the contrary defect, to the sterility of certain disdainful or jealous minds, who suffer every sprightly sally to fall to the ground, for want of knowing how to answer it. Such persons had rather wither with dullness, than suffer it to be supposed, that it has been possible to please them. They manage so well, that all who might make themselves agreeable, renounce the attempt as vain. By this means the habit of animated conversation is lost; a species of pleasure in which the French spirit triumphs, and which has scarcely ever been found with any other people, at least, with all its varieties.

Was Madame de Sévigné, though a stranger to the arts of coquetry, unacquainted with the force of love? Does she suffer no portion of the secret history of her heart to escape her in these Letters, written with so much freedom, and, as she herself expresses it, impetuosity? These are the questions asked by a sentimental reader, whilst the malignant inquirer into the virtues of women wishes to know what hers had to encounter, and whether nature had not all the honour. These researches would be more useless than those which have cost so many pains to learned biographers. Let us therefore leave the reader something to guess. It is certain that slander itself has been able to attach no weakness to Madame de Sévigné; which may be considered as a sort of phenomenon in those times of the Regency and the Civil war, when everything was love; when the illusions of the heart and the fire of the senses seemed to be the least forcible reason for this passion; when ambition, the desire of notoriety, and of taking the lead, and the spirit of faction, led away the wisest heads and the weakest minds; when intrigues, of not the most noble kind, held to attachments still less romantic; when fine women took a lover more for the sake of party, than for pleasure; in short, when all the actors in this foolish scene were the relations, friends, and intimate acquaintances of our young widow.

But besides the offers of gallants, Madame de Sévigné received many proposals of marriage, but in vain. She had not been a happy wife; she was a rich widow, and a fond mother: cultivating with success the public esteem, her own understanding, her friends, and her children, she wished for no other happiness. The happiness, however, which fell to her lot, was not without alloy. She suffered in her friendships, and saw attacks made upon her reputation.

The imprisonment, exile, and the disgrace in general, not unmerited, of Cardinal de Retz, were her first grief. She always saw in him her good genius, and an amiable man, who appreciated her better than any other person, and upon whose advancement she built the fate of one part of her family, and the hopes of the other. The memoirs of the Cardinal inform us, that his flight from the Château of Nantes was principally favoured by the Chevalier de Sévigné. She recalls to mind in one of her letters the painful situation in which these events placed her in the course of the year 1653, and the following ones [1].

In the meantime another friend occasioned her still greater uneasiness. The vainest men are the most arbitrary. The refusal of some service, which, doubtless, depended not on her, suddenly embroiled her with her cousin Bussy [2]. He had often reproached her with being too

[1] Letter 501, of 28th July, 1677, in the fourth volume.

[2] The service demanded of his cousin by Bussy, was not a loan, as we are at first led to believe; for he himself owns that, on another occasion, she had generously assisted him. But the part of the *Amours des Gaules* in which he attacks her, written in 1659, and a letter of August, 1654, (the tenth in this volume), prove that their quarrel took place between these two periods. It was precisely at this time, too, that M. Fouquet showed himself very much dissatisfied with him; whence we infer, that the good office his cousin refused him, belonged to some intrigue, for the purpose of reinstating him in the favour of the Chief-Controller.

much *taken up with virtue.* "Why," said he, "do you give yourself so much trouble about a reputation, which a calumniator may destroy?" He was himself this dangerous calumniator. In his resentment, he wrote against her the article in question, in which he respects truth merely for the sake of stabbing more deeply; in which, for want of vices to bring against her, he charges her with absurdities; in which he makes her character a sort of moral paradox, pretending that an unimpeachable conduct concealed an impure heart, and that she had at least an inclination for all the follies which she did not commit. Though the falsity of this portrait appears in his contradictions, there is no doubt, thanks to the general malignity of the world, that it made more impression at that time, than in the present day, and that he wantonly pierced a heart born for the love of virtue in all its branches, and even the renown that follows it. Long did the wound bleed: feeling hearts retain the impression of evil as well as of good; and hence the meaning of the ingenious saying, "Revenge is the gratitude for injuries." Madame de Sévigné took no revenge; she even pardoned Bussy, but it was with difficulty, and not perhaps without restriction. Frequent recollections of injuries escape her in her letters to him; and they are wanting, at least, in that bloom of confidence, which we in some degree inhale in what she says to her other friends; this is the only point in which this part of her correspondence has appeared less worthy of her.

To this affliction there succeeded the reverse of fortune which precipitated the unfortunate Fouquet from the height of his power into a perpetual prison. Here she herself paints her anxiety in her letters, in which she places herself by the side of La Fontaine, in heart as well as in style.

What can be added to this? Her letters, however, speak of nothing but the trial, and the trial did not begin till three years after Fouquet was arrested. The thunderbolt which struck him, surprised his friends, like himself, in all the illusions of his fortune. Madame de Sévigné was almost within its reach, and she had reason to tremble for herself. The Chief-Controller was brilliant, and prodigal, treating affairs of consequence lightly, and neglecting no pleasure. The amiable widow had entered into a correspondence of wit and friendly jesting with him; an innocent and very natural confidence towards one, who had given her the best proof of that sort of esteem, which a powerful and liberal-minded man does not entertain for one sex more than another. It was soon known, that among Fouquet's papers, letters were found which exposed many women of the Court. Those of Madame de Sévigné could do him no injury. They were in the hands of Le Tellier, Secretary of State, who declared them to be "the most honourable letters in the world[1];" but it is possible that her frank gaiety might have treated certain things and persons according to their deserts; and there are times when railleries pass for confederacies. A letter of Bussy's shows, that her apprehensions were sufficiently strong for her to withdraw for a time to some distance into the country[2]. The cabal, which had destroyed Fouquet, wished it to be believed, that he was supported by a powerful party. In these cases, the first blow is struck upon whatever presents itself first: this is the ordinary step in the revolutions of Courts, as well as in other revolutions; and we recognize equally in them the exercise of private revenge: two reflections that must be placed by the side of the alarm and precautions of Madame de Sévigné, to explain what appears extravagant in them.

Indeed she could not have been really implicated, since we see her soon appearing with splendour in the centre of a Court, which Louis XIV. began to render so brilliant. The entertainments of Versailles, in the years 1664 and 1665, will not be obliterated from the memory of man,

[1] *Mémoires de Bussy.* It was to him Le Tellier gave this favourable testimony. [2] He exaggerates what he had done for his cousin, though upon ill terms with her, at the time of Fouquet's fall. He adds: "You were not really in prison, but you were in S****;" meaning either the estate of Sévigné near Rennes, or perhaps Sucy-en-Brie. In Letter 437, of 22nd July, 1676, (in the third volume), she says that she spent her youth in this place.

their ingenious composition and elegant magnificence having rendered them worthy of the historical pencil with which Voltaire immortalises everything he touches. Madame de Sévigné, though formed to ornament this great theatre by her own charms, appeared at it merely to enjoy the success of her daughter, who, in the first bloom of beauty, and endowed with superior understanding and talents, was presented in 1663. Mademoiselle de Sévigné took part in the ballets in which the King himself danced before a crowded Court. In these she assumed the character of a shepherdess. Benserade, "who," says Voltaire, "had a singular talent for little complimentary pieces, in which he always made delicate and pointed allusions to the characters of the performers, to the personages of ancient or fabulous history whom they represented, or to the passions which animated the Court," wrote many verses on her upon these occasions, in which he also frequently celebrated her mother.

It will not be superfluous, we think, to observe, that it was at this very period that Madame de Sévigné acted and interested herself with so much zeal for Fouquet. The air and admiration of a Court did not produce on her their usual effect, that of inspiring forgetfulness of the unfortunate.

At the same time, other friends in disgrace experienced, in like manner, her fidelity. The Jansenists [1] then resisted the Court, the Clergy, the Parliaments, and even the Pope himself. Were certain lines, condemned by the latter, to be found or not in Jansenius? In imputing them to him, no one thought of quoting the passage from the book. Voltaire is astonished at the circumstance, as if that alone would have resolved the question. But the Pope's bull was before the eyes of the whole world, and

[1] The name given to the followers of Cornelius Jansen (1585-1638), Bishop of Ypres, France, whose book—entitled *Augustinus*—was published in 1640, and taught the doctrine of free grace. This view was contrary to that held by the Jesuits, and resulted in a long and bitter religious controversy. The Jansenists were persecuted by Louis XIV. and in 1720 they were banished from France and fled to the Netherlands, where Jansenism still exists.

there was no disagreement on the question, whether the bull made Jansenius the author of the lines. Probably Jansenius himself would not have been believed. Madame de Sévigné interested herself little in these things, except for the sake of persons. But her relations with Port-Royal were intimate. It is not so well known, and indeed is of little importance in itself, that she laid the first stone of one of the wings of this house, built at the expense of her uncle, the Chevalier de Sévigné, who had retired thither. He was tormented, no doubt, by the affair of the Formulary. Besides, the most illustrious among these illustrious recluses, the Arnauld family, were then in exile. It will be seen how deeply she was affected by their misfortunes.

The establishment of her children, and particularly the marriage of her daughter, soon became her only concern. The latter was scarcely twenty years of age, yet an event, which was to interrupt her happiness, seemed to arrive too slowly for this most unselfish mother. She had herself, however, rejected more than one opportunity. She could see few men worthy of such a daughter. She pleasantly describes her industry in raising obstacles for the purpose of discarding any of whom she augured ill. Twice was the marriage of Mademoiselle de Sévigné broken off, though very far advanced. M. de Caderousse and M. de Mérinville, two very distinguished Provençals, sought her hand. Judging by the memoirs of the times, the ill success of the first was a fortunate circumstance for her. At length, on the twenty-ninth of January, 1669, she was married to another Provençal, the Comte de Grignan. The sequel of these letters sufficiently make known the character of the husband, and the happiness of the union.

Madame de Sévigné began soon afterwards the establishment of her son, by purchasing for him a military commission. These were two great sacrifices of fortune to her at once: but she appeared so little to perceive it, that we should scruple to heighten their little merit.

Madame de Sévigné had flattered herself that by marrying her daughter to a courtier, she would spend her life with her. But M. de Grignan, who was Lieutenant-General of the government of Provence, received an order soon after his marriage, to repair thither; and in the end, he commanded almost always in the absence of the Duc de Vendôme, who was the Governor. Then began a second widowhood for Madame de Sévigné, more painful perhaps than the first; we mean the absence of her daughter, to which we owe the letters of the mother. These intervals, which she considered as her evil times, were fortunate moments for posterity: we enjoy her privations, and as soon as she is made happy, we become sufferers in our turn; and find ourselves regretting, that, for our pleasure, she was not more frequently, and for a longer period, afflicted by this separation.

From this era, the life of Madame de Sévigné is contained in the letters which are now presented to the reader. Some journeys, the loss of several friends, the campaigns, dangers, hopes, little irregularities and marriage of her son, but particularly the various fortunes of her daughter, and at length, some changes in her own health, form the only events of her life. As poor in facts, as it was rich in sentiments, it would only furnish a dry narration, if her pen did not give life to the most trifling occurrences. It is enough for us to have thrown a little light upon the hitherto unknown preliminary scene of this interesting drama; let the heroine in future speak for herself.

There remain, however, some particulars, which her letters do not supply, or which they leave us to guess at imperfectly, by trivial relations, or short hints.

The marriage of M. de Sévigné in 1684, placed this generous mother in a situation of constraint and inconvenience by the sacrifices she then made. We perceive, indistinctly, that at that time, whether to meliorate her fortune, or from other motives, her friends and even her daughter formed various plans for her [1]; there was an idea

[1] See Letter 733, of 8th July, 1685, and also Letter 736, of 1st August, 1685, both of which are in the fifth volume. It appears that the gentleman was the Duc de Luynes.

of procuring her a place at Court, and she was even advised to marry again, which she rejected as a folly that had no attractions for her.

Among other advantages she had that of preserving her exterior charms to a very late period. When Bussy applied to her the burlesque verses which Benserade addressed to the moon,

> Et toujours fraîche et toujours blonde,
> Vous vous maintenez par le monde,[1]

she was forty-six years of age, and more than fifty-two, when Madame de Scuderi wrote to Bussy: "I met Madame de Sévigné the other day, whom I think handsome still [2]. Hence this name of *Mère-beauté* (mother beauty) given her by Coulanges. Her constitution was good, and she managed it with great judgment. For some time, she was thought to have a tendency to apoplexy [3], and was sent to the waters. This alarm did not last. In thirty years the only ailment she had known was rheumatism.

She therefore experienced little of the hardest condition of women, the rapid transition from youth to age, of which nature warns them by signs, as painful as they are certain, and for which society is ill calculated to console them. But it is to those who have built their happiness upon the success of their charms, to women of gallantry or coquetry, that this crisis is the most painful. Happy all her life, by the exercise of natural and pure affections, Madame de Sévigné thought less of the ravages of time; and it was not for her that her friend Rochefoucauld had said, that "the hell of women is old age."

When death terminated her existence at the age of seventy, her illness, the result of her uneasiness and the fatigues she had endured for six months on her daughter's

[1] And ever fresh and ever fair,
The world supports you high in air, [Translation.]

[2] Collection of the *Letters of Bussy* for the year 1678. See her portrait under the name of *Sophronie* in the *Dictionnaire des Précieuses*, by Saumaise.

[3] See Letter 512, of 26th August, 1677, in the fourth volume.

account, took her by surprise, and was announced by no symptom. It was short. Madame de Sévigné in her last moments showed her head to be as sound, as her heart was irreproachable. Several letters describe to us the affliction of her friends. We cannot read the bitterness of their complaints, and the long duration of their regret, without being affected [1]. Madame de Sévigné was interred in the Collegial Chapel of Grignan. Maréchal de Muy, to whom this estate belonged, caused her coffin to be dug up and deposited in a cenotaph raised in the centre of the same chapel.

Without pretending to encroach upon the privileges of the panegyrist, we feel as if every observation, that has a tendency to illustrate Madame de Sévigné's extraordinary merit, belongs to our narrative. Premising this, we shall first insist, that she received no taint from the manners of her times, nor from the persons with whom she associated: the truest criterion of a just understanding, and of a firm and delicate soul.

During the minority of Louis XIV., when thrown into the midst of the political intrigues of so many illustrious men and women, you cannot trace in her a single trait of coquetry, or a spark of ambition.

What matters it, that she was included in the number of the *Précieuses,* that her circle was one of the most celebrated, that she lived among the wits of the Rambouillet Mansion, that she perhaps admired them? She took care not to imitate them. The romances of La Calprenède and La Scuderi delighted her, but her style does not partake of this strange taste. At every period of her life she wrote with the same ease. Better informed than the generality of the women who composed her circle, she was less pedantic than any of them; and what is remarkable, though at that time every woman of understanding attempted some literary composition, Madame de Sévigné has not left a single page written designedly for the public, or for the

[1] See the Letter 1079, of 23rd May, 1696, of M. de Grignan, her son-in-law, in the seventh volume.

sake of displaying her talent for writing. When she mentions books she would write, it is merely in jest. She affected nothing, and loved nothing by imitation.

Port-Royal, its doctors and their partisans, have all her good wishes; but this predilection never reached to enthusiasm. While pitying these poor persecuted brethren, she was the first to laugh at their prejudices, their contradictions, their pious frauds, and proved herself little worthy of the foolish honour that was paid to her, of enregistering her name in the catalogue of Jansenian authors. Besides, what had she adopted of their opinions [1]? nothing but the philosophical part: and this she followed from sentiment rather than choice. Their rigid morals, which were true stoicism, subjugate her mind; whereas the equivocal and wavering doctrines of their adversaries, alarm and fatigue it. Free will, and the subtle expedients by which the difficulties it gives birth to are eluded, perplex her imagination. Too penetrating to avoid doubts, and too sincere to disguise them, she prefers resting on the simple and convenient system of a Providence, which does everything, which is the cause of all we do, the source and limit of everything, furnishes an answer to everything, and acts incessantly for a known or for an unknown good. Her very uncertainty, in a matter forever uncertain, shows the rectitude and independence of her judgment. Strange Jansenism was hers! See her playful regret at not being able to become a devotee [2]. She laughs at all popular superstitions. The processions, shrines, chaplets, and even the fast-days, furnish her with witticisms, and entertaining stories. She does not seem to be very strongly convinced of the necessity of confession; and the eternity of torments is repugnant to her belief. She writes on the altar of her chapel, this almost heretical inscription: SOLI DEO. She speaks so freely, that a Calvinistic author appears inclined to place her in the list of his sect [3].

[1] See Letter 496, of 16th July, 1677, in the fourth volume.

[2] See Letter 493, of 3rd July, 1677, in the fourth volume.

[3] See Chauffepied's Dictionary.

At the epoch, when the conversion of Louis XIV. became as it were a signal for all who had connections with the Court; when the most able, as well as the most virtuous, adorned themselves uniformly in the exterior of bigotry; we do not see her following the common course, nor speaking less freely than before: as she took no lover in her youth, she had no director in her old age. Her cheerfulness was the same at sixty, as at twenty-five. Her life, in short, was not of the nature of those that require to be spent in penitence. She had little to regret, and nothing to expiate.

This is at least a part of what he, who so properly dignified Madame de Sévigné with the title of an *extraordinary woman,* meant to express. In fact, her character was no less original than her mind; and the union of these two singularities had made her a most rare composition.

But it was on this very account that she was in general unjustly judged, and that she experienced more censure than we might be apt to suppose. The first injury done by the censorious, is that which makes so many false reputations, the habit of attaching serious consequences to trifling incidents, of judging a whole life by a single moment, and placing to the score of character, features which originate in the imagination. A lively person frequently describes, in what she writes, only her momentary feelings; while character is made up of the habitudes of the soul.

For instance, the competition between the young Racine and the old Corneille kindled one of these little wars of opinion, of which the common effect is, that every one outruns his own sentiments. Madame de Sévigné writes in the heat of the contest; and the first stroke of her pen is converted into a literary heresy: her taste is for ever decried; as if an adventurous judgment proved a want of judgment!

The species of enthusiasm which she displays to her cousin Bussy, on the genealogy of the Rabutins, and the good Mayeuls, her ancestors, who were great lords in the twelfth century, is also severely criticised. But read what she writes to her daughter upon the same subject[1]; you will there find nothing but good sense, reducing to their just standard the advantages of high birth. At that time few persons reasoned well upon this point. But a proud relation and a vain author, first consecrates to her a principal article in his book, and then dedicates the book itself to her: and for this compliment was it not necessary to return a compliment? We could vindicate as easily her frequent exclamations respecting the nobleness of the name of Grignan, and the Royal Castle of that family, and the ancient grandeur of the Adhémars. These passages were intended for her son-in-law, whose weakness she flattered from the purest motives. All this did not prevent her from writing to her daughter with as much precision as truth: "How little honour is there in being vain!" and these were her real sentiments!

So, when the praise of Louis XIV. comes to her pen at every opportunity, and sometimes for actions not the most laudable, is it not evident that the phrases she adopts are often nothing more than eloquent precautions, a passport, as it were, for letters, the seals of which were little respected?

The reproach that is cast on her for a foolish infatuation for the Court, is not less hasty and unfounded. She goes to Versailles; she is kindly received, and perhaps flattered, because seldom there; perhaps too, there is something in the air of this place calculated to incite a sprightly woman to sprightly sallies of wit, and she gives way to an inclination, that is best appreciated where it is best understood. She returns, delighted with everyone, as everyone is delighted with her. On the instant she writes to her daughter; she hastily describes to her, her first sensation; and her pen, always tinctured with poetry, heightens still further what she has felt. The frigid mind who peruses her, takes all she says seriously. "Weakness!" he exclaims; "low-minded vanity!" And yet, who has ever judged more truly of the wretchedness of a life at Court? You will

[1] See Letter 735, of 22nd July, 1685, in the fifth volume.

find in her letters a beautiful supplement to the chapter of La Bruyère on the subject [1]. What can be more forcible than the stroke on Madame de Richelieu, that eagle of Ladies of Honour, who soared so high into the air of etiquette? "The search after truth does not perplex a poor brain half so much, as the nothings and compliments with which hers is filled."

But we have a more serious grievance to recite. Some jests, not too neatly clothed up, some words, of rather a coarse sound, which are scattered in the several volumes of her letters, have given so much offence to certain connoisseurs, that they doubt almost whether Madame de Sévigné would have been a fit associate for them. Let us endeavour to remove their fears.

Languages are purified slowly. The society which was formed in the first twenty years of the reign of Louis XIV. long admitted a familiarity of expression, which it has since proscribed. In proportion as originality remained in the characters, conversation, and particularly playful conversation, retained an air of freedom, which did not so carefully avoid the word that presented itself, as is done now. The success of a jest depended less upon the choice of terms. When Molière introduced upon the stage certain words, now excluded from polite language, he did not sacrifice to the taste of the pit so much as it has been supposed: in more than one instance he thought of the boxes. Call to mind the success of Scarron, read the ingenious Voiture, and then judge of what was called delicacy and good taste. How many admired sallies, how many sayings even of Madame de Cornuel, so well received in the highest circles, would now be deemed unbecoming in the mouth of a woman like her! The greater part of the songs of Coulanges would lose much of their witty gaiety. The first personages of the times, whether in point of rank or elegance, indulged in jests, which would appear to us of a low taste.

[1] See Letter 446, of 14th August, 1676, and also Letter 447, of 19th August, 1676, both of which are in the third volume.

Among other examples, we shall cite the word *cocu* (cuckold). Is it surprising that it should be found under the friendly and confidential pen of Madame de Sévigné, when we see it used as a common word in the *Memoirs of Cardinal de Retz,* destined for posterity; and especially when we read what passed even in the King's circle, on the occasion of Madame Loiseau (bird)? She was the wife of a rich citizen, and well known by her original repartees. The King, seeing her very near his circle, bade the Duchess de *** to ask her some question; and she asked her what bird was most subject to be made a cuckold? "A Duc, Madame," she replied [1]. It must be owned that this conceit would not succeed so well in our days, in parties that command still less respect [2], and that Madame de Sévigné jests more delicately, and more decently.

If there is a fault of her pen which cannot be denied, it is a tincture of slander. And why should it be denied? She herself tells us, that her confessor refused her absolution on account of her hatred for a certain Bishop. She very jocosely applies to herself the saying of Montaigne on the Court: "Let us take our revenge by abusing it." It is true also, that she could not boast, like Fontenelle, at the close of her life, that she had never thrown the slightest ridicule upon the least virtue. Several excellent persons, the useful d'Hacqueville, for instance, M. de La Garde, and even her good uncle Coulanges, with his minute regularity, are rallied by her with too little scruple. But what is there in common between Fontenelle and Sévigné? It

[1] *Ménagiana,* Vol. II. Madame Cornuel said of a husband who accused his wife of adultery, "He takes care to make the Parliament believe more in cuckolds than in witches."

[2] An anecdote, not less strange, is related of the most brilliant period of the Court of Louis XIV. in 1685. Madame de Coligny writes it to her father. "M. de Roquelaure adjusting his wig at a looking-glass in the apartment of the Dauphiness, the Duc de La Ferté made horns at him, as he stood behind him. M. de Roquelaure having perceived it, came to the Duchesse d'Arpajon, Lady of Honour, and told her that M. de La Ferté had exposed himself in the Princess's apartment and before her maids. The Duchesse, in great anger, went to the Maids of Honour to know what had passed; they told her; and there was a loud laugh upon the occasion."

is well known, that he was all reason, and she, on the contrary, all instinct. If this is not praise, it is, at least, an excuse. After all, the world which is so fond of slander, gives but too much cause for slander. This is the way in which we could justify her upon this article, at the same time that we would avoid supposing, as a refined critic has done, that this blind mother only indulged in certain little instances of malice to flatter the malignity of her daughter. But why absolve her from a part of this sin? We observe the pleasure she takes in it, and we can see no appearance that she wished to yield to others in any respect.

If Madame de Sévigné, however, sometimes seizes on opportunities to laugh at the expense of her neighbour, at least, she never seeks for them; and with regard to her friends, she denies herself this species of merriment. Her ready imagination, and her eager pen, never lead her away. Their malice never rouses hers. She never sacrifices one friend to another. She silences the ridiculous stories of Coulanges against Madame de Marbeuf. She takes the part of Madame de La Fayette against her son. Even her daughter has not the privilege of shaking her good will for any one whom she had found after her own heart. Accordingly, for fifty years, we do not see her lose, except by death, a single friend; a striking proof of her possessing a heart, as true as it was delicate and sensible. Her letters have no caustic spirit: neither is it the character of the witticisms that are related of her, and of which we shall insert a few here.

The Comtesse Colonne and the Duchesse de Mazarin, both flying from their husbands, passed into Provence, and came to Grignan, taking with them their diamonds, but so little clothing, that in the evening Madame de Sévigné thought she ought to make them a present of a dozen shifts, observing to them: "You are like the heroines of a romance; plenty of jewels, but no linen."

She was at church, and the creed was chanted: "Oh, how false that is!" she cried; and correcting herself, "I mean the singing, not what is sung."

Ménage observing to her *qu'il etoit enrhumé* (that he had a cold), Madame de Sévigné replied, *Je la suis aussi* (so have I). The honest grammarian began to prove to her, that she ought to use the masculine pronoun instead of the feminine, and say, *je* le *suis*. "As you please," resumed she, "but for my part, if I were to express myself so, I should fancy I had a beard." And in her letters she often violates this rule.

Some one exaggerating to her the good qualities and understanding of Pélisson, "I can see nothing but his ugliness," said she; "let his lining, therefore, be taken out for me."

Such was the person to whom we are indebted for this book; which was composed without being thought of either by herself or others, and which only became a book from the good fortune of the French language and the French nation.

A resemblance has been found between Madame de Sévigné and Montaigne; and, indeed an inscription which one may read in the first page of his *Essays,* written by a lady, might justly be applied to her: "An author who the least knows what he is going to say, and the best what he says."

She has been compared to Cicero, whose *Letters* are the best that antiquity has left us, and who, in like manner, was passionately fond of his daughter. She might also have been compared to a Roman lady, as much celebrated for the style of her letters, as for her chastity and maternal affection—to Cornelia, the mother of the Gracchi. Lastly, there are points of resemblance between La Fontaine and Sévigné. But these parallels speak her praise better than they represent her: they prove that everyone likes to trace in her the features of his favourite author.

It may be remarked, to the honour of her contemporaries, that though they had no idea of her becoming an authoress, they duly appreciated her epistolary talent. Her letters were read in circles the most renowned for taste.

Madame de Coulanges lent them to her three sisters, who have signalised the wit of the Mortemars. The Abbé Têtu paid his court with them to the Abbess de Fontévrault. By this circulation many were lost. Bussy-Rabutin enriched with them the *Memoirs* he caused to be read to the King to regain his favour, and the modesty of Madame de Sévigné took alarm at the circumstance. Madame de Maisons, distinguished at that time by her understanding, and to whom, about the year 1690, Bussy had communicated his cousin's letters, copied them. When Bouhours published his *Entretiens* (Conversations), Corbinelli wrote thus to Bussy: "Why seek for so many passages in Balzac and Voiture, when you would have found better ones in your and your cousin's letters, if you wanted examples of perspicuity, delicacy, and noble simplicity of thought?"

Accordingly, as soon as a few of these letters were printed, authors and men of the world agreed in regarding them as valuable models. From the date of Balzac's celebrity, everybody wished to write fine letters. When Voiture was in fashion, the desire was to give them a prettiness. But when those of Sévigné were read, no attempt was made to imitate her style; everyone wrote a letter as he could: and this is the way in which letters ought to be written.

The foregoing Biographical Sketch was written by M. Ph. A. Grouvelle, the last editor of, and the acknowledged highest authority on the Letters of Madame de Sévigné. It was prefixed to the last and best French edition from which it has been translated into English, and is now, with many necessary revisions and corrections, prefixed to this edition.

THE LETTERS OF MADAME DE SÉVIGNÉ

THE

LETTERS

OF

MADAME DE SÉVIGNÉ

*LETTER 1

From Madame la Marquise DE SÉVIGNÉ *to her cousin the Comte* DE BUSSY-RABUTIN.

March 15, 1647.

You are a pretty fellow, truly, not to have written to me for these two months. Have you forgotten who I am, and the rank I hold in the family? I shall make you remember this, young man; and, if you irritate me, I shall reduce you to the ranks. You knew I was on the point of lying-in; and you care no more about my health, than if I were still a girl. Well, I have to inform you, and you may storm at the intelligence as much as you please, that I am brought to bed of a boy, who shall suck hatred of you with his milk, and that I intend to have a great many more, for the sole purpose of raising you up enemies. You have not the wit, let me tell you, to do as much: you, with your progeny of girls!

But I cannot, after all, conceal my affection; nature will get the better of policy. I had resolved to scold you for your laziness, from the beginning to the end; but I do violence to my feelings, and must return to the old subject, and tell you honestly, my dear cousin, that M. de Sévigné and I both love you very much, and often talk of the pleasure it would give us to have you with us.

* Letters with an asterisk have not previously been translated.

*LETTER 2

From the Comte DE BUSSY *to Madame* DE SÉVIGNÉ.

Valence, April 12, 1647.

In answer to your letter of the fifteenth of March, I must tell you, Madame, that you take a method of reproving me, which has more the tone of a mistress, than of a cousin. Take care what you do; for when once I am resolved to suffer, I will have the indulgences of a lover, as well as the punishments. I am aware, that you are an able General, and that, in virtue of this title, I owe you due reverence; but you abuse my submission. It is true, that your anger is as prompt in subsiding, as it is in being put into commotion, and that if your letters begin with, *you are a pretty fellow*, they end with, *we love you very much, M. de Sévigné and myself.*

For the rest, my lovely cousin, do not count too much on the fertility with which you threaten me; for, know, since the law of grace, wives are not held in the estimation they formerly were; and, with some modern husbands, they are even held in no estimation at all. Be content then, if you please, with the boy you have brought into the world; it is a very laudable act: I have not the wit, I own, to do as much; and I envy this good luck of M. de Sévigné's more than anything else in the world.

---

*LETTER 3

From the Comte DE BUSSY *to Monsieur and Madame* DE SÉVIGNÉ.

Paris, November 15, 1648.

I thought, at first, of writing a separate letter to each of you; but I considered, that it would be too troublesome to send my compliments from one to the other in two letters; and I was apprehensive that a postscript might give offence; so I rejected these expedients, and have resorted to a third, which is, to address you both at the same time.

The most certain intelligence I have to communicate is, that I have been very dull since I saw you: this is surprising enough; for I have been to see the little *brunette*, who, you know, once caused a gentle fluttering in my heart: in reality, she jumped into my eyes, as they say, before I had spoken to her: her conversation, however, heals all the wounds that are made by her beauty. See her for a moment, and you cannot help loving her; see her longer, and your love is at an end. This was precisely the case with me.

But I forget to inquire after our dear uncle [1]. I beg you will entertain him with droll stories; if you do not make him laugh heartily, even though he should cough a little in consequence, you will disoblige me very much.

---

*LETTER 4

From the Comte DE BUSSY *to Madame* DE SÉVIGNÉ.

St. Denis [2], February 15, 1649.

I have long hesitated about writing to you, not knowing whether you were become my enemy, or were still my very good cousin, and whether I ought to send you a footman or a trumpeter. At last, recollecting I had heard you blame the churlishness of *Horace,* who said to his brother-in-law, that since war was declared [3] he no longer knew him, I thought the state of public affairs would not pre-

[1] Towards the end of the year 1648, Bussy-Rabutin, accompanied by M. and Madame de Sévigné, visited M. de Neuchèzes, Bishop of Châlons, at his home, the Abbey of Ferrières. The Bishop was uncle of both Madame de Sévigné and De Bussy.

[2] This was during the Civil wars of the Fronde. Bussy followed the Court, and served in the army of the Prince de Condé, who laid siege to Paris. (Voltaire, *Siècle de Louis XIV.*, chap. 4.)

[3] He alludes to the line *Albe vous a nommé, je ne vous connois plus* in Corneille's tragedy of *The Horaces.*

vent you from reading my letters; and, for my own part, I assure you, that, except as far as concerns the interest of the King, my master, I am your very humble servant.

Let us now talk a little about the war, my dear cousin: this mounting guard is cold work, and though we have plenty of fire-wood, which costs us nothing, and live well at a trifling expense, I am very tired of it notwithstanding. If it were not for the hope of rendering you some small service at the sacking of Paris, and that you would probably fall to my sole lot, I really think I should turn deserter. But this idea alleviates my sorrows.

I send this time a footman, in the name of our uncle the Grand-Prior, that he may bring me news of you, and lead back my coach-horses. Adieu, my dear cousin.

---

*LETTER 5

From the Comte DE BUSSY *to Madame* DE SÉVIGNÉ.

St. Denis, March 25, 1649.

I now treat you as an enemy, in writing to you by my trumpeter. The truth is, he is going to Maréchal de La Mothe with a request that he will send back the coach-horses of our uncle, the Grand-Prior of France, that his servants decamped with as they were coming to me. I do not ask you to use your interest in this affair, because it is as much your business as mine; but we shall judge by the success of your exertions, in what estimation you are held by your party; or rather, we shall think well or ill of your Generals, as they comply with or slight your recommendations.

I have just arrived from Brie-Comte-Robert; no poor dog was ever more tired. I have not taken off my clothes for a whole week: we are your masters, but it has cost us some trouble to be so. If you do not die with fatigue, surrender, or we shall very soon be obliged to submit on our part. In addition to my other evils, I have that of being extremely impatient to see you. If Cardinal Mazarin had such a cousin as you in Paris, I am very much deceived if peace would not be made upon any terms. I love you very much.

---

*LETTER 6

From the Comte DE BUSSY *to Madame* DE SÉVIGNÉ.

St. Denis, March 26, 1649.

So much the worse for those who have refused you, my lovely cousin; I know not whether it will turn to their advantage, but this I know, that it will not redound to their honour. For my own part, I consider the expressions of friendship I have received from you in this business, as more than an equivalent for the loss of my horses. And for your Maréchal de La Mothe, if ever he has occasion for my services, he will find me a very uncourteous Knight.

But respecting peace; what do they think of the subject in Paris? We have a sad opinion of it here; for is it not strange that both parties should so earnestly desire the event, and yet be unable to effect it?

You call me impertinent, for having sent you word that we had taken Brie. Can your Parisians deny the fact? If we had raised the siege, we should have been very much inconvenienced; your Generals, however, have had all the patience imaginable: we should be to blame to complain of them.

Will you allow me to speak freely, my beautiful cousin? As there is no danger to be feared from your party, there is no honour to be gained; they do not sufficiently dispute their ground, and we have no pleasure in conquering them. Let them surrender, or let them fight manfully: this is the first war, I believe, in which fortune had no share. When we can find you, we are sure to beat you, and neither the advantage of numbers nor of situation can for a moment balance the scale of victory.

O, my lovely cousin, how you will hate me for this! not all the fine speeches in the world will appease your wrath.

---

*LETTER 7

From the Comte DE BUSSY *to Madame* DE SÉVIGNÉ.

From the Camp at Montrond [1], July 2, 1650.

I have at length declared myself for M. le Prince; but I told you truly, my lovely cousin, it was not without great repugnance; for I serve, against my King, a Prince who does not love me. It is true, that his situation excites my pity; and I will serve him, therefore, during his imprisonment, as well as if he did love me; but should he be liberated, I will instantly quit him.

What say you to these sentiments, Madame; are they not noble, sublime? Pray let me know your opinion, and write to me often; the Cardinal shall know nothing of the matter, and if he should discover it, and send you a *lettre de cachet,* what a fine thing it would be for a woman of twenty to have the notoriety of being concerned in the important affairs of State! I own I should very much like to make you commit a crime of some kind or other. When I reflect, that we were in opposite parties last year, and continue so still, I cannot help thinking we are playing at *barriers*: but you are always the better off being permanent in Paris, while I go from St. Denis to Montrond, and in the end, I fear, shall go from Montrond to the devil.

---

*LETTER 8

From the Comte DE BUSSY *to Madame* DE SÉVIGNÉ.

Montpellier, June 16, 1654.

I have had tidings of you, Madame. Do you remember the conversation you had last winter with the Prince

[1] Bussy joined the party against the Court, after the imprisonment of the great Condé and his brothers; but he soon abandoned it. It was at that time reported, that Corbinelli (a much esteemed and close and life-long friend of Madame de Sévigné's) adjusted the difference.

de Conti, at Madame de Montausier's? He tells me he said some pretty things to you; that he found you very amiable; and that he will have a little chat with you again this winter. Take care, my charming cousin; the woman, who is not guided by interest, is sometimes led away by ambition; and she who can refuse the King's financier,[1] may be induced to yield to His Majesty's cousin. By the way in which he mentioned you, I see plainly he designs to make me his confidant. To this I suppose you will have no objection, knowing, as you do, how well I have acquitted myself of the charge in former adventures. If, after all that fortune throws in your way, I am not more successful than I have hitherto been, it will be your fault alone; but you will take care that it shall be otherwise, and, indeed, you ought to serve me in one instance at least. I think you will be somewhat embarrassed between your two rivals.

Perhaps you will be afraid to attach yourself to the service of a Prince, and my example may deter you; perhaps the person of the Chief-Controller does not please you: let me hear something of the latter, and of the progress he has made in your heart, since my departure. How many *gratis patents* has your liberty cost him? My dear cousin, you are an ungrateful little personage; but you will repay him one time or other: you are taken up with virtue, as if it were a real good; and you despise wealth, as if you could never be in want of it: we shall see you some day regretting the time you have lost; we shall see you repenting that you have misemployed your youth, at the expense of acquiring a reputation which a calumniator may destroy, and which depends more on your good fortune, than on your good conduct.

---

[1] M. Fouquet endeavoured, unsuccessfully, to obtain from Madame de Sévigné, what he was accustomed to receive from ladies of exalted rank, almost without solicitation.

*LETTER 9

From the Comte DE BUSSY *to Madame* DE SÉVIGNÉ.

Figuières, July 30, 1654.

Heavens, my lovely cousin, what a fund of wit you possess! how enchantingly you write! how adorable you are! It must be owned, that with so much prudence too, you are under an obligation to me for not loving you more than I do. Faith, I can hardly keep within the limits you have prescribed. Sometimes I blame your insensibility, sometimes I excuse it; but I always esteem you. I have reason not to displease you, and still greater reason to disobey you. What! flatter me, my dear cousin, and yet forbid me to express the extent of my affection! Well, I forbear; I must love you in your own way; but you will some day have to answer before God for the constraint I put upon my feelings, and the evils that will follow in consequence.

---

*LETTER 10

From the Comte DE BUSSY *to Madame* DE SÉVIGNÉ.

From the Camp at Verges, August 17, 1654.

You often tell me, that you would regret me if I were dead; and there is something so delightful in the idea of being regretted by you, that I would willingly die, if a few trifling considerations did not operate in a different way, and make me wish to live. As I have never caught you in an untruth, I cannot help believing you in this instance, and it is probable, that a person, whose eyes glisten with tears at the bare mention of the loss of her friend, would weep plenteously were she to lose him in reality. I believe, therefore, my charming cousin, that you love me; and I am as well pleased with your friendship, as you are with mine: not that I agree with you, that your letter, frank and kind as it is, would disgrace all the *billets-doux* that ever were written; they are things totally distinct from one another. You ought to be satisfied that your friends approve your style, without wishing to decry these sweeter productions, that have never injured you. You are ungrateful, Madame, in abusing them, after the respect they have shown you. For my part, I own myself an advocate for *billets-doux,* but not to the prejudice of your letters: as I said before, they are distinct things, they have their different beauties; your letters have their charms, and *billets-doux* have theirs; but, to speak candidly, your letters would not be so much esteemed, if you would send us sometimes a *billet-doux* instead of them.

You are strangely inveterate, my cousin, against flirts. I do not know whether you will be so when you are fifty; but at all events I shall exercise myself now and then, as an enamoured swain to some beauty or other, that I may act the part with you, if you should happen to change your mind: till then, I shall only entertain for you the purest friendship in the world, since you will have nothing more.

I am glad you are satisfied with the Chief-Controller; it is a proof that he is returning to reason, and does not take things to heart so much as he used to do. When you will not comply with our wishes, we are obliged to yield to yours; we are too happy in being on the list of your friends. Nobody but yourself, in the whole kingdom, could bring a lover to be content with friendship; there are few who continue upon good terms, when they cannot agree to love one another; and that woman, I am persuaded, must have extraordinary merit, who does not convert a disappointed lover into an enemy.

---

*LETTER 11

From Madame DE SÉVIGNÉ *to the Comte* DE BUSSY.

Livry, June 26, 1655.

I had no doubt that you would take some opportunity of bidding me adieu, either at my own house or from the Camp at Landrecy. As I am not a woman of ceremony, I am content with the latter; and have not even thought of being angry, that you failed in coming to me, before you set out. Your reasons presented themselves naturally to my mind, even before you informed me of them; and I am too reasonable to think it strange that you should sleep at a *bagnio* the night before your departure [1]. I am very accommodating to public liberty, and provided these baths be not under my own roof, I am content; my fastidiousness does not extend so far as to wish them banished from the city.

I have not stirred from this desert, since your departure; and, to speak frankly, I am not much afflicted to find you are with the army. I should be an unworthy cousin of so brave a cousin, if I were sorry to see you, during the present campaign, at the head of the finest regiment in France, and in so glorious a post as the one you hold. I dare say you would disown any sentiments less worthy than these; I leave weaker and more tender feelings to the true *bagnio* gentry. Everyone loves in his own way. I profess to be heroic as well as you, and am proud to boast of these sentiments. Some women, perhaps, would think this a little in the old Roman style, and *would thank God they were not Romans, that they might still preserve some feelings of humanity* [2]. But on this subject I can assure them I am not so inhuman as they suppose; and, with all my

[1] Bussy, who was from home when Madame de Sévigné sent to him, wrote her word that he slept that night at the baths; an expression which his cousin did not fail to interpret literally.

[2] Madame de Sévigné parodied the first portion of this quotation from Corneille's tragedy of *The Horaces*.

heroism, I wish your safe return as passionately as they can do. I trust, my dear cousin, you will not doubt the truth of this, nor that I fervently pray your life may be spared. This is the adieu you would have received from me in person, and which I now beg you to accept from here, as I have accepted yours from Landrecy.

---

*LETTER 12

From Madame DE SÉVIGNÉ *to the Comte* DE BUSSY.

Paris, July 14, 1655.

Will you always disgrace your relations? Will you never be weary of making yourself the subject of conversation in every campaign? Do you imagine it can give us pleasure to hear that M. de Turenne has sent word to Court, that you have done nothing worthy of notice at Landrecy[1]? This is really very mortifying to us, and you may easily comprehend how deeply I feel the affronts you bring upon your family. But I know not why I thus amuse myself, for I have no leisure to carry on the jest. I must tell you, therefore, that I am delighted with the success which has attended your exploits. I wrote you a long letter from Livry which I fear you have not received. I should be sorry if it were lost, for you would laugh heartily at its contents.

I was yesterday at Madame de Montglas's; she had just received a letter from you, as also had Madame de Gouville. I expected one likewise, but was disappointed. I suppose you were unwilling to effect too many wonders at once. I am not sorry, however, and shall some day claim a whole cargo for myself. Adieu, my cousin; the *Gazette* speaks of you but slightly, which has given offence to many, and to me especially, for no one can be so much interested in your affairs as myself.

---

[1] Mere jesting. Bussy had merited and obtained the praises of Turenne.

*LETTER 13

From Madame DE SÉVIGNÉ *to the Comte* DE BUSSY.

Paris, July 19, 1655.

This is the third time I have written to you since you left Paris; a sufficient proof that I have nothing upon my mind against you. I received your farewell letter from Landrecy while I was at Livry, and answered it immediately. I see plainly that my letter has never reached you, and I am extremely vexed at it; for, besides its being written with becoming affection, it was in my opinion a very pretty composition; and as it was designed for you only, I am wroth that another should have the pleasure of reading it. I have since written to you by the servant you dispatched here with letters to some of your favourites.[1] I did not amuse myself by quarrelling with you for not remembering me at the same time; but wrote you a line or two at full speed, which, however incoherent, would inform you of the pleasure I received from the success of your regiment at Landrecy. This intelligence came to us in the most acceptable manner possible, by some of the Court, who assured us, that Cardinal Mazarin had spoken very handsomely of you to the King, who afterwards joined with the whole Court in extolling your conduct. You may conceive that my joy was not inconsiderable at hearing all this: but to return to my story. This was the subject of my second letter, and five or six days after I received one from you, full of complaints against me. You see, however, my poor cousin, with how little justice you complain; and hence I draw this fine moral reflection, that we should never condemn a person unheard. This is my justification; another perhaps would have expressed the same thing in fewer words; you must bear with my imperfections, in consideration of my friendship: every

[1] Mesdames de Montglas and de Gouville.

one has his peculiar style; mine, as you see, is by no means laconic.

I never remember to have read anything more entertaining than your description of your leave-taking with your mistress. What you say on the subject of love is so pretty, and so true, that I am astonished I never had the wit to say the same thing, though it has passed in my mind a thousand times. I have even sometimes fancied that friendship does pretty much the same, and, in its way, has its *recommencements* also. But though it is civil of you to tell me the particulars of this affair, I am not inclined to return the compliment, and make you a similar confidence in what passes between the Chief-Controller and me. I should be grieved to have the power of saying anything in the least resembling it. I have always in his company the same circumspection, and the same fears; and these considerably retard the progress he would make in my affection. I think, in the end, he will be weary of renewing a subject in which he is so little likely to succeed. I have seen him but twice during the past six weeks, on account of a journey I had to take. This is all I can, and indeed all I have to tell you upon this subject. Be as careful of my secret as I am of yours; it is as much your interest as mine to be so.

A word of Bartet's [1] adventure. I dare say it has very much amused you; for my part, I thought it a well contrived scheme. A certain lady is accused of busying herself in discovering whether it was intended as an affront, as she had heard the suffering party say it was a mere trifle. He now, it is said, begins to feel the disgrace, and would rather not have been shaved. Adieu, my dear cousin; this is neither a good letter, nor an answer worthy of yours: we are not always in the same humour. I have been indisposed for this week past, and have in consequence

[1] She alludes to M. Bartet. The Duc de Candale, provoked at something he had said, caused half his head to be shaved, and one of his mustachios. As Bartet was Secretary to the King's Cabinet, it might appear a daring act; but it savoured of the licence that prevailed during the Civil wars of the Regency.

lost all my vivacity. Love me always; I do my duty, and sincerely wish you a happy return.

---

*LETTER 14

From the Comte DE BUSSY *to Madame* DE SÉVIGNÉ.

From the Camp at Angres, October 7, 1655.

I am very glad, Madame, to receive assurances from you that the Chief-Controller is disposed to think me in the right in the affair between us. This does not fail to surprise me; and it appears to me very extraordinary, that he had rather complain of Madame de Martel than of me.

Cardinal Mazarin has been a second time to the army, to examine the strength of Condé and Saint-Guilain, that these places may be in a state of security, and that he may do without us till the spring. His Eminence has behaved very handsomely to me, having given me a thousand crowns to finish my campaign.

Chatting with M. de Turenne, two or three days ago, I chanced to mention your name. He asked me, if I saw you sometimes. I told him that I did; that we were of the same family, and were first cousins and that there was no woman I saw oftener than you. He knew you, he said, and had been twenty times to your house without finding you at home. He added, that he esteemed you highly, and that, as a proof of it,[1] *he was anxious to see you, although as a rule he did not have anything to do with women; I told him that you had spoken of him to me, that you had been informed of his courtesy towards yourself, and that you had expressed your appreciation of it to me.*

Now we are upon this subject, Madame, I must tell you, I do not believe there is a person in the world more

[1] In this place something has always been wanting in the text in every edition, but the missing portion has been supplied in this edition and is printed above in italics.

generally beloved than yourself. You are the delight of human nature; in ancient times, altars would have been raised to you; for you surely would have been created the goddess of some attribute or other. In these days, we are not so lavish of incense: we are content with saying, that you are the most virtuous and lovely woman of your age. I know many Princes of the blood, foreign Princes, Lords, Governors, Ministers of State, and Philosophers, who would even twirl the distaff for your sake. What more would you have? You can surely go no further, unless you invade the cloisters, and add even Monks to the number of your adorers.

---

*LETTER 15

From the Comte DE BUSSY *to Madame* DE SÉVIGNÉ.

Noyon, November 7, 1655.

I wait here the coming of the Messiah, that is, the orders for the winter quarters, with great impatience. I am not very dull, considering the time of year. No offence, my dear cousin, I hope; for I feel as if I ought always to be dull, when I am not in your company. I rise late, I go to bed early; I walk out, I come in; I put myself in a passion, I cool again; I pray to God, I sin against him; and with all this, the days are short enough.

As soon as I have leave of absence, I shall go and pay my respects at Compèigne; if I am to be stationed this winter upon the frontiers, I shall be eager to set out, and perhaps shall not have time to bid you adieu; but at all events I shall write to you, and wherever I go, I shall love you with all my heart.

I beg you will give my regards to all my rivals, however numerous they may be.

---

*LETTER 16

From Madame DE SÉVIGNÉ *to the Comte* DE BUSSY.

Paris, November 25, 1655.

You affect great things, M. le Comte: under the pretence that you write like a second Cicero, you believe yourself entitled to ridicule people; the passage you emphasized, in reality, made me laugh heartily; but I am astonished that you found no other equally ludicrous; for, in the way I wrote to you, it is a miracle that you comprehended my meaning; and I see plainly, that either you have a greater share of wit, or that my letter is better, than I imagined. I am glad, however, you have profited by my advice.

I am told, that you have asked leave to stay at the frontiers: as you know, my poor Comte, that mine is a blunt and honest sort of love, I am desirous your request may be granted: this is the road, it is said, to preferment, and you know how interested I am in your welfare; but I shall be pleased either way. If you remain, true friendship will be rewarded; if you will return, affectionate friendship will be satisfied.

Madame de Roquelaure has returned, so handsome, that she yesterday completely challenged the Louvre: this kindled such jealousy in the beauties who were present, that they have resolved, out of spite, she shall not be a party at any of the *after-suppers,* and you know how gay and pleasant they are. Madame de Fiennes would have kept her there yesterday, but it was understood by the Queen's answer, that her presence would be dispensed with.

Adieu, my dear cousin; believe me to be the most faithful friend you have in the world.

---

*LETTER 17

From the Comte DE BUSSY *to Madame* DE SÉVIGNÉ.

From the Camp at Blecy, August 4, 1657.

Your letter is very entertaining, my beautiful cousin; it delighted me exceedingly. What a happiness it is to have a friend who possesses so much good sense! Nothing can be more just than what you say. Whatever politeness I may owe you, I always, as you know, speak my mind freely, and never say what I do not mean: you know, too, that I pique myself a little upon my judgment, since I have even presumed to criticise Chapelain, and have sometimes justly blamed both his sentiments and his style.

I enclose you the copy of a letter I have written to the Marquise d'Uxelles. She sent me word, that if I was an admirer of fine eyes and white teeth, she was equally an admirer of a tender, respectful, and timid lover, and that, not finding me of that description, I might consider myself rejected: she afterwards relented; and when I told her I should quit the chase if she discouraged me, and that she would never catch me again, unless she surprised me under the disguise of Madame la Maréchale; she wrote to me not to despair, and promised to surrender when she arrived at the dignity, the desire of which, by her own account, has almost devoured her.

I have won eight hundred louis within these four or five days; if I stop here, it is because I am feared as a favourite of fortune, and can no longer find any one who will venture to play with me.

Would you know the life of a soldier? It is this. When the army is on its march, we work like horses; when it halts, nothing can exceed our idleness. We are always in extremes. For three or four days, perhaps, we do not close our eyes, or else for three or four days we never quit our beds; we feast, or we starve. Adieu, my beautiful cousin.

[The following Letters, relating to the trial of M. Fouquet, were addressed to the Marquis de Pomponne, who was afterwards Minister of Foreign Affairs.

The trial of Fouquet was not the least curious and least interesting event of the reign of Louis XIV. The plan of ruining him was laid with such odious art, and the conduct of his enemies, many of whom were his judges, was so inveterate, that it would have been impossible not to have been interested for him, even had he been more criminal than he really was. Accused and tried for financial peculations, he was sentenced to banishment for a crime against the State. His crime was a vague plan of resistance and flight into a foreign country, which he had set down upon paper five years before, when the factions of the Fronde divided France, and when he thought he had reason to complain of the ingratitude of Cardinal Mazarin. This plan, which he had wholly forgotten, was found among the papers that were seized at his house.

It is well known, that Louis XIV. was led to believe that Fouquet was a dangerous man. A guard of fifty musketeers were appointed to conduct him to the citadel of Pignerol, the King having changed the sentence of banishment into perpetual imprisonment. It was still apprehended that he had formidable friends. Among these were Pelisson and La Fontaine; one defended him eloquently, and the other bewailed his misfortunes in a very beautiful and pathetic Elegy, in which he even went so far, as to ask the King to pardon him.]

*LETTER 18

From Madame DE SÉVIGNÉ *to M.* DE POMPONNE.

To-day, Monday, November the seventeenth, 1664, M. Fouquet was brought a second time before the Chancellor. He seated himself without ceremony upon the *sellette* [1], as he had done the first time. The Chancellor began by bidding him hold up his hand; he replied, that he had already assigned the reasons which prevented him from taking the oath. The Chancellor then made a long speech to prove the legal authority of the Court, that it had been established by the King, and that the warrants had been confirmed by the Parliament.

M. Fouquet replied, that things were often done under the name of legal authority, which were found upon reflection to be unjust.

[1] Stool on which a prisoner sits.

The Chancellor interrupted him, "What! do you mean to say that the King abuses his power?" M. Fouquet replied, "It is you, Sir, who say it, not I: this was not my idea, and, in my present situation, I cannot but wonder at your wishing to implicate me still further with His Majesty; but, Sir, you yourself well know that we may be mistaken. When you sign a sentence, you believe it just, yet the next day you annul that sentence: thus you see it is possible to change our opinion."

"But," said the Chancellor, "though you will not acknowledge the power of the Court, you answer and put interrogatories, and you are now upon the *sellette*."—"It is true, I am so," he replied, "but it is not voluntarily; I am brought here against my will; it is a power I must obey, and a mortification which God has inflicted upon me, and which I receive from his hands: after the services I have rendered, and the offices I have had the honour to hold, I might have been spared this humiliation."

The Chancellor then continued the examination respecting the pension of the *gabelles*[1], to which the replies of M. Fouquet were extremely satisfactory. The examination will proceed, and I shall send you a faithful account of it; I am anxious to know whether my letters come safely to your hands.

Your sister, who is with our ladies at the Faubourg, has signed[2]; she is now with the community, and seems perfectly satisfied.

Your aunt does not appear at all displeased with her; I did not think it was she who had taken the leap, but some other person. You know, of course, of our defeat at Gigeri[3], and as those who formed the plan wish to throw the failure upon those who executed it, they intend to bring Gadagne to trial: there are some who will be satisfied with nothing less than his head; but the public is persuaded that he could not have advised otherwise than

[1] The Excise upon Salt.

[2] The Formulary: see the first note to the next letter.

[3] The first expedition against Algiers.

he did. M. d'Alet, who excommunicated the subaltern officers of the King, who were for compelling the clergy to sign, is very much talked of here. This will ruin him with your father, while it will bring him into favour with Père Annat [1].

Adieu: the desire of gossiping has seized me, but I must not yield to it: the narrative style should be concise.

---

*LETTER 19

From Madame DE SÉVIGNÉ *to M.* DE POMPONNE.

Thursday, November 20, 1664.

M. Fouquet was examined this morning respecting the gold mark; he answered extremely well; several of the judges bowed to him; the Chancellor reproved them, and said, that, as he was a Breton, it was not the custom. "It is because you are Bretons that you bow so low to M. Fouquet." In returning on foot from the Arsenal, M. Fouquet asked what the workmen were doing: he was told they were making the vase of a fountain; he went to them, and gave his opinion, and afterwards returned smiling to d'Artagnan. "You wonder, no doubt," said he, "at my interfering; but I formerly understood these things well."—The friends of M. Fouquet, and I among the rest, are pleased at this delightful composure: others call it affectation: such is the world. Madame Fouquet, his mother, has given the Queen a plaster, that has cured her convulsions, which, properly speaking, were nothing but the vapours.

Many, believing what they wish, imagine that the Queen will, on this account, intercede with His Majesty to pardon the unfortunate prisoner; but I, who hear a great deal of the kindness of this country, do not believe a word of it. The fame the plaster has earned is wonder-

[1] A Jesuit, confessor of Louis XIV.

ful; everybody says that Madame Fouquet is a Saint, and has the power of working miracles.

To-day, Friday, the twenty-first, M. Fouquet has been questioned respecting the Wax and Sugar taxes. At certain objections that were raised, and which appeared to him ridiculous, he lost his temper. This was going a little too far, and there was a haughtiness in his manner that gave offence. He will correct himself; for this mode of proceeding is by no means advisable; but patience will sometimes escape; it seems to me as if I should have done the same.

I have been at Sainte-Marie, where I saw your aunt, who appeared to be swallowed up in devotion; she was at mass, and in quite a religious ecstasy. Your sister was looking very pretty; fine eyes, and great animation: the poor child fainted this morning: she is very much indisposed: her aunt is uniformly kind to her. M. de Paris has given her a sort of defeasance, which gained her heart, and induced her to sign the wicked Formulary [1]. I have not mentioned the subject to either of them: M. de Paris [2] had forbidden it. But I must give you an idea of prejudice: our sisters of Sainte-Marie said to me, "God be praised, who has at length touched the heart of this poor child! she is now in the way of obedience and salvation." From thence I went to Port Royal, where I found a certain great recluse [3] of your acquaintance, who accosted me with "Well, this silly goose has signed: God, in short, has abandoned her; she is lost."—I thought I should have died with laughing, when I reflected on the different effects of prejudice: in this, you see the world in its true mirror. I think extremes should always be avoided.

Saturday evening. M. Fouquet entered the Cham-

[1] This relates to the condemnation of the five propositions of Jansenius: the clergy of France protested against them, and drew up a Formulary, which the nuns of Port Royal and many others refused to sign; this refusal, in the end, caused their dispersion.

[2] The then Archbishop of Paris was the sage Péréfixe.

[3] No doubt the celebrated doctor Arnauld d'Andilly.

ber this morning, and was interrogated upon the subject of Town-tolls; he was attacked weakly and defended himself ably. Between you and I, this is not the worst part of the business. Some good angel must have informed him, that he had carried himself too proudly; for he altered his manner to-day, and the judges altered theirs, by not bowing to him. The examination will not be resumed till Wednesday; and I shall not write to you till then. I have only to add, that if you continue to pity me so much, for the trouble I take in writing to you, and desire me not to go on, I shall think my letters tire you, and that you do not like the fatigue of answering them; but I promise not to write such long ones in future, and I absolve you from answering them, though I prize your letters highly. After these declarations, I should think you would not attempt to interrupt the course of my bulletins. In flattering myself that I contribute a little to your pleasure, I add greatly to my own. I have so few opportunities of proving my friendship and esteem for you, that I must not neglect such as present themselves. Pray make my compliments to your family and your neighbours. The Queen is much better.

---

*LETTER 20

From Madame DE SÉVIGNÉ *to M.* DE POMPONNE.

Monday, November 24, 1664.

If I know my own heart, it is I who am the party obliged, by your receiving so kindly the information I send you. Do you think I have no pleasure in writing to you? Believe me, I have a great deal, and am as much gratified in writing, as you can be in reading what I write. The sentiments you entertain upon the subject of my letter are very natural; hope is common to us all, without our knowing why; but it supports the heart. I dined at Sainte-Marie de Saint-Antoine two days ago; the Lady Abbess related to me the particulars of four visits she has received from Puis *** [1], within the last three months, at which I am very much astonished. He came to tell her, that the now blessed Bishop of Geneva (St. François de Sales) had been so extremely kind to him during his illness last summer, that he could not help feeling most strongly the obligations he owed him; and he requested her to obtain the prayers of the community for the deceased. He gave her, for the accomplishment of his holy purpose, a thousand crowns, and entreated her to show him the Bishop's heart. When he was at the *grille,* he fell upon his knees, and remained full a quarter of an hour, bathed in tears, apostrophising this heart, and praying for a spark of the divine fire which had consumed it. The Lady Abbess also melted into tears; and gave him the relics of the deceased, with which he hurried away. During these visits, he appeared so earnest about his salvation, so disgusted with the Court, so transported with the idea of his conversion, that a person more clear-sighted than the Abbess would have been deceived. She contrived to introduce the subject of Fouquet; he answered her as a man who was interested in nothing but religion; that he was not sufficiently known; that justice would be done him, agreeably to the will of God, if from no other consideration. I never was more surprised than at this conversation. If you ask me what I think of it, I must answer, that I do not know; that it is perfectly unintelligible to me; that I cannot see the drift of this comedy, nor, if it is not a comedy, how the steps he has since taken are to be reconciled with his fine speeches.

Time must explain all this, for it is at present perfectly enigmatical. Do not mention it, for the Lady Abbess desired me not to make the circumstance known.

I have seen M. Fouquet's mother. She told me she had sent the plaster to the Queen by Madame de Charost [2].

[1] This name appears to have been altered, and ought, as will be seen farther on, to have been Pussort.

[2] Fouquet's daughter.

The effect was certainly wonderful: in less than an hour the Queen felt her head relieved, and so great a discharge of offensive matter took place, that had it remained it might have suffocated her in the next fit. The Queen said aloud, that it was this matter which had occasioned the convulsions of the preceding night, and that Madame de Fouquet had cured her. The Queen Mother thought the same, and said so to the King, who did not attend to her. The physicians, who had not been consulted in applying the plaster, withheld their sentiments on the subject, but made their court at the expense of truth. The same day these poor women threw themselves at the feet of the King, who took no notice of them. Everybody is acquainted with the circumstance of the cure; but no one knows what will come of it: we must wait for what is to follow with patience.

(Wednesday, November 26.)

M. Fouquet was interrogated again this morning, but the Chancellor's manner was changed; it seems as if he were ashamed of receiving his lesson every day from Boucherat [1]. He told the Reporter to read the article, upon which he wished to examine the accused; and the reading lasted so long, that it was half past ten o'clock before it was finished. He then said, "Let Fouquet be brought in;" but corrected himself immediately, by saying "M. Fouquet;" as, however, he had not directed the prisoner to be sent for, he was still at the Bastille. A messenger was then dispatched for him, and he arrived at eleven o'clock. He was questioned respecting the Town-tolls, and answered extremely well; but he was a little at a loss as to certain dates, which would have injured him considerably, if the examiner had been skillful and awake; but, instead of this, the Chancellor was gently dozing. This was observed by M. Fouquet, who would have laughed heartily,

[1] Boucherat, then Master of Requests, and afterwards Chancellor, had been appointed to put the seals on the papers of the Chief-Controller. He was on the Commission charged with the prosecution.

if he had dared. At length, the Chancellor roused himself, and continued the examination; and though M. Fouquet rested too much on a prop, that might have failed him, the event proved that he knew what he was about; for, in his misfortune, he has certain little advantages that belong exclusively to himself. If they go on so slowly every day, the trial will last a long time.

I shall write to you every evening; but I shall not send my letter till Saturday or Sunday evening: it will give you an account of the proceedings of Thursday, Friday, and Saturday, and I will contrive that you shall receive one on Thursday, informing you of the proceedings of Monday, Tuesday, and Wednesday: in this way your letters will not be long detained. I conjure you to give my compliments to your recluse, and to your better half. I say nothing of your dear neighbour; it will soon be my turn to give you news of her myself.

---

*LETTER 21

From Madame DE SÉVIGNÉ *to M.* DE POMPONNE.

Thursday, November 27, 1664.

The examination upon the subject of the Town-tolls was resumed to-day. The Chancellor kindly endeavoured to drive M. Fouquet to extremities, and to embarrass him, but he did not succeed. M. Fouquet acquitted himself admirably: he did not come into the Chamber of Justice till eleven o'clock, because the Chancellor made the Reporter read as before; but in spite of this parade of justice, he said the worst he could of our poor friend. The Reporter[1] always took his part, because the Chancellor evidently leaned to the other side of the question. At last, he said, "Here is a charge to which the accused will not be able to answer."—"And here, Sir," said the Reporter,

[1] The Reporter was M. d'Ormesson, one of the most respectable magistrates of his time.

"is a plaster that will cure the weakness;" he made an excellent justification of him, and then added: "In the place in which I stand, Sir, I shall always speak the truth, in whatever form it presents itself to me."

This allusion to a plaster called forth a smile from the audience, as it reminded them of the one that has lately made so much noise at Court. The accused was then brought in; he only remained an hour in Court; and, on his leaving it, M. d'Ormesson was complimented by several persons upon his firmness.

I must relate to you what I myself did. Some ladies proposed to me to accompany them to a house exactly opposite the Arsenal, where we could see the return of our poor friend. I was masked [1]; but my eye caught him the moment he was in view. M. d'Artagnan was at his side, and fifty musketeers about thirty or forty steps behind him. He appeared thoughtful. The moment I saw him, my legs trembled, and my heart beat so violently, that I could scarcely support myself. In approaching us to re-enter his dungeon, M. d'Artagnan pointed out to him that we were there, and he saluted us with the same delightful smile you have so often witnessed. I do not believe he recognised me; but, I own, I was strangely affected, when I saw him enter the little door. If you knew the misfortune of having a heart like mine, I am sure you would pity me; but from what I know of you, I do not think you have much the advantage of me in this point. I have been to see your dear neighbour. I pity you as much at losing her, as I rejoice at her being with us. We have had a good deal of conversation upon the subject of our poor friend; she has seen Sapho [2], who has considerably

[1] It was still the custom for ladies to wear masks when they went abroad; a custom which is retained in Corneille's plays, and which was brought from Italy by the Medicis, with many other customs equally disagreeable. These masks of black velvet, to which the *loups* succeeded, were intended as a preservative to the complexion.

[2] Mademoiselle Scuderi, sister of the author, known under this name by an unfortunate fertility of imagination: a woman who had more wit than her writings display, though they display a great deal.

raised her spirits. I shall go there to-morrow, to recruit my own; for I often feel the want of consolation; it is not, that I do not hear a thousand things, that should inspire hope; but, alas! my imagination is so lively, that everything, which is uncertain, destroys me.

Friday, November 28.

The Court opened early this morning. The Chancellor said he had now to speak of the four loans: d'Ormesson observed, that it was a very unimportant affair, and one upon which no blame could be attached to M. Fouquet, as he had declared from the beginning. An attempt was made to contradict him: he begged leave to explain the matter according to his own view of it, and desired his colleagues to listen to him. The Court was attentive, and he convinced them that it was a very trifling business. The accused was then ordered to be brought in; it was eleven o'clock. You will remark that he has never been more than an hour upon the *sellette*. The Chancellor still wished to speak of the loans. M. Fouquet requested he might be allowed to state what he had omitted the day before, respecting the Town-tolls; leave was given him, and he said wonders. The Chancellor asked him, "Have you had your acquittance for the disbursement of this sum?" He replied that he had, but that it was conjointly with other things, which he had marked, and which will come in their course. "But," said the Chancellor, "at the time you received these acquittances, you had not incurred the expenses?"—"True," replied M. Fouquet, "but the sums were set apart for the purpose."—"This is not enough," said the Chancellor.—"Pardon me, Sir," said M. Fouquet: "when I gave you your appointments, for instance, I sometimes received the acquittance a month beforehand, and as the sum was set apart, it was exactly the same, as if it had been paid."—"That is true," said the Chancellor; "I was much indebted to you."—M. Fouquet replied, that he had no intention to reproach him, and that he was at that time happy to serve him; but the circumstance had occurred to his mind, as an instance in point, and he could not help making use of it.

The Court has closed till Monday. They seem determined to prolong the affair as much as possible. Puis *** has promised to give the accused as few opportunities of speaking as he can. The fact is, they are afraid of him. They would therefore interrogate him summarily, and even pass over some of the articles; but he is determined they shall not do this, nor will he suffer them to judge his cause without his being permitted to justify himself upon every separate head of accusation. Puis* * * is in continual apprehension of offending Petit[1]. He excused himself the other day by saying that M. Fouquet had certainly spoken too long, but that he had no means of interrupting him. Chamillart is constantly behind the screen, whenever the examinations take place: he hears all that is said, and offers to go to the judges, and explain the reasons by which he is led to draw such opposite conclusions. All this is irregular, and shows a strong inveteracy against the unfortunate prisoner. I own I have no longer any hope. Adieu, Sir, till Monday. I wish you could see my heart; you would then be convinced of the sincerity of a friendship which you profess to prize.

---

*LETTER 22

From Madame DE SÉVIGNÉ *to M.* DE POMPONNE.

(Monday, December 1, 1664.)

Two days ago, every one believed that it was intended to protract M. Fouquet's affair as much as possible; but now the reverse of this appears to be the case, and the interrogations are hurried over in a most extraordinary manner. This morning, the Chancellor took his paper and read, as he would an inventory, ten heads of accusation,

[1] See note, page 33.

without giving the accused time to reply. M. Fouquet said, "I do not wish, Sir, to prolong the business; but I entreat you to give me time to answer the charges that are brought against me: you question me, and it appears as if you did not wish me to reply; but it is of consequence to me to speak. There are many articles I must explain; and it is but justice that I should answer to all those which are formally alleged against me." The Court was then obliged to attend, contrary to the wishes of the ill-disposed, who could not bear to hear him defend himself so ably. He answered extremely well to every accusation. The trial will now go on, but will be conducted so rapidly, that I expect the examination will close this week. I have just been supping at the Nevers Mansion; the mistress of the house and I conversed a good deal upon this subject. We are uneasy to a degree, which you only can comprehend, for I have just received your letter; it surpasses even my own feelings upon the subject. You put my modesty to too great a trial, in asking me, upon what terms I am with you and your dear recluse. It seems to me, that I see him, and hear him say what you tell me: I am quite piqued that it was not I who *metamorphosed Pierrot to Tartuffe*[1]; it was so natural, that if I had half the wit you ascribe to me, it would have flowed mechanically from my pen.

I must relate to you a little anecdote, which is perfectly true, and which cannot fail to amuse you. The King has lately employed himself in making verses; Messieurs de Saint-Aignan and Dangeau put him in the way of it. He wrote a little madrigal the other day, with which he was not much pleased. One morning he said to the Maréchal de Gramont, "M. le Maréchal, read this little madrigal, if you please, and tell me if you ever saw so silly a one: because it is known, that I have lately been fond of poetry, they bring me all the nonsense that is written."—The Maréchal, having read it, said to the King, "Your Majesty is an excellent judge of everything: this is certainly, without exception, the most silly and ridiculous

[1] The Chancellor Seguier's name was Pierre.

madrigal I ever read."—The King laughed, and continued, "Must not the writer be a great fool?"—"There is no other name for him," said the Maréchal.—"O!" said the King, "how delighted I am that you have spoken your sentiments so freely! I am myself the author of it."—"Ah, Sire, what treason have I uttered! I entreat Your Majesty to give it me again. I read it hastily."—"No, M. le Maréchal; the first sentiments are always the most natural."—The King was very much entertained at this little frolic; but those about him thought it the most cruel thing that could be done to an old courtier. For myself, I love to make reflections, and I wish the King would reflect in like manner on this adventure, that he might see how far he is from knowing the truth. We are upon the point of experiencing a still more painful instance of royal delusion, in the repurchase of our Bonds, at an expense that will send us all to the workhouse: the emotion it occasions is great, but the hardship is still greater. Do you not think this is undertaking too much at once? The loss of a part of my income is not the point that affects me the most.

Tuesday, December 2.

Our dear unfortunate friend spoke for two hours this morning, but so uncommonly well, that several persons could not help expressing their admiration. Among others, M. de Renard said, "This man, it must be owned, is incomparable; he never spoke so well in the Parliament; he maintains his self-possession better than he has ever done." The subject was the six millions, and his own expenses. Nothing could exceed what he said. I shall write to you on Thursday and on Friday: these will be the last days of the examination, and I shall go on to the end.

God grant my last letter may contain the information I so ardently wish. Adieu, my dear Sir: desire our recluse (Arnauld) to pray for our poor friend. I heartily embrace you both, and, for modesty's sake, I include your wife.

Tranquillity reigns throughout the family of the unfortunate Fouquet. It is said, that M. de Nesmond declared on his death-bed, that his greatest sorrow was that he had not challenged these two judges; that if he had lived to the end of the trial he would have repaired his fault, and that he prayed God to pardon his error.

Tuesday, December 2.

M. Fouquet, as I observed before, spoke to-day two whole hours, upon the subject of the six millions: he commanded attention, and performed wonders. Everyone was affected in his way. Pussort made gestures of disbelief and disapprobation, that shocked every honest man in Court.

When M. Fouquet had done, M. Pussort rose impetuously, and said, "Thank God, it can never be said that he has not had his belly-full of talk."—What say you to this speech? was it not worthy of a judge? It is said that the Chancellor is very much alarmed at the erysipelas that occasioned the death of M. de Nesmond, fearing there may be a repetition of the judgment in store for himself. If the apprehension could inspire him with the sentiments of a man about to appear before God, it would be something: but it will be said of him, I fear, as of Argante, *e mori come visse* [1]: he died as he lived.

Wednesday, December 3.

I have received your letter; it has proved to me that I have not obliged a person who is ungrateful; nothing can be more kind, nothing more gratifying. I must be wholly exempt from vanity to be insensible to such praises. I assure you, I am delighted at the good opinion you entertain of my heart, and I further assure you, without meaning compliment for compliment, that my esteem for you infinitely surpasses the power of ordinary language

[1] *Gerusalemme Liberata*, canto 19; the verse runs thus:
Moriva Argante, e tal moria qual visse.

to express, and that I experience real pleasure and consolation in being able to inform you of events, in which we are both so much interested. I am very glad your dear recluse takes his part in them: I supposed you would make them known also to your incomparable neighbour. You gratify me extremely in telling me, that I have made some progress in her heart; there is no one in whose affections I would more gladly establish myself, and when I would indulge in a little gaiety, I think of her, and her Enchanted Palace. But I return to business, from which I have been insensibly led, to tell you of the sentiments I entertain for yourself and your amiable friend.

M. Fouquet was upon the *sellette* again to-day. The Abbé d'Effiat bowed to him, as he passed. In returning his bow, he said to him, with the same enchanting smile we have so often observed, "Sir, I am your very humble servant." The Abbé was so much affected, that he could not speak.

As soon as M. Fouquet was in the Chamber, the Chancellor desired him to be seated. He replied, "Sir, you took advantage yesterday of my placing myself upon the *sellette*: you infer from my doing so, that I acknowledge the authority of the Court; as that is the case, I beg leave to stand." The Chancellor then told him he might withdraw. M. Fouquet replied, "I do not mean by this, to advance any new objection: I only wish, to make my protestation, as usual, and, the charge being cited against me, to be permitted to reply."

This was agreed to; he then seated himself, and the examination respecting the pension of the *gabelles* was resumed, to which he replied admirably. If this mode continue, the interrogations will be favourable to him. The spirit and firmness he displays are the subject of general conversation in Paris. He has asked one thing of a friend, which makes me tremble: he has entreated him to let him know his sentence, whether favourable or otherwise, in some private way by signal, the instant it is pronounced, that he may have time to reconcile himself to his fate before it be announced to him officially; adding, that if he has half an hour to prepare himself, he will hear without emotion the worst that can be told him. This has made me weep, and I am certain it will affect you also very painfully.

There were few persons at the examination, on account of the Queen's illness; she was supposed to be dying, but is now somewhat better. Yesterday evening she received the viaticum. It was the most affecting and solemn spectacle that can be imagined, to see the King and the whole Court going for the Holy Sacrament, and conducting it to the palace. It was received with a profusion of lights. The Queen made an effort to rise, and took it with a devotion that reduced every one to tears. It was not without difficulty that she had been brought to consent; the King was the only one who could make her listen to reason: to every other person she said, that she was very willing to receive the communion, but not the viaticum: it was full two hours before she could be prevailed upon.

The general approbation that is given to M. Fouquet's answers, is very grating to Petit[1]. It is even thought he will engage Puis* * * to feign illness, in order to interrupt the torrent of admiration, and to have time himself to take breath at this, and other instances of his ill success. I am the most obedient servant of the dear recluse, of your lady, and the adorable Amalthée.

---

[1] Petit is a feigned name, meant either for Le Tellier or Colbert. With regard to Puis***, as, from the sense of the expressions, he must be one of the judges against Fouquet, there is little doubt that Pussort is the person alluded to; and what is said of him in the preceding Letters must be so understood.

It may further be remarked, that the conduct of Colbert and Le Tellier, in this business, was extremely well characterized, by a criticism of the great Turenne, who interested himself warmly for Fouquet. To some one who blamed the violence of Colbert, and praised the moderation of Le Tellier, Turenne replied, "True, Sir; M. Colbert has most desire that he should be hanged, and M. Le Tellier most fear lest he should not be."

*LETTER 23

From Madame DE SÉVIGNÉ *to M.* DE POMPONNE.

Thursday, December 4, 1664.

At length the examinations are over. M. Fouquet entered the Chamber this morning. The Chancellor ordered his *accusation* to be read throughout. M. Fouquet spoke first upon the subject. "I believe, Sir," said he, "you can derive nothing from this document, but the effect it has just produced, of overwhelming me with confusion."—The Chancellor replied, "You have yourself heard and seen by it, that your regard for the State, which you have so much insisted upon in Court, was not so considerable, but that you would have embroiled it, from one end to the other."—"Sir," replied M. Fouquet, "this idea occurred to me only in the depth of the despair in which the Cardinal often placed me; especially when, after contributing more than any man in the world to his return to France, I found myself repaid by the basest ingratitude. I had a letter from himself, and one from the Queen-Mother, in proof of what I say; but they have been taken away with my papers, as have several other letters. It is to be lamented, that I did not burn this unfortunate paper, which had so completely escaped my mind and my memory, that I have been nearly two years without thinking of it, or knowing even that it existed. However this affair may terminate, I disown it with my whole heart, and I entreat you, Sir, to believe, that my regard for the person and service of the King, has never been in the slightest degree diminished."—"It is very difficult to believe this," said the Chancellor, "when we see such contrary sentiments expressed at a different period."—M. Fouquet replied, "At no period, Sir, even though at the hazard of my life, have I ever abandoned the King's person; and, at the time in question, you, Sir, were at the head of the Council of his enemies, and your relations gave free passage to the army against him."

The Chancellor felt this stroke; but our poor friend was irritated, and therefore not quite master of himself. The subject of his expenses was afterwards introduced. "I undertake," said he, "to prove, that I have not incurred a single expense, which, either by means of my private income, with which the Cardinal was well acquainted, or my appointments, or my wife's fortune, I was not able to afford; and if I do not prove this satisfactorily, I consent to be treated with the utmost ignominy."—In short, this interrogation lasted two hours; M. Fouquet defended himself ably, but with a degree of warmth and petulance; the reading of the *accusation* having ruffled him exceedingly.

When he had left the Court, the Chancellor said, "This is the last time we shall interrogate him." M. Poncet then went up to the Chancellor, and said, "You have made no mention, Sir, of the proofs there are that he had attempted to put his project against the State into execution."—The Chancellor replied, "They are not, Sir, sufficiently strong; he would have refuted them too easily."—Upon which Sainte-Hélène and Pussort said, "Everyone is not of that opinion."—This is a subject to muse upon. The rest to-morrow.

Friday, December 5.

This morning the subject of the Requests was mentioned, which are of little importance except that there are persons, not ill disposed, who wish the sentence to refer to them. The business on the side of the prosecution is at an end. It is now M. d'Ormesson's turn to speak; he is to recapitulate the several matters. This will occupy the whole of the next week, during which the time we shall pass can scarcely be called living. For myself, you would hardly know me, and I do not think I can hold out so long. M. d'Ormesson has desired me not to see him again till the business is over: he is in the conclave, and will have intercourse with no one. He affects great reserve; he listens to me, but does not answer. I had the pleasure, in bidding him adieu, to acquaint him with my sentiments. I will inform you of all I hear. God grant my last tidings may be good: I desire it fervently. I assure you we are all very much to be pitied. I mean you and I, and all who, like ourselves, are interested in the event. Adieu, my dear Sir: I am so dull this evening, and my heart is so much oppressed, that I must conclude.

---

*LETTER 24

From Madame DE SÉVIGNÉ *to M.* DE POMPONNE.

Tuesday, December 9, 1664.

I assure you the days pass very tediously; suspense is extremely painful; but it is an evil to which the whole family of the unfortunate prisoner is habituated. I have seen, and cannot sufficiently express my admiration of them. It seems as if they had never known, never read, the events that have taken place in former times; what surprises me most is, that Sapho is just like the rest; she, whose understanding and penetration are unlimited. When I reflect upon this circumstance, I persuade myself, or, at least, I wish to persuade myself, that they know more of the matter than I do. When I reason too with others, on whose judgment I can rely, and who are less prejudiced, because less interested, I find all our measures so just, that it will be really a miracle, if the business does not terminate according to our wishes. We are sometimes only lost by a single voice, but that voice is everything. I remember, however, the *recusations,* respecting which these poor women thought themselves so sure, and we lost them by five to seventeen; since that time their confidence has been my distrust. Yet I have a little spark of hope in my heart; I hardly know whence it comes, nor whither it would lead, nor is it sufficient to make me sleep in peace. I talked over this affair yesterday with Madame du Plessis [1]: I can see nobody, but those who will converse with me on the subject, and who are of the same opinion as myself. She hopes, as I do, without knowing the reason. "Why do you hope?"—"Because I do:" this is our answer: a notable one, it must be confessed. I told her, with the greatest sincerity in the world, that if the sentence should be in conformity to our wishes, the height of my joy would be to dispatch instantly a man on horseback with the pleasing intelligence to you; and that the pleasure of picturing the delight I should give you, would render my own delight complete. She perfectly agreed with me; and our imagination gave us more than a quarter of an hour's holiday on the occasion. I must correct my last day's report of the examination respecting the project against the State. I related it to you exactly as I heard it; but the same person has since tasked his memory, and told it to me over again more accurately. Everybody has heard it from the different judges. After M. Fouquet had said, that the only effect that could be drawn from this *accusation,* was the confusion the reading of it had occasioned him, the Chancellor observed, "You cannot deny that this is a crime against the State."—"I confess, Sir," he replied, "that it is a foolish and extravagant thing, but not a crime against the State. I entreat you, gentlemen," said he, turning towards the judges, "to suffer me to explain what constitutes a State crime: not that I consider you less capable of defining it than myself; but I have had more time perhaps than you to examine the question. A crime against the State, is when a person, holding an important office, and being in the secrets of a Prince, suddenly goes over to the side of his enemy, engages his whole family in the same interests, opens the gates of a city, of which he is

[1] Madame du Plessis-Guénégaud. It does not seem possible that it could be Madame du Plessis Bellière, the intimate friend of Fouquet. He had commissioned her to take his papers from his house at St. Mandé. She was not in time to execute it. She was at first exiled, and afterwards recalled. She died in 1705, aged 100 years.

the Governor, to the foe, shuts them against his lawful Sovereign, and reveals to his enemy the secrets of the State. This, gentlemen, is what is called a State crime."—The Chancellor did not know which way to look, and the judges could scarcely refrain from laughter. This is the truth without any embellishment. You will agree with me, that nothing could be more spirited, more delicate in its satire, and at the same time more diverting.

The whole kingdom knows and admires the prisoner's reply on this occasion. He afterwards entered minutely into his defence, and said what I told you before. I should have been quite unhappy, if you had not known this circumstance, and our dear friend would have lost much by it. This morning M. d'Ormesson began the recapitulation. He spoke well and clearly. On Thursday he will give his opinion; his colleague will then speak for two days: it will take several more for the rest to give their opinions. Some of the judges say, that they will enlarge a great deal upon the subject, so that we have to languish in expectation till next week. In this state of suspense we can scarcely be said to live.

Wednesday, December 10.

M. d'Ormesson has continued the recapitulation: he has done wonders, that is, he has spoken with extraordinary clearness, intelligence, and ability. Pussort interrupted him five or six times, with no other intention than to embarrass him, and prevent his speaking so well: he said to him in one instance, where his argument went strongly in favour of M. Fouquet, "Sir, we shall speak after you, we shall speak after you."

---

*LETTER 25

From Madame DE SÉVIGNÉ *to M.* DE POMPONNE.

Thursday, December 11, 1664.

M. d'Ormesson has not yet finished. When he came to the article of the gold mark, Pussort said, "This speaks strongly against the accused."—"It may be so," said M. d'Ormesson, "but there are no proofs."—"What!" said Pussort, "have not the two officers been examined?"—"No," replied M. d'Ormesson.—"It cannot be," said Pussort.—"I can find no such thing in the proceedings," said M. d'Ormesson.—Upon this, Pussort rose in a fury, and said, "Sir, you ought rather to say, I find here a very gross omission."—M. d'Ormesson made no answer, but if Pussort had addressed another word to him, he would have replied, "I am here, Sir, as a judge, and not as an informer." You may remember what I once said to you at Fresne, that M. d'Ormesson would not discover the omission till there was no remedy. The Chancellor also interrupted M. d'Ormesson several times: he told him it was not necessary to speak of the project. This must be from malice; for many will suppose it a great crime, and the Chancellor would be glad that the proofs, which are truly ridiculous, should be withheld, that the idea which prevails might not be weakened. As, however, it is one of the articles of the indictment, M. d'Ormesson will not omit it. He will finish to-morrow. Sainte-Hélène will speak on Saturday. On Monday the two Reporters will give their opinion, and on Tuesday, the whole committee will assemble early in the morning, and not separate till judgment be passed. I tremble when I think of that day. The hopes of the family are very sanguine. Foucault goes about everywhere, and shows a writing of the King's, in which he is made to say, that he should think it very improper if any of the judges leaned towards the prisoner, from the circumstance of his papers being taken away:

that it was he who ordered it to be done: that there is not one that can be of use to the prisoner in his defence; that they are papers that relate merely to his office; and that he makes this known, that the judges may not draw improper inferences. What say you to this magnanimous proceeding? Are you not grieved that a Prince, who would love justice and truth if he were left to himself, should be prevailed upon to act thus? He said the other day at his levee, that Fouquet was a dangerous man: this has been put into his head by some one. In short, our enemies no longer keep within bounds; they run at full speed; threats, promises, everything is resorted to; but if God be on our side, we shall be stronger than they. You will perhaps have another letter from me: if we have good news, I shall dispatch an express to you, with all possible expedition; but how I shall act, or what will become of me, in any other case, I am at a loss to conjecture. A thousand compliments to our recluse, and to your better half. Pray earnestly to God for our friend.

Saturday, December 13.

After having fixed and changed, and fixed and changed again, it was at length resolved, that M. d'Ormesson should give his opinion to-day: that Sunday might pass over, and Sainte-Hélène begin anew on Monday, which would make a stronger impression. M. d'Ormesson's opinion was, that the accused should be sentenced to perpetual banishment, and his property confiscated to the King. M. d'Ormesson has by this means established his reputation as a judge. This sentence is a little severe [1], but let us pray that no worse counsel may be given; it is always glorious to be the first in an assault.

---

[1] Severe as it was, the King aggravated the punishment still more. Fouquet's dilapidations were certainly criminal, but Cardinal Mazarin gave less, and took much more. The licentiousness of the times, and the force of example, were an excuse, if any excuse could be made.

*LETTER 26

From Madame de Sévigné *to M.* de Pomponne.

Wednesday, December 17, 1664.

You languish, my dear friend, after the intelligence, and so do we. I was sorry I sent you word that judgment would be pronounced on Tuesday; for, not hearing from me, you must have thought it was all over; but our hopes are as strong as ever. I informed you, on Saturday, in what way M. d'Ormesson had reported the cause, and how he had voted; but I did not sufficiently express the extraordinary esteem he has acquired by his conduct in this business. I have heard several of his profession say, that his speech was a master-piece; that he explained himself with great clearness, and rested his opinion upon the most convincing arguments: it was eloquence and grace combined. In short, no man had ever a finer opportunity of making himself known, and no man ever made a better use of it. If he had wished to open his door to congratulations, his house would have been crowded; but he was too modest for this, and kept out of the way. His colleague, Sainte-Hélène, indignant at his success, spoke on Monday and Tuesday: he resumed the summation of the case weakly and miserably, reading what he had to say, without adding any new circumstance, or giving a different turn to it: he voted, but did not assign his reasons, that M. Fouquet should lose his head for his crime against the State; and to gain votes on his side, he played the Normand, and alleged, that it was probable the King, who alone could do it, would remit the sentence and pardon him. It was yesterday he performed this brilliant action, at which we were as much grieved, as we had before been satisfied with the conduct of M. d'Ormesson.

This morning Pussort spoke for four hours, but with so much vehemence, fury, rage, and rancour, that several of the judges were shocked; and it is thought his intemperance will do more good than harm to our poor friend. He even redoubled his violence towards the end, and said, upon the subject of the crime against the State, that the example of a certain Spaniard, who had so great a horror for a rebel, that he ordered his house to be burned, because Charles de Bourbon had passed through it, ought to make us blush at our moderation; that we had much greater reason to hold in abhorrence the crime of M. Fouquet; that the halter and the gibbet were the only proper punishments for him; but that, in consideration of the high offices he had held, and the noble families to which he was related, he would relax his opinion, and vote with M. de Sainte-Hélène, that he be beheaded.

What say you to this moderation? Is it because he is the uncle of M. Colbert, and was excepted against, that he conducts himself so generously? For my part, I can scarcely contain myself, when I think of this scandalous proceeding. I do not know whether judgment will be pronounced to-morrow, or the business be protracted to the end of the week. We have still many difficulties to encounter; but perhaps some one will side with M. d'Ormesson, whose opinion at present stands alone.

But I have to beg your attention to two or three little incidents, which are no less extraordinary than true. In the first place, then, a comet made its appearance, about four days ago. It was announced, at first, by some women only, who were laughed at for their pains; but it has now been seen by everyone. M. d'Artagnan sat up last night, and saw it very distinctly. M. de Neuré, a great astronomer, says it is of considerable magnitude. M. du Foin has seen it, with three or four other learned men. I have not seen it myself, but I intend sitting up to-night for the purpose: it appears about three o'clock. I tell you of this, ignorant whether you will be pleased or displeased with the intelligence.

Berrier, in the literal sense of the word, is become mad; he has been bled profusely, and is in a perfect frenzy. He raves of wheels and gibbets, and has even mentioned particular trees: he declares he is going to be hanged, and makes so dreadful a noise, that his keepers are obliged to chain him. This is evidently a judgment of Providence, and a very just one. A criminal of the name of Lamothe, who was in prison, and about to be tried, has deposed, that Messieurs de Bezemaux and Chamillard [1], and B*** (they add also Pussort, or Poncet, but of him I am not so certain) urged him several times to implicate M. Fouquet and Lorme; promising if he would do so, that they would obtain his pardon; but he refused, and published the circumstance in Court, before his trial took place. He was condemned to the galleys. The wife and mother of M. Fouquet have procured a copy of the deposition, and will present it to-morrow at the Chamber. Perhaps it will not be received, because the judges are now giving their opinions; but it may be made known, and must produce a strong impression on the Court. Is not all this very extraordinary?

I must tell you also of an heroic act of Masnau. He had been dangerously ill for a whole week of a bladder complaint; he took a variety of medicines, and was at last bled at midnight. The next morning, at seven o'clock, he insisted on being carried to the Chamber of Justice, where he suffered the most excruciating pain. The Chancellor saw him turn pale, and said, "This is not a fit place for you, Sir; you had better retire."—"True, Sir," he replied, "but I may as well die here." The Chancellor perceiving him ready to faint, and finding him bent upon remaining, said, "Well, Sir, retire; we will wait for you." Upon this he went out for a quarter of an hour, during which time he passed two stones, of so enormous a size, that it might be considered as a miracle, if men were deserving that God should work miracles in their favour. This worthy man then returned into Court, gay and cheerful, everyone astonished at the adventure.

This is all I know. Everybody is interested in this

[1] M. de Boucherat was one of the Commissioners: the other B*** is, no doubt, Berrier.

weighty affair. Nothing else is talked of. Men reason, infer, calculate, pity, fear, wish, hate, admire, are overwhelmed: in short, my poor dear, our present situation is a most singular one; but the resignation and firmness of our dear unfortunate friend is perfectly heavenly. He knows every day what passes, and every day volumes might be written in his praise. I beg you to thank your father[1] for the gratifying note he has written me, and the charming works he sent me. I have read them, though my head feels, alas, as if it were split into pieces. Tell him I am delighted he loves me a little, a great deal, I mean, and that I love him still more. I have received your last letter; alas! you overpay so abundantly the trifling services I render you, that I remain your debtor.

---

*LETTER 27

From Madame DE SÉVIGNÉ *to M.* DE POMPONNE.

Friday, December 19, 1664.

This is a day which gives us great hopes; but I must go back in my story. I told you that M. Pussort had on Wednesday voted for the death of our friend; on Thursday, Nogués, Gisaucourt, Fériol, and Héraut, voted in the same way. Roquesante concluded the day, and, after speaking well for an hour, sided with M. d'Ormesson. This morning our hopes have sailed before the wind; for several votes that were doubtful have been given; La Toison, Masnau, Verdier, La Baume, and Catinat, and all in favour of M. d'Ormesson's opinion. It was then Poncet's turn to speak; but thinking that those who remained were almost all disposed to be lenient, he would not begin, though it was only eleven o'clock. It is thought, he wishes to consult with some one what he shall say, and that he is not willing to bring disgrace upon himself, and consign a man to death unnecessarily. Such is our present situa-

[1] Arnauld d'Andilly, the translator of *Josephus*.

tion, and though so favourable a one, our joy is not complete; for you must know, that M. Colbert is so enraged, that we expect some unjust and atrocious proceeding in consequence, that will plunge us again into despair. But for this, my poor dear, we should have the satisfaction of seeing our friend, though unfortunate, yet safe, as far as his life is concerned, which is a great thing. We shall see what will happen to-morrow. We are now seven to six. Le Feron, Moussy, Brillac, Bernard, Renard, Voisin, Pontchartrain, and the Chancellor, have not yet voted; but of these, we shall have by far the greater number.

Saturday.

Fall on your knees, Sir, and return thanks to God; the life of our poor friend is saved. Thirteen were of M. d'Ormesson's opinion, and nine of Sainte-Hélène's. I am almost wild with joy [1].

Sunday evening.

I was sadly afraid some other person would have the pleasure of communicating to you the joyful tidings. My courier was not very diligent; he said, on setting out, that he would sleep no where but at Livry; he assures me, however, he was the first that arrived. Heavens! how gratifying must the intelligence have been to you! how inconceivably sweet are the moments that relieve the heart on a sudden from the anguish of so painful a suspense! It will be a long time before I shall lose the joy I received yester-

[1] Names of the Committee who judged Fouquet:

(*Favourable*)

D'Ormesson.	Le Feron.	Pontchartrain.	Brillac.
Bernard.	Roquesante.	Moussy.	La Baume.
Masnau.	Catinat.	La Toison.	Renard.
		Verdier.	

(*Adverse*)

St. Hélène.	Poncet.	Feriol.
Héraut.	Gisaucourt.	Voisin.
Pussort.	The Chancellor.	Nogués.

day; it was, in reality, too great, too much almost for me to bear. The poor man learned the news by signals, a few moments after judgment was pronounced, and I dare say felt it in all its extent. This morning the King sent the Chevalier du Guet to the mother and wife of M. Fouquet, recommending them both to go to Montluçon in Auvergne, the Marquis and Marquise de Charost to Ancenis, and the young Fouquet to Joinville in Champagne. The good old lady sent word to the King, that she was seventy-two years of age; that she besought His Majesty not to deprive her of her only remaining son, the support of her life, which apparently was drawing near its close. The prisoner does not yet know his sentence. It is said he will be taken to-morrow to Pignerol, for the King has changed his banishment into imprisonment. His wife, contrary to all rule, is not permitted to see him. But let not this proceeding abate the least particle of your joy: mine, if possible, is increased; for I see in this more clearly the greatness of our victory. I shall faithfully relate to you the sequel of this curious history. I have given you what has passed to-day; the rest to-morrow.

Monday evening.

This morning, at ten o'clock, M. Fouquet was conducted to the Chapel of the Bastille. Foucault held the sentence in his hand. "You must tell me your name, Sir," said he, "that I may know whom I address." M. Fouquet replied, "You know very well who I am; and as for my name, I will not give it here, as I refused to give it in the Chamber of Justice; by the same rule also, I protest against the sentence you are going to read to me." What passed being written down, Foucault put on his hat, and read the sentence; M. Fouquet heard it uncovered. Pecquet and Lavalée [1] were afterwards separated from him,

[1] His physician and his servant.

and the cries and tears of these poor men melted every heart that was not of iron; they made so strange a noise, that M. d'Artagnan was obliged to go and comfort them; for it seemed to them, as if a sentence of death had just been read to their master. They were both lodged in the Bastille, and it is not known what will be done with them.

M. Fouquet went to the apartment of M. d'Artagnan: while he was there, he saw M. d'Ormesson, who came for some documents that were in the hands of M. d'Artagnan, pass by the window. On perceiving him, M. Fouquet saluted him with an open countenance, expressive of joy and gratitude: he even cried out to him, that he was his very humble servant. M. d'Ormesson returned the salutation with very great civility, and came with grief of heart to tell me what had passed.

At eleven o'clock a coach was ready, into which M. Fouquet entered, with four guards. M. d'Artagnan was on horseback with fifty musketeers; he will escort him to Pignerol, where he will leave him in prison, in the care of a man of the name of Saint-Mars, who is a very honest fellow: he will have fifty soldiers to guard his prisoner. I do not know whether another servant has been allowed our friend; you can form no idea how cruel the circumstance of taking Pecquet and Lavalée from him appears to everyone: some even go so far as to draw dreadful inferences from it. May God preserve him, as he has hitherto done: in him we must put our trust, and leave our friend to the protection of that Providence which has been so gracious to him. They still refuse him his wife, but have permitted the mother to remain at Parc, with the Abbess her daughter. L'Ecuyer will follow his sister-in-law: he has declared that he has no other means of subsistence. M. and Madame de Charost are going immediately to Ancenis. M. Bailly, the attorney general, has been turned out of office, for having said to Gisaucourt, before judgment was pronounced, that he ought to retrieve the honour of the Grand Council, which would be disgraced if Chamillard, Pussort, and himself acted together in the business. I am sorry for this upon your account; it is a rigorous measure. *Tantæne animis cœlestibus iræ?*[1]

But no, it does not mount so high as that. Such harsh and low revenge cannot proceed from a heart like that of our monarch. His name is used, and, as you see, profaned. I will let you know the rest: how much better we could converse upon these things! it is impossible to communicate by letter all we have to say. Adieu, my poor dear sir, I have not so much modesty as you, and, without taking refuge in the crowd, I assure you I love and esteem you highly.—I have seen the comet; its train is of a beautiful length. I partly found my hopes on it. A thousand compliments to your dear wife.

Tuesday.

I send you something to amuse you for a few minutes. You will certainly find it worth reading. It is charity to entertain you both in your solitude. If the friendship I bear the father and the son were a remedy against dullness, it is an evil of which you would never have to complain. I am just come from a place where, it seems, I have renewed this sentiment, by talking of you with five or six persons, male and female, who, like me, rank themselves among your friends; it was at the Nevers Mansion. Your wife was of the party; she will tell you of the delightful little comedians we met there. I believe our dear friend has arrived, but I have had no certain intelligence. It is only known, that M. d'Artagnan, continuing his obliging manners, gave him the necessary fur clothing, that he might pass the mountains without inconvenience. I know also that M. d'Artagnan has received letters from the King, and that he told M. Fouquet to keep up his spirits and his courage, and that everything would go well. We are always looking forward to some mitigation, and I in particular: hope has been too kind for me to abandon it.

[1] Virgil's Æneid, lib. i.

Whenever I see the King at our ballets, these two lines of Tasso come into my head:

> *Goffredo ascolta, e in rigida sembianza*
> *Porge più di timor che di speranza*[1].
>
> GERUSALEMME LIBERATA, *cant.* v, *verse* 35.

But I take care not to despond: we must follow the example of our poor prisoner; he is tranquil and gay; let us be so too. It will give me real pleasure to see you here. I cannot think your exile will be of long duration. Assure your good father of my affection; I cannot help expressing myself thus; and let me know your opinion of the stanzas. Some of them are admired, as well as some of the couplets.

---

*LETTER 28

From Madame DE SÉVIGNÉ *to M.* DE POMPONNE.

Thursday evening, January —, 1665.

At length, the mother, the daughter-in-law, and the brother have obtained leave to be together; they are going to Montluçon in the heart of Auvergne. The mother had permission to go to Parc-aux-Dames to her daughter, but her daughter-in-law has prevailed on her to accompany her. M. and Madame de Charost are on their way to Ancenis. Pecquet and Lavalée are still in the Bastille. Can anything be more dreadful than this injustice? They have given M. Fouquet another servant. M. d'Artagnan was his only comfort on his journey. It is said, that the person who is to have the care of him at Pignerol is a very worthy creature. God grant he may be so! or rather, God protect our friend! He has already protected him so visibly, that we ought to think he has an especial care of him. La Forêt, his old esquire, accosted him as he was going away. "I am delighted to see you," said Fouquet to him: "I know

[1] Godfrey attends, and with a brow severe
But little gives to hope, and much to fear.
Hoole's Translation.

your fidelity and affection: tell my wife and mother not to despair, that my courage remains, and that I am in good health."—Is not this admirable? Adieu, my dear sir; let us be like him; let us have courage, and dwell on the joy occasioned by the glorious sentence of Saturday.

Madame de Grignan, (*Angélique-Claire d'Angennes, M. de Grignan's first wife*) is dead.

Friday evening.

It seems, by your too much overflowing thanks, as if you were giving me my dismissal; but I will not take it yet. I intend to write to you whenever I please, and as soon as I have the verses from Pont-neuf, and the others, I shall send them to you. Our dear friend is still upon the road: it was reported, that he had been ill; everybody exclaimed: "What! already?"—It was reported also, that M. d'Artagnan had sent to Court to know what he was to do with his sick prisoner, and that he had been answered unfeelingly, that he must proceed with him, however ill he might be. This is all false: but it shows the general feeling, and the danger of furnishing materials with which to build whatever horrid castles we please. Pecquet and Lavalée are still in the Bastille: this treatment is truly unaccountable. The Chamber will resume after the Epiphany.

I should think the poor exiles must have arrived at the place of their destination ere this. When our poor friend has reached his, I will inform you; for we must follow him to Pignerol: would to God we could bring him thence to the place we wish [1]! And how much longer, my poor dear, will be your exile? I often think of this. A thousand compliments to your father. I have been told your wife is here: I shall call upon her. I supped last night with one of your lady friends, and we talked of paying you a visit.

---

[1] It was the general opinion that Fouquet died in prison in the year 1680. See Voltaire's *Le Siècle de Louis XIV.*, and the note at the beginning of Letter 614, dated April 3, 1680, in Volume IV.

*LETTER 29

From the Comte DE BUSSY *to Madame* DE SÉVIGNÉ.

Forléans, November 21, 1666.

I was yesterday at Bourbilly [1]. Never, my lovely cousin, was I so much surprised. I thought the house beautiful, and when I endeavoured to discover the reason of this, after the long dislike I had taken to it, I found that it arose from your absence. In reality, you and Mademoiselle de Sévigné make every object appear frightful that surrounds you; and you played this trick, for two whole years, to your house. This is a fact; and I advise you therefore, if ever you dispose of it, to make the bargain through your agent, for your presence would very much lessen its value.

In approaching it, the sun, which had not shone for two days, made its appearance, and, conjointly with your farmer, did very handsomely the honours of the house; one preparing me an excellent repast, and the other gilding the apartments, which the Christophles and the Guys had been pleased to decorate with their arms. My family accompanied me, and were all as much pleased with the place as myself. The living Rabutins, seeing so many escutcheons, held themselves in greater estimation, perceiving the consequence which the dead Rabutins attached to their blood. But an involuntary fit of laughter seized us, when we saw the good man Christophle on his knees, who, after distributing his arms in a thousand places, and in a thousand different ways, had at last brought them together in a coat. This is indeed pushing the love of his name as far as it can go. You believe, no doubt, my dear cousin, that this Christophle had a seal, and that his arms

[1] An estate with a fine manor-house belonging to Madame de Sévigné. It was the principal *manoir* of the branch of the Rabutin-Chantal family to which Madame de Sévigné belonged and of which she was the last heiress. It is believed she was born here.

were also engraved upon his plate, his harness, and his carriage. For my part, I would take my oath on it.

---

*LETTER 30

From Madame DE SÉVIGNÉ *to the Comte* DE BUSSY.

Paris, May 20, 1667.

I received a letter from you, my dear cousin, when I was in Brittany, in which you talked of our ancestors the Rabutins, and of the beauty of Bourbilly. But as I had heard from Paris that you were expected there, and as I had hoped myself to arrive much sooner, I deferred writing to you; and now I find you are not coming at all. You know that nothing is now talked of but war. The whole Court is at Camp, and the whole Camp is at Court; and every place being a desert, I prefer the desert of Livry forest, where I shall pass the summer,

En attendant que nos guerriers
Reviennent couverts de lauriers [1].

There are two lines for you, but I do not know whether I have heard them before, or have just made them. As it is a matter of no great importance, I shall resume the thread of my prose. My heart has been very favourably inclined towards you, since I have seen so many people eager to begin, or rather to revive, a business in which you acquired so much honour during the time you were able to engage in it. It is a sad thing for a man of courage to be confined at home, when there are such great doings in Flanders [2]. As you feel, no doubt, all that a man of spirit and valour can feel, it is imprudent in me to revive so painful a subject, I hope you will forgive me, in consideration of the great interest I take in your affairs.

[1] Waiting the return of our warriors covered with laurels.
[Translation.]

[2] Bussy had been exiled to his estates.

It is said you have written to the King. Send me a copy of your letter, and give me a little information respecting your mode of life, what sort of things amuse you, and whether the alterations you are making in your house do not contribute a good deal towards it. I have spent the winter in Brittany, where I have planted a great number of trees, and a labyrinth, that will require Ariadne's clue to find the way out of it. I have also purchased some land, to which I have said as usual, "I shall convert you into a park." I have extended my walks at a trifling expense. My daughter sends you a thousand remembrances. I also beg to send mine to all your family.

---

*LETTER 31

From Madame DE SÉVIGNÉ *to the Comte* DE BUSSY.

Paris, June 6, 1668.

I wrote to you the last; why have you not answered my letter? I have been expecting to hear from you, and have at length found the Italian proverb true; *chi offende, non perdona*—the offender never pardons.

Madame d'Epoisses has informed me that part of a cornice fell upon your head, and hurt you considerably. If you were well, and I dared exercise a little wicked wit upon the occasion, I should tell you, that they are not trifling ornaments like these that injure the heads of husbands in general; and that it would be a fortunate circumstance for them, if they met with no worse evil than the fall of a cornice. But I will not talk nonsense; I will first know how you are, and assure you, that the same reason which made me languid when you were bled, gives me the headache from your accident. The ties of relationship cannot I think be carried farther than this.

My daughter was on the point of marriage. The affair

is broken off, I hardly know why. She kisses your hand: I do the same to your whole family. Have you done anything yet with regard to the Court? Pray let me know how you stand there.

---

*LETTER 32

From Madame DE SÉVIGNÉ *to the Comte* DE BUSSY.

Paris, July 26, 1668.

I begin by thanking you, my dear cousin, for your letters to the King: they would afford me pleasure even if they were written by a stranger: they have awakened in me sentiments of pity, and I should think they must produce the same effect on our Sovereign. It is true, he does not bear the name of Rabutin, as I do.

The prettiest girl in France sends her compliments to you. This title is due to her; I am, however, weary of doing the honours of it. She is more worthy than ever of your esteem and friendship.

You do not know, I believe, that my son has gone to Candia with M. de Roannes, and the Comte de Saint-Paul. He consulted M. de Turenne, Cardinal de Retz, and M. de La Rochefoucauld upon this: most important personages! and they all approved it so highly, that it was fixed upon, and rumoured abroad, before I knew anything of the matter. In short, he is gone. I have wept bitterly, for it is a source of great grief to me. I shall not have a moment's rest during his voyage. I see all its dangers, and terrify myself to death: but, alas, I am wholly out of the question; for, in things of this nature, mothers have no voice. Adieu.

---

*LETTER 33

From Madame DE SÉVIGNÉ *to the Comte* DE BUSSY.

Paris, September 4, 1668.

Rise, Comte; I will not kill you, while prostrate at my feet; and take your sword, to resume the combat. But it is better that I should give you life, and that we should live in peace[1]. I exact but one condition, that you own the thing as it has happened. This is a very generous proceeding on my part: you can no longer call me a little brute.

M. de Montausier has just been appointed Governor to the Dauphin.

Je t'ai comblé de biens, je t'en veux accabler[2].

Adieu, Comte. Now I have conquered you, I shall everywhere proclaim that you are the bravest man in France, and whenever extraordinary duels are mentioned, I shall relate ours. My daughter sends her compliments. The idea you express of her good fortune in the late affair is some consolation to us.

---

*LETTER 34

From the Comte DE BUSSY *to Madame* DE SÉVIGNÉ.

Chaseu, September 7, 1668.

Nothing can be more generous, Madame, than the action you have just performed. Yes, I will proclaim it everywhere: but I could not have supposed you had been able to express yourself so well on the subject, and

[1] Bussy and his cousin had frequent quarrels: the reason has before been given. The new difference to which she alludes seems to have been a slight one.

[2] I have loaded thee with favours, I will add to the burden. [Translation.]

conclude you had some affair of this kind in Brittany, which taught you the language. Is it not a pity that we should have been so long at variance, and thereby have lost so many follies which we should have embellished so well, and which would have amused us so highly? For though neither of us has been dumb, it seems as if we had each tried to lower the other, and said things we should not have said at another time.

---

*LETTER 35

From Madame DE SÉVIGNÉ *to the Comte* DE BUSSY.

Paris, December 4, 1668.

Have you not received the letter, Sir, in which I gave you life, disdaining to kill you at my feet? I expected an answer to this noble action; but you have thought it unworthy your notice: you have contented yourself with rising from the ground, and taking your sword, as I commanded you to do. I hope you will never again employ it against me.

I must tell you a piece of news, that will, I am sure, give you pleasure. It is, that the prettiest girl in France is going to be married, not to the handsomest youth, but to one of the worthiest men in the kingdom, to M. de Grignan, whom you have long known. All his wives died to give place to your cousin, and, through extraordinary kindness, even his father and mother died too; so that knowing him to be richer than ever, and finding him besides, by birth, situation, and good qualities, everything we could wish, we have not trafficked with him, as is customary, on the occasion, but confided in the two families that have gone before us. He seems very well pleased with the alliance, and, as soon as we have heard from his uncle the Archbishop of Arles, his other uncle the Bishop of Usèz being on the spot, the business will be finished; probably before the end of the year. As I am a lover of decorum, I could not fail asking your advice and approbation. The public seems pleased: this is a great deal; for we are such fools as to be almost always governed by its opinion.

LETTER 36

From Cardinal DE RETZ *to Madame* DE SÉVIGNÉ.

Commerci, December 20, 1668.

If the interests of Madame de Meckelbourg[1], and those of Maréchal d'Albret, are alike indifferent to you, Madame, I shall solicit in behalf of the Cavalier, because I have four times the regard for him, that I have for the Lady; but if it be your desire that I should solicit for the Lady, I will do it with the greatest readiness, because I esteem you four million times more than I do the Cavalier; if you would have me observe a neutrality, I shall do so inviolably. In short, you have only to speak, to be implicitly obeyed. I am not in the least surprised at the apprehensions my niece[2] is under; I have long perceived that she degenerates: but however great you describe her shudderings at the thought of the important day of conclusion[3], I much question whether they equal mine for the consequences, since I have seen by a letter of yours, that you have neither had, nor wish to have, any explanations, but leave all to destiny; which, by the by, is often very ungrateful, and little deserving of the confidence we place in it. I find myself beyond comparison more sensible to what regards you and that dear child, than to

[1] Elisabeth-Angélique de Montmorency, widow of Gaspard de Coligni, Duc de Châtillon: and married again in February 1664, to Christian-Louis, Duc de Meckelbourg. This is the famous Duchess de Châtillon, a very full account of whom is given in *Amours des Gaules*.

[2] Mademoiselle de Sévigné, afterwards Comtesse de Grignan.

[3] This relates to the marriage of Mademoiselle de Sévigné with Monsieur le Comte de Grignan, which was solemnised the 29th of January following.

anything that ever related to myself however nearly.

You must blame, Madame, neither the Cardinal Datary[1], nor me, that nothing has yet been done for Corbinelli. A person belonging to the Datary's office, in whom I had confidence, has made use of my name to obtain a great many favours, and has deceived me in three or four very important instances; if he has acted by Corbinelli as he has done by several others on the same occasion, I question whether the name of Corbinelli has been even mentioned since my first letter. It is not a fortnight since this same man wrote me full details of this affair, and of some others that I had recommended to his care; and I have discovered two falsities in the account he sent me; not with regard to Corbinelli, indeed; but finding he has told me lies concerning the others, I imagine he may have done the same with regard to him also: I shall take care to remedy this to the utmost of my power by the first post: you cannot think what vexation it has given me.

---

*LETTER 37

From Madame DE SÉVIGNÉ *to the Comte* DE BUSSY.

Paris, January 7, 1669.

It is as true, that I did not receive your answer to the letter in which I gave you life, as that I was in pain, lest, with the best intention possible to pardon you, I had unintentionally killed you, being little accustomed to wield a sword. This was the only good reason I could assign to myself for your silence. In the meantime, you had written, though your letter had never reached me. Allow me still to regret the circumstance. You always write pleasantly; and if I had wished to lose any portion of your correspondence, it would not have been that letter. I am glad you approve of the marriage with M. de Grignan:

[1] The chief officer in the Pope's Chancery, at Rome.

he is a very good man, and very gentlemanly; has wealth, rank, holds a high office, and is much esteemed and respected by the world. What more is necessary? I think we are fortunate, and as you are of the same opinion, sign the deed I send you, and be assured, my dear cousin, that if it depended on me, you should be first at the entertainment. How admirably well you would act your part! Since you left us, I have heard no wit equal to yours, and I have said to myself a thousand times, "Good heavens, what a difference!"—War [1] is talked of, and it is said the King will take the field in person. Shall we not see you again in a character that you have so well sustained?

*LETTER 38

From the Comte DE BUSSY *to Madame* DE SÉVIGNÉ.

Chaseu, January 22, 1669.

I do you justice, my lovely cousin, in the same way that you have done justice to me. I wrote to you, and you did not receive my letter: it is all true. I am also much obliged by the uneasiness you have felt lest you had unintentionally killed me, and I must tell you, that you are not so unskillful as you supposed. When you gave me my life, you kissed the point of your sword, and I rose from the ground enamoured with your generosity. Had it, however, been otherwise, I should not have been the first you had killed undesignedly. Though you were to use your eyes less skillfully than a sword, there are people so awkward, that they would run headlong into destruction; and we know whose hearts you have pierced, almost without knowing that such persons were in existence.

[1] It was a vague report. No idea was yet entertained of breaking the peace of Aix-la-Chapelle, concluded only seven months before. But it was in contemplation to interfere in the quarrel between the Comte Palatin and the Duc de Lorraine, and force the latter to lay down his arms.

*LETTER 39

From Madame DE SÉVIGNÉ *to the Comte* DE BUSSY.

Paris, April 16, 1670.

I have received your letter, my dear cousin; you are always courteous and amiable; and I need not look deep into my heart for feelings of kindness towards you. I thank you for having opened the door of our correspondence, which had been closed. Some accident or other is always happening to us; but the heart is good, and we will some day laugh at our little dissensions. Let us return to our cousin, M. Frémiot; was it not kind of the good President to bequeath to me his property at his death? I had no idea of such a thing: I had a great affection for him, which, added to my present feelings of gratitude, makes me truly grieved.[1] It is a shame, as you say, that a wife should be able to survive such a husband. Even I can do no more. Adieu. I wish you patience to triumph over your misfortunes. You will not let me speak of my daughter; but I will in defiance of you. She is with child, and is still here: her husband is in Provence.

---

*LETTER 40

From M. DE CORBINELLI *to the Comte* DE BUSSY.

Paris, May 17, 1670.

Madame de Sévigné and I owe you each a letter, but we have determined to make one serve for both. I shall therefore say for myself, that one of the greatest pleasures I have experienced here, has been the thought of my returning to you.

Yes, yes, we will make moral and political reflections; we will take for granted the twofold disgrace, that you

[1] Madame de Sévigné valued her part of this legacy at one hundred thousand livres.

have mentioned to Madame de Sévigné. I came here to examine into the truth of this, and I find it exactly as you represented it. Some imagine they are well at Court, and are on the point of becoming like us; others think they are like us, and are on the point of becoming favourites; and others again are neither one thing nor the other, and ruin themselves courageously by waiting for some decided calamity. I will relate to you the particulars of the story of the Petites-Maisons; and will prove to you demonstratively, that those who think they have reason to pity, ought to envy you. Believe what I say: we will talk this over in Languedoc.

I have many other things to tell you, to make my company bearable for a few days. Prepare, therefore, to acknowledge that you are obliged to the King for having banished you from Court, or you will be the most ungrateful of mankind.

---

*LETTER 41

From Madame DE SÉVIGNÉ *to the Comte* DE BUSSY.

Paris, June 17, 1670.

Be it so, M. le Comte; I shall write to you only when you write to me, or when I am in the humour to write. This, I think, is rule sufficient for conduct so little orderly as ours. It is a miracle if we are good in the main, without being particular with regard to externals. I envy you the pleasure you have in view of seeing Corbinelli. My pleasure is departing; for I shall soon lose him. I am very much grieved at this, for his turn of mind is very similar to my own, and I shall find nothing to console me for his absence. He loves me exactly as I wish to be loved; in losing him, therefore, I lose in a measure, the charm of my existence. I wonder by what compulsion his destiny leads him at the distance of two hundred leagues from me; his interest makes me consent to it against my own. Adieu,

Comte: let us continue to write to each other, and let us take courage against our enemies. Think you that I am without courage? I beg my compliments to your ladies. Madame de Grignan sends hers, with a very good grace. I am not accustomed to the enlargement of her shape, and am as much shocked at it as you can be.

---

*LETTER 42

From Madame DE SÉVIGNÉ *to her son-in-law the Comte* DE GRIGNAN [1].

Paris, Wednesday 25 June, 1670.

You have written me the most charming letter in the world. I should have answered it much sooner, had I not known that you were traversing your Province. I should likewise have sent you the music you desired, but have not yet been able to procure it: in the meantime let me tell you that I love you most affectionately, and if that is capable of giving you the satisfaction you assure me it does, you ought to be the most contented man in the world. You must certainly be so in the correspondence you carry on with my daughter; it appears to me very animated on her part, and I do not think any one can love another more than she does you. I hope to return her to you safe and sound, with a little one the same, or I will burn my books. I am not very skillful indeed myself; but I can ask advice, and follow it, and my daughter on her side takes all possible care of herself.

I have a thousand compliments to send you from M. de La Rochefoucauld [2] and his son [3]; they have received all your letters. Madame de La Fayette [4] returns you

[1] Monsieur de Grignan had been some time in Provence, whither he had been obliged to repair on the King's service; and Madame de Grignan remained at Paris on account of her being with child.

[2] François, Duc de La Rochefoucauld, author of *Maxims*.

[3] The Prince de Marsillac.

[4] Marie-Madeleine Fioche de La Vergne, Comtesse de La Fayette.

many thanks for your remembrance of her, as do my aunt[1] and the Abbé[2], who is very fond of your wife; this I assure you is no small matter, for if she were not extremely prudent, he would show his dislike without the least reserve.

If an opportunity should offer of being serviceable to a gentleman of your country, whose name is ***, I beg you would embrace it; you cannot give me a more agreeable proof of your friendship. You promised me a Canonship for his brother; you know all his family. The poor youth was particularly attached to Monsieur Fouquet[3]; he was convicted of having conveyed a letter to Madame Fouquet, from her husband, for which he was condemned to the galleys for five years, a very extraordinary punishment: you know he is one of the best creatures living, and as fit for the galleys, as to fly in the air.

Brancas[4] expresses himself satisfied with you, and does not intend to spare you when he shall have occasion for your services. He thinks you can never acquit yourself of the obligation you are under to him for giving you so charming a wife, and one who loves you so tenderly. Adieu, my dear Comte; I embrace you with all the affection of my heart.

---

*LETTER 43

From Madame DE SÉVIGNÉ *to the Comte* DE BUSSY.

Paris, July 6, 1670.

I hasten to write to you, in order to efface from your mind as speedily as possible the vexation which my last

[1] Henriette de Coulanges, Marquise de La Trousse, sister of Marie de Coulanges, the mother of Madame de Sévigné.

[2] Christophe de Coulanges, Abbot (or Abbé) of Notre-Dame, Livry; uncle of Madame de Sévigné.

[3] Nicolas Fouquet, Chief-Controller of the Finances, who was banished from Court by the artifice and intrigues of M. Colbert.

[4] Charles, Comte de Brancas, Chevalier d'honneur to Queen Anne of Austria; who was remarkable for his great absence of mind.

letter occasioned you. I had no sooner written it, than I repented having done so. M. de Corbinelli would have prevented my sending it; but I was not willing it should be lost, naughty as it was; and I thought I should not lose you by it, as you did not lose me when your offence was still greater. We cannot destroy kindred: our chains stretch a little sometimes, but they never break. I know this by experience, and was therefore willing to risk my packet. It is true, I was in an ill humour. My spirit was high, and I could not make it bend. I dipped my pen in gall, and it composed a foolish bitter letter, for which I beg a thousand pardons. If you had entered my room an hour afterwards, I should have joined with you in laughing at my folly. Now then we are friends: you would be fortunate if we were quits; but, on this score, how much more do I owe you than I shall ever repay! M. de Corbinelli will tell you how I am; notwithstanding my grey hairs [1], he will revive perhaps your old partiality for me. He loves me truly, and I swear I love nobody more than I love him. His mind, his heart, his sentiments, please me in the highest degree. This blessing I owe to you: but for you I should not have been acquainted with him. You will soon see him: you will have pleasure in conversing with him. He will inform you of the death of MADAME [2], and that with her have died all the gaiety, charms, and pleasures of the Court. Adieu, Comte; no animosity: let us quarrel and plague each other no more. I have been a little to blame, but who, in this world, is perfect? I am glad I have appeased you, on my daughter's

[1] Madame de Sévigné at this time was only 44 years old!

[2] Henrietta, daughter of Charles I., King of England, and grand-daughter of Henry the Great, a Princess dear to France by her understanding and her charms, who died in the prime of life. Thus Voltaire expresses himself. He believed her death natural, contrary to the opinion of all his contemporaries, contrary even to the prejudice this Princess herself evinced on her death-bed: we are led to believe that, in this instance, as in many others, he displayed his superior knowledge as well as superior judgment. We shall say more on the subject of her death.

account. Ask M. de Corbinelli how handsome she is. Show him my letter, and he will see, that if I inflict wounds, I heal them.

---

*LETTER 44

From the Comte DE BUSSY *to Madame* DE SÉVIGNÉ.

Chaseu, July 10, 1670.

I am very glad, my charming cousin, that you own yourself in the wrong. It is a proof of a good heart, and obliges me to think you less so than I had supposed you were. The letter I have just received from you is as agreeable, as the preceding one was the reverse. Your penitence is so pleasing, that I give you leave to offend me again, provided you make me the same amends. Tell me, then, how much you are indebted to me; and hasten your payments, that we may be quits. I assure you, the death of MADAME has very much grieved me. You know how highly I once stood in her favour. My disgrace also drew a thousand attentions from her, which I will some day relate to you. If anything is capable of detaching those from the world who are the most strongly wedded to it, it is the reflections arising from events like the present one. For my part, it is a great consolation to me under my misfortune, to see that those who have the power of driving others to madness, and who by their rank are out of the reach of reprisals, are not secure from the strokes of Providence. I am wholly appeased, for Madame de Grignan's sake; what M. de Corbinelli may tell me cannot increase my affection for her, unless he were to assure me she was at variance with her husband; for then I should love her more than my life. Adieu, my charming cousin: we will quarrel no more. Though you assure me the ties of kindred stretch a little sometimes, but never break, I would not have you trust too much to them; more happens sometimes in an hour than in a year; for my part, I love gentleness: like the brother of Arnolphe, *I am all sugar and honey.* [1]

LETTER 45

From Madame DE SÉVIGNÉ *to the Comte* DE GRIGNAN.

Paris, Wednesday, August 6, 1670.

Is it not true, that I have given you the prettiest wife in the world? and can anyone be more prudent, more regular in her conduct? Can anyone love you more, have more Christian sentiments, long more ardently to be with you, or attend more strictly to the duties of her station? It is ridiculous enough to say all this of my own daughter; but I admire her as other people do, and perhaps more, as I am more an eye-witness of her behaviour; and to own the truth to you, whatever good opinion I had of her as to the principal points, I never thought she would have been so exact as she is in all the minuter ones. I assure you, everybody does her justice, and she loses none of the praises which are so much her due.

It is an old maxim of mine, and what may perhaps one day or other pull an old house about my ears, that the public is neither foolish nor unjust: Madame de Grignan has too much reason to be contented with it, to dispute that point with me at present. She has been under inconceivable distress about your health; I heartily rejoice at your recovery, as well for the love I bear to you, as the affection I have for her. I beg, if you expect any more attacks from your ailment, that you will prevail on it to desist, at least, till your wife is brought to bed. She is every day making complaint at being detained here; and declares with a very serious face, that it was great

[1] He has confounded *Arnolphe* in *L'Ecole des Femmes* with *Ariste* in *L'Ecole des Maris,* see Act I, scene 2 of the latter.

cruelty to separate her from you. It looks as if we had taken pleasure in sending you two hundred leagues from her. I desire you will in your next endeavour to make her easy on this head, and let her know the pleasure you have in the thoughts of her lying-in so agreeably where she is. It was absolutely impossible for her to have accompanied you in the condition in which she was; and nothing can be better for her health, and indeed for her reputation, than to lie-in where the best assistance is to be had, and to remain in a place where her conduct has been so very much admired. If, after all this, she will become a giddy creature and a fool, it will be a twelvemonth, at least, before it will be credited; so good an opinion has everybody of her prudence. I call all the Grignans that are here to witness the truth of what I say. I have not a little joy in it, upon your account; for I love you most sincerely, and am charmed to find that the event has so completely justified your choice. I shall tell you no news; that would be infringing my daughter's rights; I only conjure you to be assured that no one can be more affectionately interested in everything that concerns you.

LETTER 46

From Madame DE SÉVIGNÉ *to the Comte* DE GRIGNAN.

Paris, Friday, August 15, 1670.

When I write to you so frequently, you must remember, that it is on condition, that you do not answer me. Relying on this, I shall proceed to tell you that I am heartily rejoiced at the many honours that are conferred on you. It appears to me, that the Commandant has less share in them than M. de Grignan himself; and I think I see a partiality for you that another would not experience.

I find there is so brisk a correspondence kept up between a certain lady and you, that it would be ridiculous to give you any news. I have not so much as a hope of acquainting you that she loves you; her every action, her whole conduct, with all her little anxieties and cares about you, tell it plainly enough. I am very delicate on the point of friendship, and pretend to know something about it, and I own to you that I am perfectly satisfied with what I see, and could not wish it to be greater. Enjoy this pleasure to the utmost, and never be ungrateful. If there is any little vacant place in your heart, allow me the pleasure of occupying it; for, I assure you, you hold a very considerable one in mine. I do not tell you how much care I take of your dear half; how I watch over her health, and how heartily I wish the vessel safely unladen in port: if you know what it is to love, you will easily judge of my feelings. Would to God your poor wife was as happy as the little Deville[1]! She has just been brought to bed of a boy, who looks as if he were three months old. "Ah!" said my daughter just now, "how vexed am I! little Deville has taken my boy from me: two such never can come together in one house." I have given my daughter a book for you; you will find it admirable; it is written by an intimate friend[2] of Pascal's; nothing but what is perfect comes from that quarter: pray read it with attention. I have sent you likewise some beautiful airs, till I can get the other music. Do not lose your voice; preserve your fine tenor: in a word, continue to be amiable, since you are so much loved.

LETTER 47

From Madame DE SÉVIGNÉ *to the Comte* DE GRIGNAN.

Paris, Friday, September 12, 1670.

I do not write with a design to establish a correspondence with you; no, I should be cautious how I did that,

[1] M. de Grignan's housekeeper.

[2] Monsieur Nicole.

knowing how much you have already upon your hands from Madame de Grignan. I really pity you for having such long letters to read: I never saw anything so impetuous; and I believe from my heart that you would gladly have her with you, to be delivered from them; to such straits has her importunity reduced you. She has just retired to a corner of the room, with a little table and a desk before her; not thinking M. de Coulanges, or myself, personages worthy of approaching her; she is perfectly enraged at your having written to me: I never saw such an envious, jealous little creature in my life. However, I defy her, let her do what she will, to interrupt our friendship. You have a great part in the care I take of her health, and whenever I reflect upon the pleasure you will feel in having a wife and a child, both full of life and spirit, I redouble my attentions to procure you this gratification. I hope all matters will go well. We begin to think, that this same child will certainly be a boy. Adieu, my dear. I positively forbid you to write to me; but I entreat you to love me.

From Monsieur DE COULANGES [1] *to the Comte* DE GRIGNAN.

(Enclosed in Madame DE SÉVIGNÉ*'s Letter.)*

You may say and do as you please, Sir, but I cannot help telling you that I am extremely pleased that you like the Controller of Lyons, and his wife [2]. They are both of them highly delighted with you: and everybody, my sister-in-law [3] not excepted, writes us a thousand handsome things of you. Do not take the trouble of answering me; only give me leave, as I happen to be here while the

[1] Philippe Emmanuel de Coulanges, Master of the Requests, so well known in the gay world for his wit, humour, and the singular talent he had for a jovial song. He was first cousin of M. de Sévigné.

[2] Monsieur and Madame du Gué-Bagnols, whose eldest daughter was married to M. de Coulanges.

[3] Mademoiselle du Gué-Bagnols, who was afterwards married to Monsieur du Gué-Bagnols, Controller of Flanders, her own cousin.

good folks are writing to you, to assure you, there is no one more devoted to your service than myself.

Your wife is as handsome as an angel; she lives the life of an angel; and, if it please God, she will be brought to bed as happily as an angel. This is all I have to say to you at present. As you seem to like my sister-in-law, I wish you would get her a good match in your Province: she is a niece of M. Le Tellier, and first cousin of M. de Louvois.

LETTER 48

From Madame DE SÉVIGNÉ *to the Comte* DE GRIGNAN.

Paris, Wednesday, November 19, 1670.

Madame de Puisieux [1] says, that if you have such a fancy for a son, you should have taken the pains to get one: I must own, I think what she says is very just and reasonable. You left a little girl in our hands, and a little girl we return you. Never was labour so favourable! You must know that my daughter and I went last Saturday to take a walk in the Arsenal: she felt some slight pains: when we came home I was for sending for Madame Robinette, but she would by no means agree to it. We supped, and everything was well. She ate pretty heartily. The Coadjutor [2] and I were for giving her chamber a little the air of a lying-in woman's, but she opposed it, and so firmly, that we thought her indisposition but a passing fit of the colic. At last, as I was going to send for Robinette, the pains came on stronger, and continued in such a manner! her cries were so violent, so piercing! that we presently found she was in labour. But the worst of it was, there was no midwife. We none of us knew what we did; for my part, I was perfectly wild. My daughter

[1] Charlotte d'Estampes-Valançai, Marquise de Puisieux.

[2] Jean Baptiste Adhémar de Monteil, Coadjutor of Arles, brother of M. de Grignan.

cried out for assistance, and for the midwife, and not without reason, poor girl; for we sent in all haste for the one that laid Deville, and she had not been in the room a quarter of an hour before the event took place. And just at that instant Pecquet came in, who assisted to lay her. When all was over Robinette arrived, and was quite surprised; for she had been employed in setting everything in order about the Duchess, thinking she had that night good at least. Hélène [1] at first whispered me, "Madame, it is a boy." I told this to the Coadjutor; but when we came to examine a little nearer into matters, behold it was a girl! We were a little disconcerted, and ashamed of ourselves, when we came to reflect, that we had been all the summer making *des béguins au Saint-Père* [2], as La Fontaine says, and that after all our hopes, *La Signora met au monde une fille.* I assure you this has lowered our crests a little, and nothing comforts us but my daughter's being so perfectly well. She has had no milk-fever. The child has been christened by the name of Marie-Blanche [3]; the Coadjutor standing for Monsieur d'Arles [4], and I for myself. Here is a detail now that would be very tiresome, if it were about indifferent things, but we are fond of hearing every little circumstance that relates to those we love. The premier President of Provence [5] came here from St.-Germain purposely to make his compliments on the occasion. I never saw truer marks of friendship. But what have I yet to tell you? Dare I do it? I flatter myself that the knowledge of your dear wife being so perfectly well, will in some measure comfort you; but our amiable Duchess de Saint-Simon [6] lies so dangerously ill of the small-pox, that her life is despaired of. Adieu, my

[1] One of Madame de Sévigné's maids.

[2] See La Fontaine's Conte de *l'Hermite.*

[3] The same who was afterwards a nun in the Convent of St. Marie d'Aix, and died there at the age of 62.

[4] François Adhémar de Monteil, Archbishop of Arles, Usher of the King's orders, uncle of M. de Grignan.

[5] Monsieur de Forbin d'Oppède.

[6] Diane-Henriette de Budos, Duchess de Saint-Simon.

dear friend; I leave your poor heart to make something out of all these different sentiments. You know mine with regard to yourself long since. Malicious folks will have it, that Blanche d'Adhémar is not likely to be the greatest beauty in the world; and the same people add, that she very much resembles you. If that be the case, you will hardly doubt of my loving her dearly.

LETTER 49

From Madame DE SÉVIGNÉ *to the Comte* DE GRIGNAN.

Paris, Wednesday, November 26, 1670.

You have a letter from your dear wife. It is mere folly therefore to give myself the trouble of writing to you! but it is only to let you know, that the Duchess de Saint-Simon is out of danger. The day I wrote to you she had received all the sacraments, and it was not expected that she could live two days. Now you may, without interruption, enjoy all the pleasure the knowledge of my daughter's good health can afford you. She has just received a piece of news which is very agreeable to her. She believed young Noirmoutier[1] would be blind. She had made many Christian and moral reflections upon the occasion; and felt all the pity and concern so deplorable an accident could excite; when, all of a sudden, she received a message, acquainting her that he could see perfectly well, and that his poor eyes, which had been in a manner washed out of his head by a violent defluxion, had very luckily recovered their places again, as if nothing had been the matter. Upon this she desires to know what she is to do with her reflections; and complains that they have broken in upon her chain of thoughts; and that it shows very little consideration to come with such news to her before the nine days are up: in short, we have laughed so

[1] Antoine-François de La Trémoille, Duc de Noirmoutier. He was then 18 years of age.

heartily at this oddity, that we were afraid she would have made herself ill with it.

Monsieur Le Grand and Maréchal de Bellefonds are to have a race next Monday in the wood of Boulogne, with horses that outstrip the wind. The bet is no less than three thousand pistoles.

LETTER 50

From Madame DE SÉVIGNÉ *to the Comte* DE GRIGNAN.

Paris, Friday, November 28, 1670.

Let us hear no more, I beseech you, of this wife of yours; we love her beyond all bounds of reason. She is very well, and I now write to you wholly on my own account. I want to talk to you about Monsieur de Marseilles [1], to beg you, by all the confidence you have in me, to follow my advice in your conduct respecting him. I know the manners of the Provençals, and the pleasure they take in fomenting divisions, insomuch that if we are not continually upon our guard against the discourse of these gentry, we are insensibly led away by their sentiments, which are often very false and unjust. I can assure you that time, or other reasons, have made a great alteration in Monsieur de Marseilles' temper; for some days he has been extremely mild; and, provided you do not treat him as an enemy, you will not find him one. Let us take him at his word, till we discover that he does something to contradict it; nothing is so capable of overturning a good intention as to show a distrust of it; to be suspected for an enemy, is often sufficient to make a person become one: everything is then at an end, and there are no longer any measures to keep. Whereas confidence prompts to good actions; we are agreeably affected with the good opinion of others, and cannot readily bring ourselves to

[1] Toussaint de Forbin-Janson, Bishop of Marseilles, afterwards Bishop and Comte de Beauvais, Cardinal, and Grand Almoner of France.

forfeit it. In God's name, open your heart, and you will perhaps be surprised by a behaviour that you at present little expect. I never can think this man conceals any rancour in his heart, under so many professions of friendship as he has made us, and of which we had better be the dupes, than entertain false or injurious suspicions. Follow my advice; it is not mine only; several very able heads recommend this conduct to you, and give you assurances that you will not be deceived. Your family is persuaded of it. We see better into these things than you; so many persons who love you, and have just pretensions to good sense and discernment, can scarcely be mistaken.

I wrote you the other day, that the premier President of Provence had come purposely, on hearing of your wife's being brought to bed, to make her his compliments. Nothing can be more obliging, or show a greater interest in your concerns. We have seen him again to-day, and he spoke to us in the most frank and kindly manner possible, about the affair you have proposed to the Assembly (of the States of Provence). He told us, that you had orders sent you to call them together, and that he had written to you, to communicate his advice on the occasion; advice which we all thought very good. As we can only know men at first by their words, we should always believe them till they contradict their words by their actions: we find sometimes that those we have taken for enemies are not so; and we are then heartily ashamed of having been mistaken. It is sufficient to be ready to hate where we have reason for hatred. Adieu, my dear Comte, I have truth on my side, which makes me so importunate.

Madame de Coulanges [1] writes me word, that you love me: though this is no news to me, yet I ought to be pleased that your friendship for me can resist absence and the charms of Provence, and is so ready to show itself on all occasions.

I heartily thank you for your kindness to ***. I have received a great many handsome compliments on the

[1] Madame de Coulanges was at that time at Lyons.

occasion. The King has had compassion on him; he is no longer in the galleys [1], but enjoys his liberty, and lives comfortably in Marseilles. We cannot too much applaud His Majesty for this act of goodness and justice.

LETTER 51

From Madame DE SÉVIGNÉ *to the Comte* DE GRIGNAN.

Paris, Wednesday, December 3, 1670.

Alas! is it then my lot to acquaint you with the death of the Duchess of Saint-Simon, of the small-pox, after continuing eighteen days in a state sometimes recovering, sometimes hopeless? She died yesterday, and has left everybody in the greatest affliction for the loss of so amiable a woman. For myself, I am affected by it to the last degree. You know the great regard I always had for her; if you had the same, this melancholy news must trouble you.

Father Bourdaloue preaches divinely at the Tuileries. We were much mistaken in thinking that he would not make a figure out of his tennis-court; he surpasses infinitely all we have heard of him.

Adieu, my dearest Comte; your brother has preached lately, and has met with general and unfeigned approbation.

LETTER 52

From Madame DE SÉVIGNÉ *to the Comte* DE GRIGNAN.

Paris, Wednesday, December 10, 1670.

Madame de Coulanges has told me several times, that you love me sincerely, that you talk of me, that you wish me with you. As I made the first advances towards this

[1] See Letter 42, of 25th June, 1670, in this volume.

friendship, and wooed you the first, you may judge how happy I am to find that you return the partiality I have so long had for you. All that you write of your daughter is admirable, and I had no doubt that the good health of the mother would comfort you for your disappointment. The joy I should have had in acquainting you with the birth of a son, would have been too great, it would have been showering too many blessings at once, and the pleasure I naturally take in being the messenger of good news, would have been carried to excess. I shall soon be in the same condition you saw me in last year. I must love you extremely to send my daughter to you at this inclement season of the year. How foolish it is to leave a good mother, with whom you assure me she is very well satisfied, to run after a man at the farthest end of France! I give you my word, nothing can be more indecorous than such behaviour. I do believe you were greatly concerned at the death of the amiable Duchess. I was so afflicted myself, that I stood in need of comfort while I was writing to you about it.

My daughter desires me to acquaint you with the marriage of Monsieur de Nevers [1]; that Monsieur de Nevers, who was so difficult to be caught, who used to slip so unexpectedly through the hands of the fair, is at length going to wed. And whom think you? Not Mademoiselle d'Houdancourt, nor yet Mademoiselle de Grancei, but the young, the handsome, the modest Mademoiselle de Thianges [2], who was brought up at the Abbaye-aux-Bois. Madame de Montespan [3] is going to have the wedding solemnised at her house next Sunday; she acts as mother on the occasion, and receives the honours as such. The King restored Monsieur de Nevers to all his posts; so that this *belle,* though she does not bring him a penny of for-

[1] Philippe-Julien-Mazarini-Mancini, Duc de Nevers.

[2] Diane-Gabrielle de Damas, daughter of Claude Léonor, Marquis de Thianges, and Gabrielle de Rochechouart-Mortemar, sister of Madame de Montespan.

[3] Then mistress of Louis XIV.

tune, will be worth more to him than the richest heiress in France. Madame de Montespan does wonders in everything.

I forbid you to write to me: write to my daughter, and leave me to the freedom of writing to you, without embarking you in a train of answers, which would rob me of the pleasure I have in acquainting you with every little trifle. Continue to love me, my dear Comte; I dispense with your honouring my motherly dignity, but you must love me; and assure yourself that there is not a place in the world where you are so dearly beloved as you are here.

Do not fail writing to Madame de Brissac[1]. I saw her to-day: she is in a great deal of affliction. She mentioned the concern she imagined you would be in at hearing of her mother's death.

Monsieur de Foix is sometimes at death's door, sometimes a little better; I would not answer for the lives of those who have the small-pox this year.

A young son of the Landgrave de Hesse has just died here of a fever, for want of being bled. His lady mother charged him, when she went away, not to suffer himself to be bled by anyone in Paris. He would not be bled; and so he died.

Noirmoutier is irrecoverably blind; Madame de Grignan's old reflections may now come into play again. The Court is here, and the King is so heartily tired of it, that he intends going to Versailles three or four times at least every week.

The Maréchal de La Ferté says the most unaccountable things! The other day he presented the Comte de St. Paul[2], and *le petit Bon*[3] to his wife, as two young persons very proper to be introduced to the ladies. He made the Comte de St. Paul some reproaches for having

[1] Gabrielle-Louise de Saint-Simon, Duchess de Brissac, daughter of Claude, Duc de Saint-Simon, and of Diane-Henriette de Budos.

[2] Afterwards Duc de Longueville.

[3] A name given to the Comte de Fiesque.

been so long without coming to see him. The Comte made answer, that he had been several times at his house, and that he supposed his servants had not acquainted him with it.

LETTER 53

From Madame DE SÉVIGNÉ *to her cousin Monsieur* DE COULANGES.

Paris, Monday, December 15, 1670.

I am going to tell you a thing the most astonishing, the most surprising, the most marvellous, the most miraculous, the most magnificent, the most confounding, the most unheard of, the most singular, the most extraordinary, the most incredible, the most unforeseen, the greatest, the least, the rarest, the most common, the most public, the most private till to-day, the most brilliant, the most enviable; in short, a thing of which there is but one example in past ages, and that not an exact one either; a thing that we cannot believe in Paris; how then will it gain credit at Lyons? a thing which makes everybody cry, "Lord have mercy upon us!" a thing which causes the greatest joy to Madame de Rohan and Madame d'Hauterive; a thing, in fine, which is to happen on Sunday next, when those who are present will doubt the evidence of their senses; a thing which, though it is to be done on Sunday, yet perhaps will be not finished on Monday. I cannot bring myself to tell it you: guess what it is. I give you three times to do it in. What, not a word to throw at a dog? Well then, I find I must tell you. Monsieur de Lauzun[1] is to be married next Sunday at the Louvre, to . . . . . ., pray guess to whom! I give you four times to do it in, I give you six, I give you a hundred. Says Madame de Coulanges, "It is really very hard to

[1] Antoine Nompar de Caumont, Marquis de Puiguilhem, afterwards Duc de Lauzun.

PHILIPPES EMANUEL
DE COULANGES.

Peint par Ferdinand Fire du Cabinet de Mme la Mise de Clermont Montoisen. Gravé par C. MF. Dien

guess: perhaps it is Madame de La Vallière." Indeed, Madame, it is not. "It is Mademoiselle de Retz, then." No, nor she neither; you are extremely provincial. "Lord bless me," say you, "what stupid wretches we are! it is Mademoiselle Colbert all the while." Nay, now you are still further from the mark. "Why then it must certainly be Mademoiselle de Créqui." You have it not yet. Well, I find I must tell you at last. He is to be married next Sunday, at the Louvre, with the King's leave, to Mademoiselle, Mademoiselle de . . . . . ., Mademoiselle . . . . . . guess, pray guess her name: he is to be married to Mademoiselle, the great Mademoiselle; Mademoiselle, daughter of the late MONSIEUR [1]; Mademoiselle, grand-daughter of HENRI IV.; Mademoiselle d'Eu, Mademoiselle de Dombes, Mademoiselle de Montpensier, Mademoiselle d'Orléans, Mademoiselle, the King's first cousin, Mademoiselle, destined to the throne, Mademoiselle, the only match in France that was worthy of MONSIEUR. What glorious matter for talk! If you should burst forth like a bedlamite, say we have told you a lie, that it is false, that we are making a jest of you, and that a pretty jest it is without wit or invention; in short, if you abuse us, we shall think you quite in the right; for we have done just the same things ourselves. Farewell, you will find by the letters you receive this post, whether we tell you truth or not.

---

*LETTER 54

From Madame DE SÉVIGNÉ *to the Comte* DE BUSSY.

Paris, December 19, 1670.

M. de Plombières [2] is here, to whom I have spoken of you with pleasure and pain. I do not tell you how much I am grieved at the change in your fortune, it would be

[1] Gaston de France, Duc d'Orléans, brother of Louis XIII.

[2] This name is not indicated in the letter but by a P. He was a particular friend of Bussy-Rabutin's.

like fishing for acknowledgments. I am in despair when I see people happy. This is not a very noble feeling; but how when our friends are unhappy can one support thunderstrokes of bliss in others? I thank you for your congratulations on the safe delivery of my daughter; it is too much, a third daughter for M. de Grignan. I am very glad you amuse yourself with our noble and ancient genealogy and chivalry: it is a circumstance that gives me real pleasure. The letter you have done me the honour to write, by way of dedication to our genealogy, is very flattering and very obliging. I must be perfect, that is, wholly free from vanity, to be insensible to such well-seasoned praise. It is so delicate, and so happily turned, that, without great care, it would be impossible not to give way to the delicious feelings it excites, and to believe, however exaggerated, that it is not in some degree just. You ought always, my dear cousin, to have been thus blind; for I have constantly loved you, and have never deserved your hatred. Let us say no more on the subject: you have made amends for the past, and in so handsome and natural a way, that I am now very willing to hold myself your debtor. Adieu, Comte: it is a great pity fate should have separated us. We were intended to inhabit the same city; it seems to me, as if we understood each other at half a word. I do not enjoy myself without you, and if I ever laugh, it is only a forced laugh. M. de Plombières appears to me very much interested for you. I wish, as Maréchal de Gramont says, that I could put what is in his head, into the head of another person whom I could name.

LETTER 55

From Madame DE SÉVIGNÉ *to Monsieur* DE COULANGES.

Paris, Friday, December 19, 1670.

What is called falling from the clouds, happened last night at the Tuileries; but I must go farther back. You have already shared in the joy, the transport, the ecstasies, of the Princess and her happy lover. It was just as I told you, the affair was made public on Monday. Tuesday was passed in talking, astonishment, and compliments. Wednesday Mademoiselle made a deed of gift to Monsieur de Lauzun, investing him with certain titles, names, and dignities, necessary to be inserted in the marriage-contract, which was drawn up that day. She gave him then, till she could give him something better, four Duchies; the first was that of Comte d'Eu, which entitles him to rank as first peer of France; the Dukedom of Montpensier, which title he bore all that day; the Dukedom of Saint-Fargeau; and the Dukedom of Châtellerault: the whole valued at twenty-two millions. The contract was then drawn up, and he took the name of Montpensier. Thursday morning, which was yesterday, Mademoiselle was in expectation of the King's signing the contract, as he had said he would do; but, about seven o'clock in the evening, the Queen, Monsieur, and several old dotards who were about him, had so persuaded His Majesty that his reputation would suffer in this affair, that, sending for Mademoiselle and Monsieur de Lauzun, he announced to them, before the Prince, that he forbad them absolutely to think any further of this marriage. Monsieur de Lauzun received the prohibition with all the respect, submission, firmness, and, at the same time, despair, that could be expected in so great a reverse of fortune. As for Mademoiselle, she gave a loose to her feelings, and burst into tears, cries, lamentations, and the most violent expressions of grief; she keeps her bed all day long, and takes nothing within her lips but a little broth. What a fine dream is here! what a glorious subject for a tragedy, or romance, but especially talking and reasoning eternally! This is what we do day and night, morning and evening, without end, and without intermission; we hope you do the same, *E frà tanto vi bacio le mani* [1].

---

[1] And with this I kiss your hand. [Translation.]

LETTER 56

From Madame DE SÉVIGNÉ *to Monsieur* DE COULANGES.

Paris, Wednesday, December 24, 1670.

You are now perfectly acquainted with the romantic story of Mademoiselle and of Monsieur de Lauzun. It is a story well adapted for a tragedy, and in all the rules of the theatre; we laid out the acts and scenes the other day. We took four days instead of four and twenty hours, and the piece was complete. Never was such a change seen in so short a time; never was there known so general an emotion. You certainly never received so extraordinary a piece of intelligence before. M. de Lauzun behaved admirably; he supported his misfortune with such courage and intrepidity, and at the same time showed so deep a sorrow, mixed with such profound respect, that he has gained the admiration of everybody. His loss is doubtless great, but then the King's favour, which he has by this means preserved, is likewise great; so that, upon the whole, his condition does not seem so very deplorable. Mademoiselle too has behaved extremely well on her side. She has wept much and bitterly; but yesterday, for the first time, she returned to pay her duty at the Louvre, after having received the visits of everyone there: so the affair is ended and is all over. Adieu.

LETTER 57

From Madame DE SÉVIGNÉ *to Monsieur* DE COULANGES.

Paris, Wednesday, December 31, 1670.

I have received your answers to my letters. I can easily conceive the astonishment you were in at what passed between the fifteenth and twentieth of this month; the subject called for it all. I admire likewise your penetration and judgment, in imagining so great a machine could never support itself from Monday to Sunday. Modesty prevents my launching out in your praise on this head, because I said and thought exactly as you did. I told my daughter on Monday, "This will never go on as it should do till Sunday; I will wager, notwithstanding this wedding seems to be sure, that it will never come to a conclusion." In effect the sky was overcast on Thursday morning, and about ten o'clock, as I told you, the cloud burst. That very day I went about nine in the morning to pay my respects to Mademoiselle, having been informed that she was to go out of town to be married, and that the Coadjutor of Rheims [1] was to perform the ceremony. These were the resolves on Wednesday night, but matters had been determined otherwise at the Louvre ever since Tuesday. Mademoiselle was writing; she made me place myself on my knees at her bedside; she told me to whom she was writing, and upon what subject, and also of the fine presents she had made the night before, and the titles she had conferred; and as there was no match in any of the Courts of Europe for her, she was resolved, she said, to provide for herself. She related to me, word for word, a conversation she had had with the King, and appeared overcome with joy, to think how happy she should make a man of merit. She mentioned, with a great deal of tenderness, the worth and gratitude of M. de Lauzun. To all which I made her this answer: "Upon my word, Mademoiselle, you seem quite happy! but why was not this affair finished at once last Monday? Do not you perceive that the delay will give time and opportunity to the whole kingdom to talk, and that it is absolutely tempting God, and the King, to protract an affair of so extraordinary a nature as this is to so distant a period?" She allowed me to be in the right, but was so sure of success, that what I said made little or no impression on her at the time. She repeated the many amiable qualities of Monsieur de Lauzun, and the noble house he was descended

[1] Charles-Maurice Le Tellier.

from. To which I replied in these lines of Corneille's *Polyeucte*:

> Je ne la puis du moins blâmer d'un mauvais choix,
> Polyeucte a du nom, et sort du sang des rois. [1]

Upon which she embraced me tenderly. Our conversation lasted above an hour. It is impossible to repeat all that passed between us, but I may without vanity say, that my company was agreeable to her, for her heart was so full, that she was glad of anyone to unburden it to. At ten o'clock she devoted her time to the nobility, who crowded to pay their compliments to her. She waited all the morning for news from Court, but none came. All the afternoon she amused herself with putting M. de Montpensier's apartment in order, which she did with her own hands. You know what happened at night. The next morning, which was Friday, I waited upon her, and found her in bed; her grief redoubled at seeing me; she called me to her, embraced me, and whelmed me with her tears. "Ah!" said she, "you remember what you said to me yesterday. What foresight! what cruel foresight!" In short she made me weep, to see her weep so violently. I have seen her twice since; she still continues in great affliction, but behaves to me as to a person who sympathised with her in her distress; in which she is not mistaken, for I really feel sentiments for her that are seldom felt for persons of such superior rank. This however between us two and Madame de Coulanges; for you are sensible that this chit-chat would appear ridiculous to others.

---

[1] Her choice of him no one can surely blame,
Who springs from Kings, and boasts a noble name.
[*Translation.*]

LETTER 58

From Madame de Sévigné *to the Comte* de Grignan.

Paris, Friday, January 16, 1671.

Alas! the poor dear child is still with me, for it was utterly impossible for her, do what she would, to have set out the tenth of this month, as she all along hoped and intended to do. The rains have been, and are still, so very violent, that it would have been downright folly to have attempted it. The rivers are overflowed; the roads are all under water; and the carriage-tracks so covered, that she would have run the risk of being overturned in every ford. In short, things are in such a state that Madame de Rochefort, who is at her country-seat, and is absolutely wild to be in Paris, where she is expected with the greatest impatience by her husband and mother, does not dare to venture till the roads are a little safer. Indeed the winter is perfectly dreadful. We have not had an hour's frost, but there has been a continual deluge of rain every day. Not a boat can pass under any of the bridges; the arches of the Pont-Neuf are in a manner choked up. In short, it is something more than common. I own to you, that seeing the season so very inclement, I warmly opposed her setting out. I would not stop her, for the cold, the dirt, or the fatigues of the journey; but methinks I would not have her drowned. Yet, strong as the reasons are for her stay, nothing could have prevailed on her had not the Coadjutor, who is to go with her, been engaged to perform the marriage ceremony of his cousin d'Harcourt [1], which is to be solemnised at the Louvre; Monsieur de Lionne is to stand proxy. The King has spoken to the Coadjutor upon this subject; but the affair has been put off day after day, and may not be finished this week. My poor daughter is in such extreme impatience to be gone,

[1] Marie-Angélique-Henriette de Lorraine, married the 7th February 1671, to Nugno-Alvarès Péreíra de Mello, Duc de Cadaval in Portugal.

that the time she now passes with us cannot be called living; and if the Coadjutor does not disengage himself from this same wedding, I think I see her ready to commit an act of folly, by setting out without him. It would be so extraordinary to go by herself, and so happy on the contrary to have a brother-in-law to accompany her, that I shall do all in my power to prevent their separation. In the meantime, the waters may be a little drained off. But I can assure you that I have no sort of pleasure in her company. I know she must leave us: all that passes now is mere ceremony and preparation; we make no parties, we take no amusement, our hearts are heavy, and we talk of nothing but rains, bad roads, and dreadful stories of persons who have lost their lives in attempting to pass them. In a word, though I love her to the degree you are sensible of, our present condition is insupportably disagreeable. The last few days have passed without the least satisfaction. I am infinitely obliged to you, my dear Comte, for all the kindness and compassion you feel for me. You can judge better than any other person what I suffer, and am likely to suffer. But I should be sorry that the joy you will have in seeing her should be damped by any reflections of that sort. These are the changes and vexations with which life is chequered. Adieu, my dearest Comte, I overwhelm you with the length of my letters; but I flatter myself you know from what source it springs.

LETTER 59

From Madame DE SÉVIGNÉ *to the Comte* DE BUSSY.

Paris, January 23, 1671.

Once more, I very much approve your intention of writing a little history of our family. To you, I wish the continuance of your philosophy, and to myself, the continuance of your friendship. The latter cannot be destroyed, let us do what we will: it is of a good sort, and is rooted in our bones. My daughter sends you a thousand remembrances and adieus. She is going to that hateful Provence. I am inconsolable at the separation. I embrace my dear nieces.

LETTER 60

From Madame DE SÉVIGNÉ *to her daughter Madame* DE GRIGNAN.

Paris, Friday, February 6, 1671.

My affliction would be light indeed if I were capable of giving you a description of it. I shall not therefore attempt it. I search everywhere in vain for my dear child; I see her not! and every step she takes carries her still farther from me! I returned to Saint-Marie half dead, weeping all the way; I thought my very heart and soul had been torn from me. Good God! how cruel a separation is this! I begged to be alone; they led me into Madame du Housset's apartment, where they made a fire. *Agnès* stayed with me, but without speaking a word, for that was our agreement. I passed five whole hours in this manner, without ceasing to sigh or sob: every thought brought death with it. I wrote to M. de Grignan, you may easily guess in what style. Then I went to Madame de La Fayette's, who renewed my sorrows by the interest she took in them. She was alone, indisposed, and in affliction for the death of a sister: the very situation I could have wished her to be in. Monsieur de La Rochefoucauld came; they talked to me of nothing but you, how much reason I had to be concerned, and of their intending to speak in a proper manner to *Mellusine*[1]. You may take my word that she will have it pretty handsomely: d'Hacqueville will give you a full account of the affair. About eight o'clock I came home, but, ah! think what I felt on

[1] Madame de Marans, sister of Mademoiselle de Montalais, Maid of Honour, and chief favourite of Princess Henrietta of England.

going up stairs! That room which I used to enter with such pleasure, was open to me indeed, but I found everything in it disordered and desolate, and your sweet little girl there, who put me so in mind of my own. Think what I suffered! the night passed in mournful vigils, and the returning light found me in the same state of despondency. The afternoon I passed with Madame de La Troche[1] at the Arsenal. In the evening I received your letters, which renewed the violence of my first emotions. I shall finish what I am now writing this evening at M. de Coulanges', where I shall pick up some news for you; though, from the concern you have left everyone in behind you, I might, if I would, fill my letter with compliments.

Friday night.

The news that I am now about to impart to you, I learned at Madame de Lavardin's. Madame de La Fayette told me, that she and M. de La Rochefoucauld had yesterday a conversation with *Mellusine,* the particulars of which cannot easily be committed to writing: but you may suppose that she was very much confounded at the consciousness of her wicked behaviour, which was laid open to her without the least reserve. She thinks herself very happy in what was offered her, and very readily came into it; which is, that she shall for the future observe a strict silence, and on this condition, no more will be said to her of the affair. You have friends here who have interested themselves in the warmest manner in your behalf: I do not find one who has not a very great love and esteem for you, and who does not sympathise with me in my grief. I have not yet been anywhere but at Madame de La Fayette's. All our friends strive to find me out, and get me with them; but I dread it like death. I entreat you, my dear child, to take care of your health; preserve it for my

[1] Marie Godde de Varennes, widow of the Marquis de La Troche, of the House of Savonière in Anjou. She had a son a Maréchal-de-Camp, who was killed the 18th September 1691, at the battle of Leuze; and was an officer of great merit.

sake, and do not give way to those cruel neglects, which may have fatal consequences. I embrace you with a tenderness that is not to be equalled; no offence, I hope, to the most tender.

The marriage articles between Mademoiselle d'Houdancourt and Monsieur de Ventadour were signed this morning. The Abbé de Chambonnas also was this morning nominated to the Bishopric of Lodève. The Princess [1] will set out on Ash-Wednesday for Châteauroux, where the Prince is desirous she should make some stay. M. de La Marguerie succeeds M. d'Estampes, who is dead, in his place in the Council. Madame de Mazarin comes to Paris to-night; the King has declared himself her protector, and has sent a carriage, with a military escort, to bring her from Lis.

I have a piece of ingratitude to inform you of that will not displease you, and of which I shall make a liberal use when I write my book upon that subject. Maréchal d'Albret has detected Madame d'Heudicourt not only in a commerce of gallantry with Monsieur de Béthune, which he would hitherto never credit, but likewise in having reported of Madame Scarron and him the worst things imaginable. She has endeavoured to do them both all the ill offices that were in her power; which has been proved so clearly, that Madame Scarron and all the Richelieu family have resolved to see her no more. Here is a woman fallen indeed! however, she has this consolation, that she has contributed largely to bring it upon her herself.

LETTER 61

From Madame DE SÉVIGNÉ *to Madame* DE GRIGNAN.

Paris, Monday, February 9, 1671.

I receive your letters in the same way in which you received my ring. I am in tears while I read them. My

[1] Claire Clementina de Maille Brezé, Princess de Condé.

heart seems ready to burst. Bystanders would think that you had treated me ill in your letters, or were sick, or that some accident had happened to you; whereas everything is the reverse. You love me, my dear child, you love me, and you tell me so in a manner that makes my tears flow in torrents. You continue your journey without any disagreeable accident. To know this, is the thing I could the most desire: and yet am I in this deplorable condition! And do you then take a pleasure in thinking of me? in talking of me? and have more satisfaction in writing your sentiments to me than in telling them? In whatever way they come, they meet with a reception, the warmth of which can only be known to those who love as I do. In expressing yourself thus, you make me feel the greatest tenderness for you, that is possible to be felt: and if you think of me, be assured that I, on my side, am continually thinking of you. Mine is what the devotees call an habitual thought; it is what we ought to have for the Divine Being, were we to do our duty. Nothing is capable of diverting me from it. I see your carriage continually driving on, never, never to come nearer to me; I fancy myself on the road, and am always in apprehensions of the carriage overturning. I am almost distracted at the violent rains we have had the last three days, and am frightened to death at the thoughts of the Rhône. I have at this instant a map before me; I know every place you sleep at. To-night you are at Nevers, Sunday you will be at Lyons, where you will receive this letter. I could only write to you at Moulins by Madame de Guénégaud. I have had but two letters from you; perhaps a third is on the road; they are my only comfort. I ask for no other. I am utterly incapable of seeing much company at a time; I may recover the feeling hereafter, but it is out of the question now. The Duchesses de Verneuil and d'Arpajon have used all their endeavours to divert me, for which I am much obliged to them: never surely were there better people than in this country. I was all the day on Saturday at Madame de Villars, talking of you, and weeping, she takes a great share in my sorrow [1]. Yesterday I heard Monsieur d'Agen [2] preach, and was at Madame de Puisieux and Madame du Pui-du-Fou's, who both send you a thousand remembrances. This evening I shall sup tête-à-tête [3] in the Faubourg. These are my carnivals. I have a mass said for you every day. This is no superstitious devotion. I have seen Adhémar [4] but for a moment; I am going to write to him, and thank him for his bed; for which I am more obliged to him even than you are. If you would give me real pleasure, take care of your health, sleep in that little snug bed, eat broth, and exert that courage which I want. Continue to write to me. The friendships you left behind you here, are all increased; and I should never have done with compliments, if I were to tell you how much everyone is concerned about your health.

Mademoiselle d'Harcourt was married the day before yesterday; there was a grand *souper en maigre* given to the whole family. Yesterday there was a grand ball, and at night a supper for the King and Queen, and ladies of the Court, who were extremely brilliant on the occasion; it was one of the most splendid entertainments that could possibly be seen.

Madame d'Heudicourt is gone off in the greatest despair. She had lost all her friends, and was fully convicted

[1] Marie Gigault de Bellefonds, Marquise de Villars, mother of the late Maréchal of that name.

[2] Claude Joli, a celebrated preacher, afterwards Bishop of Agen.

[3] With Madame de La Fayette.

[4] Joseph Adhémar de Monteil, brother of M. de Grignan, known at first by the name of Adhémar, was, after the death of Charles-Philippe-d'Adhémar his brother, which happened the 6th of February 1672, called the Chevalier de Grignan; but being afterwards married to N. . . . d'Oraison, he resumed the name of Comte Adhémar. In 1675 he was Colonel of a regiment of horse, at the head of which he signalised himself on several occasions, particularly at the battle of Altenheim. He was made Maréchal-de-Camp in 1688: and, had not repeated attacks of the gout prevented him from continuing in the service, he would doubtless, from his reputation, merit, and illustrious birth, have obtained the most considerable military honours. He died without issue the 19th November 1713, at the age of sixty-nine.

of what Madame Scarron had so long defended her against, and, in short, of every kind of treachery imaginable. Let me know when you have received my letters. I shall seal this presently.

Monday night.

I shall make up my packet before I go to the Faubourg, and shall direct it to the Controller at Lyons. I am charmed with the distinction you observe in your letters respecting me. Ah, my dear, I deserve it, for the distinguishing love I bear you.

I must now tell you what I learned concerning the entertainment yesterday. The courtyards belonging to the Guise Mansion were illuminated with upwards of two thousand lamps. The Queen went first of all into the apartment of Madame de Guise, which was lighted and decorated in a most sumptuous manner; the ladies of the Court were all ranged round Her Majesty on their knees, without any distinction of rank. Supper was served in that apartment. There were forty ladies at table; the supper was very magnificent. The King entered, and looked gravely round the room, without sitting down to table. After supper the company went to an upper apartment, where everything was prepared for the ball. The King led out the Queen, and honoured the assembly by dancing three or four *courantes,* and then returned to the Louvre with his usual attendants. Mademoiselle was not there. This is all I know of the entertainment.

I am resolved to see the countryman from Sully, who brought me your letter yesterday. I intend to give him something to drink. I look upon him as a happy creature in having seen you. Ah, what would I give could I see you but for a moment! and how do I regret the moments I have lost! I form *dragons* [1] to myself as well as other people. Dirval [2] has heard of the affair of *Mellusine*; he

[1] A familiar expression between the mother and daughter, for vexation or anxiety.

[2] The Comte d'Avaux.

says, you are rightly served; that he told you of the jests she made of you at the first lying-in, but you would not hear a word of it; from which time he never came near you. That creature has long spoken ill of you, but nothing could persuade you of it but your own eyes. And our Coadjutor too, will you not make it up with him for my sake? Do you not yet find him to be *Seigneur Corbeau?* I earnestly wish to see you friends again. Ah, my dear child, for heaven's sake, tell me, is every possible care taken of you? But there is no believing you in what relates to your health. So, you would not make use of this bed? This is just like not letting me send for Madame Robinette. Adieu, my dearest child! the only passion of my soul, the joy and anxiety of my life!

LETTER 62

From Madame DE SÉVIGNÉ *to Madame* DE GRIGNAN.

Paris, Wednesday, February 11, 1671.

I have received but three of those delightful letters that so affect my heart. One is still on the road. If I were not so fond of them, and loth to lose anything that you write me, I should not think I had lost much; for nothing can be wished for beyond what I find in those I have already received. In the first place, they are well written, and are besides so tender, so natural, that it is impossible not to believe everything contained in them; Distrust itself would here stand convinced. They wear that air of truth which, as I have always maintained, carries authority with it; while falsehood and lies skulk under a load of words, without having the power of persuasion; the more they attempt to show themselves, the more they are entangled. Your expressions are sincere, and they appear so; they are used only to explain your meaning, and receive an irresistible force from their noble simplicity. Such, my dear child, do your letters appear to me.

If my words have the same power as yours, I am confident the truths they convey must have had their usual effect with you. I will not have you say, that I was a curtain that concealed you; so much the worse if I concealed you; you appear still more amiable now that curtain is drawn aside; you require to be discovered to appear in your true perfection. This is what we have said a thousand times of you. As for me, I appear to myself quite naked, divested of everything that made me agreeable: I am ashamed to appear in society; and notwithstanding the endeavours that have been used to bring me back to it, I have latterly been like one just come out of the woods; nor could I be otherwise. Few are worthy of understanding what I feel; I have sought those chosen few, and avoided all others. I have seen Guitaud and his wife; they have a great regard for you; write me a word or two for them. Two or three of the Grignans came to see me yesterday. I have given Adhémar a thousand thanks for lending you his bed. We did not examine how far it might have been his interest to have disturbed your quiet, rather than to have contributed to it; we had not spirits to support the jest; but were very happy that the bed had proved so good a one. I fancy you are at Moulins today; if so, you will receive one of my letters. I did not write to you at Briare; if I had, it must have been on that cruel Wednesday, the very day you set off; and I was so overwhelmed with grief, that I was incapable even of tasting the consolation of writing to you. This is the third letter; my second is at Lyons. Be sure you let me know if you receive them. When at a distance, we no longer laugh at a letter beginning with, *I received yours, etc.* The thought of your going still further and further from me, and of seeing the carriage continually driving on, is what harrows me most. You are always going on, and at last, as you say, you will find yourself at two hundred leagues' distance from me; resolved therefore not to suffer such injustice without repaying it in my turn, I shall set myself about removing further off too, and shall do it so effectually, as to make it three hundred. A very pretty distance, you will say! And would it not be a step highly worthy the love I have for you, to undertake to traverse all France to find you out? I am delighted at the reconciliation between you and the Coadjutor; you know how necessary I always thought it to the happiness of your life. Preserve this treasure with care: you own yourself charmed with his goodness; let him see you are not ungrateful. I shall soon finish my letter; perhaps when you get to Lyons you will be so giddy with the honours you will receive there, that you will not find time to read it; find enough however, I beseech you, to let me hear of you, and whether you embark upon that horrible Rhône.

Wednesday night.

I have this moment received yours from Nogent; it was given me by a very honest fellow, whom I questioned as much as I could; but your letter is worth more than anything that could have been told me. It was but justice, my dear, that you should be the first to make me smile, after having caused me so many tears. What you tell me of Monsieur Busche is quite original; it is what may be called a genuine stroke of eloquence. I did laugh then, I own, and I should be ashamed of it, had I done anything else than cry for this week past. I met this Monsieur Busche in the street when he was bringing your horses for you to set out; I stopped him, and all in tears asked him his name; which he told me. "Monsieur Busche," said I, sobbing all the while, "I recommend my daughter to your care; do not, dear Monsieur Busche, do not overturn her; and when you have taken her safely to Lyons, if you will call upon me with the agreeable news, I will give you something to drink." I shall therefore certainly do so. What you say of him has greatly added to the respect I had for him before. But you are not well; you have not slept lately. Chocolate will do you good; but then you have no chocolate-pot: I have thought of that twenty times; what will you do? Ah, my poor child, you are not mistaken in thinking my mind is always employed about you. If you were to see me, you would see me continually seeking those who love to talk of you; if you were to hear me, you would hear me continually talking of you myself. I have not yet seen any of those who want to divert me; that is, in other words, who want to prevent my thinking of you; for I am angry with them for it. Farewell, my lovely child, continue to write to me, and to love me.

LETTER 63

From Madame DE SÉVIGNÉ *to Madame* DE GRIGNAN.

Paris, Thursday, February 12, 1671.

This is only a line precursory, for I shall not write to you till to-morrow; but I wish you to know what I have just heard.

Yesterday the President Amelot, after having made a great number of visits, towards night found himself a little out of sorts, and was soon afterwards seized with a violent apoplectic fit, of which he died about eight o'clock this morning. I would have you write to his wife; the whole family are in the greatest affliction.

The Duchess de La Vallière sent a letter to the King, the contents of which have not transpired, and then a message by the Maréchal de Bellefonds, to say, "that she would have quitted the Court, after having lost the honour of his good opinion, had she been able to prevail with herself to see him no more; but that her weakness on that head had been so great, that she was scarcely capable even now of making a sacrifice of it to her God: she was resolved, however, that the remains of the passion she had felt for him should constitute part of her penance, and, as she had devoted her youth to him, it could not be thought much if the rest of her life were spent in cares for her own salvation." The King wept bitterly, and sent Monsieur Colbert to Chaillot, to beg her to come directly to Versailles, that he might speak to her once more. Monsieur Colbert accordingly conducted her thither. The King had a whole hour's conversation with her, and wept a great deal. Madame de Montespan ran with open arms, and tears in her eyes, to receive her. We do not rightly understand all this. Some say she will remain at Versailles, and continue about the Court; others that she will return to Chaillot. We shall see.

LETTER 64

From Madame DE SÉVIGNÉ *to Madame* DE GRIGNAN.

Friday, February 13, 1671.
At Monsieur de Coulanges' house.

Monsieur de Coulanges wishes me to write to you once more at Lyons. I conjure you, my dear child, if you think of taking boat, to go down to the Pont-Saint-Esprit. Have pity on me, and take care of yourself if you would have me live. You have so thoroughly convinced me of the love you have for me, that I think, out of regard to my ease, you will not hazard your own safety. Pray let me know how you conduct your bark. Ah, how dear, how precious to me is that little bark, which the Rhône so cruelly carries away from me!

I hear there have been fine doings, but it is only by hearsay, for I did not see it. I have been so unsociable that I could not bear four people at a time in a room. I was in the chimney-corner at Madame de La Fayette's. *Mellusine's* affair is in the hands of Langlade [1], after having passed through those of Monsieur de La Rochefoucauld and d'Hacqueville. I assure you she is very much confounded and thoroughly despised by all who have the honour of knowing her. I have not seen Madame d'Arpajon yet: her contented and happy mien does not suit me.

[1] A person particularly attached to the House of Bouillon, and who was afterwards made Secretary of the Cabinet.

It was thought that the ball on Shrove-Tuesday would have been put off; never was so universal a dullness. I believe your absence occasioned it. Good heavens, what a number of compliments have I to make you! how many good wishes! how many longings to hear from you! what praises bestowed on you! I should never have done were I to name all the good people, male and female, by whom you are loved, esteemed and adored; but, when you have put them all together, be assured, my dear child, they are nothing in comparison to what I feel for you. I never lose sight of you a moment, I think of you incessantly, and in such a manner! I embraced your little girl, and she kissed me again; and she acted your part in this scene extremely well. Do you know I love the dear creature, when I think to whom she belongs?

LETTER 65

From Madame DE SÉVIGNÉ *to Madame* DE GRIGNAN.

Paris, Wednesday, February 18, 1671.

I entreat you, my dear child, to be careful of your eyes. Mine, as you know, will be at your service till they close for ever. You must be aware, my love, that in the manner in which you write, there is no reading your letters without tears. To the natural tenderness and affection I have for you, join the little circumstance of my being persuaded that you love me with equal warmth, and judge what I must feel. Wicked girl! why do you ever conceal from me the precious treasures you are mistress of? Are you afraid I should die with joy? Ought you not rather to be afraid I should die with grief, lest I should ever see it otherwise? D'Hacqueville will witness for me the deplorable state he once saw me in; but let me quit these melancholy reflections, and enjoy a blessing without which life would be heavy and insupportable. These are not words, but truths. Madame de Guénégaud has told me of the condition she saw you in on my account; retain the cause, I conjure you; but no more tears; they are not so good for you as for me. I am now become pretty reasonable! I keep up my spirits upon occasion, and am sometimes for four or five hours together like another person; but a small matter makes me relapse; a remembrance, a place, a word, a thought half smothered, but especially a letter from you, or even one of my own while I am writing, or any person who speaks of you; these are the rocks and quicksands of my fortitude, and they very frequently fall in my way. I see Madame de Villars frequently; I am fond of being with her, because she enters into my sentiments; she sends you a thousand good wishes. Madame de La Fayette too is sensible of my fondness for you; and greatly touched with the tenderness you show me in return. I am generally at home with my family; sometimes however I pass an evening here, from weariness, but not often. I have seen poor Madame Amelot also; she weeps well; I am an excellent judge of weeping. I go to hear Mascaron[1] and Bourdaloue preach: they seem to strive who shall surpass the other.—Well, I think I have sent you a great deal of news: I long to hear some from you, and how you find yourself at Lyons. To say the truth, I think of nothing else. You have put me upon informing myself about the masquerade on Shrove-Tuesday. I am told that a great man, greater by some inches than any other man, had ordered a remarkable costume to be made for him, and after all would not wear it; for he learned by chance that a certain lady, with whose person he was not acquainted, and to whom he never spoke a word in his life, would not be at the assembly[2]. And now I must say with Voiture, that your absence has been the death of no one as yet, except myself; not but that the carnival has been excessively dull; you may take the honour of it, if you please; for my part, I thought it was upon your

[1] Jules Mascaron, Priest of the Oratory, nominated in 1671 to the Bishopric of Tulle.

[2] She probably refers to the King and Madame de Montespan.

account; only that it did not appear dull enough for the absence of one like you. This letter I shall send direct to Provence. I embrace M. de Grignan, and die with impatience to hear from you. As soon as I receive one letter I am impatient for another; I only breathe while I am receiving them.

You tell me wonders of the tomb of Monsieur de Montmorency, and the beauty of the Mesdemoiselles de Valençai. You write extremely well, no one better; never quit the natural; you have a turn for it, and it forms a complete style. I have made your compliments to Madame de La Fayette, and to Monsieur de La Rochefoucauld and Langlade; they all esteem and love you, and would be ready to serve you on every occasion. I think your songs charming, I knew the style perfectly. Ah, my dear child, how I long to see you for a while, to hear you speak, to embrace you, nay, to see you pass at a distance only, if the rest be too much to ask! This is one of those thoughts which I never attempt to suppress. I begin to grow weary of being without you; I feel the uneasiness of mind this separation gives me, in the same manner as I should a disease of the body. I cannot sufficiently thank you for the many letters you have written me on the road. These little attentions are gratifying, and have their full effect, I assure you. Nothing of this kind is lost upon me; it can proceed only from real friendship; otherwise it would be more agreeable to go to bed, and take one's rest. I am under no small impatience to hear from you, both from Rouane and Lyons: the idea of your being upon the water troubles me, and I long to know how the furious Rhône appeared to you, in comparison to our peaceable Loire, which you have honoured with so many civilities! How kind it is of you to remember it as one of your old friends! Alas! what is it I do not remember? The least trifles are of the greatest value to me! I have a thousand *dragons!* How are things altered! I never used to return hither but with impatience and pleasure; and now, look as long as I will, I can see nothing of you! And is it possible, to live with the reflection, that, do what we will, we can no where find the child that was so dear to the heart? I will soon convince you of my sentiments, by going in search of her.

The Dauphin has been ill, but is better. The Court will be at Versailles till Monday. Madame de La Vallière is perfectly reinstated there. The King received her with tears of joy, and she has had several tender conversations with him. All this is a little incomprehensible, but we must be silent. The news of this year does not hold good from one post to another. I have compliments for you without end. I see your little one every day, I would fain have her straight; but am not without apprehension. It would be droll enough that a child of yours and M. de Grignan should not be well made. I have some skill in these matters; perhaps, however, I am taking needless precautions.

LETTER 66

From Madame DE SÉVIGNÉ *to Madame* DE GRIGNAN.

Friday, February 20, 1671.

I cannot express how desirous I am to hear from you. Consider, my dear, I have not had a letter since that from la Palice: I know nothing of the rest of your journey to Lyons, nor of your route to Provence. I am very certain that there are letters for me; but then I want them, and they do not come. I have nothing left to comfort and amuse me, but writing to you.

You must know, that Wednesday night last, after I came from M. de Coulanges', where we had been making up our packets for the post, I began to think of going to bed. That is nothing very extraordinary, you will say; but what follows is so. About three o'clock in the morning I was wakened with a cry of Thieves! Fire! and it seemed so near, and grew so loud, that I had not the least doubt of its being in the house; I even fancied I heard them talking to my little grand-daughter. I imagined she was burned to death, and in that apprehension got up without a light, trembling in such a manner that I could scarcely stand. I ran directly to her room, which is the room that was yours, and found everything quiet; but I saw Guitaud's house all in flames, and the fire spreading to Madame de Vauvineux's. The flames cast a light over our courtyard and that of Guitaud's, that made them look shocking. All was outcry, hurry, and confusion, and the beams and joists falling down, made a dreadful noise. I immediately ordered our doors to be opened, and my people to give assistance. Monsieur de Guitaud sent me a casket of valuables, which I secured in my cabinet, and then went into the street, to gape like the rest. There I found Monsieur and Madame Guitaud in a manner naked; Madame de Vauvineux, the Venetian Ambassador, and all his people; with little Vauvineux [1], whom they were carrying fast asleep to the Ambassador's house, with a great deal of moveables and plate. Madame de Vauvineux had removed all her goods. As for our house, I knew it was as safe as if it had been on an island, but I was greatly concerned for my poor neighbours. Madame Guêton and her brother gave some excellent directions, but we were all in consternation; the fire was so fierce that there was no approaching it, and no one supposed it would cease till it had burnt poor Guitaud's house entirely down. Guitaud himself was a melancholy object; he was for flying to save his mother, who was in the midst of the flames, as he supposed, in the upper part of the house; but his wife clung about him, and held him as tightly as she could. He was in the greatest distress between the grief of not being able to save his mother, and the fear of injuring his wife, who was nearly five months with child. At last he begged me to lay hold of her, which I did, and he went in search of his mother, who, he found, had passed through

[1] Charlotte-Elisabeth de Cochefilet, married in 1679 to Charles de Rohan, Prince de Guémené, Duc de Montbason.

you can possibly write, I am sure you will. Heavens! how great is my desire to hear of you, and how dear are you to my heart!

The Comte de St. Paul is now Monsieur de Longueville: last Monday night his brother made over all his estate to him, which amounts to near three hundred thousand livres a year, together with his rich furniture and jewels, and the Longueville Mansion; so that he is now one of the best matches in France. It will be a good thing for Madame de Marans, if she can get him. I dearly love M. de Grignan, but shall not answer his last letter. Can he want anything, having you with him? M. Vallot[1] died this morning.

LETTER 68

From Madame DE SÉVIGNÉ *to Madame* DE GRIGNAN.

Paris, Friday, February 27, 1671.

There is nothing certain this year, not even the death of M. Vallot, which I now contradict. He is quite well, and instead of dying, as was told me, he took a pill which set him upon his legs again. He has told the King, that he considers M. du Chesnai du Mans as the most skillful physician in the world. Madame de Mazarin set out for Rome two days ago. Monsieur de Nevers and his lady are not to go there till the summer. The husband of Madame de Mazarin complained bitterly to the King, of his wife being sent to Rome without his consent; he said it was a thing unheard of, to take a woman from the authority of her husband, and assign her a pension of twenty-four thousand livres a year, and a present of twelve thousand francs besides, to enable her to take a journey that was contrary both to his wish and his honour. His Majesty gave him the hearing, but as the journey had been resolved upon beforehand, and everything settled, nothing

[1] First physician to the King.

further came of it. As for his wife, whenever anything was said to her about making matters up with her husband, she always turned it off with a laugh, and answered, as in the time of the Civil war, *No Mazarin! no Mazarin!*

With regard to Madame de La Vallière we are very sorry we cannot oblige you in sending her back to Chaillot; but she is better than ever at Court; and so you must resolve to let her stay there. The Duc de Longueville is now called the Abbé d'Orléans, and the Comte de St. Paul takes the title of Duc de Longueville. Monsieur de Duras has the same command during the expedition to Flanders this year, as M. de Lauzun had the last, which is so much the better for him, as the number of troops will be nearly double. The King has made Mademoiselle de La Mothe, one of the Queen's Maids of Honour, a present of two hundred thousand francs, which will soon get her a husband. Monsieur de Lauzun has refused the *bâton* of Maréchal of France, which the King was pleased to offer him. He said he had not merited it; that, had he served for it, he should esteem it as the greatest honour; but he was resolved not to accept it but in the common way. D'Hacqueville has by his interest procured six thousand livres a year for Cardinal de Retz; it is from the same fund as the pension given to the Cardinal de Bouillon, except that he is not obliged to the clergy for it.

LETTER 69

From Madame DE SÉVIGNÉ *to Madame* DE GRIGNAN.

Paris, Friday night, February 27, 1671.

The Rhône, my dear child, hangs strangely about my heart; I believe you are safe over it, but still I should be better pleased to hear it from yourself, and wait for the intelligence with an impatience of a piece with all the rest. We suppose you got to Arles last Saturday: we suppose that Monsieur de Grignan came as far as Saint-

Esprit to meet you: we suppose he was overjoyed to see you, and have you with him again: we suppose you made your entry into Aix on Wednesday; and then we suppose you were very much tired. For heaven's sake, rest yourself, keep in bed, and recover yourself, and let me know just exactly how you are. Your remembrance makes the fortune of those whom you favour with it: all the rest languish for it. Your line to my aunt cannot be repaid as yet; but we are very far from forgetting you. I have been told a thousand horrible stories about that villainous mountain Tarare: Oh, how I hate it! They say there is another road that must be passed, where the wheels are in the air, and the coach is dragged along by its top. I cannot bear the thought! however, it is all at an end now.

Madame DE SÉVIGNÉ'S *reply to the Letter from Vienne.*

I have that dear letter at last! Do you not see how I receive it? and with what emotion I read it? You will hardly expect me to be indifferent on the occasion. The rank you hold in point of beauty certainly subjects you to many fatigues. If you were not so handsome you might take your rest. You must determine: your submission gives me uneasiness: do not yield so much on this point; there is nothing so amiable as beauty: it is a present from the Deity, which we ought to preserve with the utmost care. You know what pleasure I take in your beauty; I interest myself in it from a principle of self-love, and earnestly recommend it to your care for my sake; for I figure to myself that the people of Provence will look upon me as a very clever personage to have produced that fine face, with all its sweetness and regularity. You seem to be displeased that your nose is not awry; for my part, who am in my senses, I am extremely glad of it. Do you not think M. de Coulanges and I must be conjurers to guess so patly everything you do? You do not seem surprised at the banks of the Rhône, you think them beautiful, and that the river is mere water only, like other rivers: for my part, I have very strange notions of it; and am ready to cry out with the poet:

> "Mille sources de sang forment cette rivière,
> Qui, trainant des corps morts et de vieux ossements,
> Au lieu de murmurer, fait des gémissements."[1]

Langlade will give you an account of his visit to *Mellusine*; but in the meantime I must tell you, that he went for the purpose of speaking his mind to her: he did it more readily than anyone else would have done. She is, I assure you, very much mortified, and very much abashed: I saw her the other day, and she had not a word to say for herself. Your absence has increased the affection of all your friends: but this absence must not last too long; and whatever aversion you may have to travelling, you must think of nothing but preparing to encounter and endure its fatigues. I have told M. de La Rochefoucauld what you think of the fatigues of others, and the attention you pay them: he has given me a thousand remembrances for you, in so kind a tone, and accompanied by such delicate praises, that he is worthy your regard.

I shall make your compliments to Madame de Villars; she has begged to be named in my letters. I thank you for mentioning Brancas. You doubtless saw your aunt[2] at St. Esprit, and were received like a Queen: I beg, my dear, you will let me know all about it, and tell me something of Monsieur de Grignan and Monsieur d'Arles[3]. You know that we have laid it down as a maxim, that though trifling details are disagreeable from those who are indifferent to us, they are pleasing from those we love. I leave you to guess in which of these lights you stand with me. Mascaron and Bourdaloue give me in turn a

[1] "This river is formed by a thousand streams of blood, which, dragging in its course the bodies of dead men, sends forth groans instead of murmurs."—Lines of Philippe Habert, in his *Temple of Death*.

[2] Anne d'Ornano, wife of François de Lorraine, Comte d'Harcourt, and sister of Marguerite d'Ornano, mother of Monsieur de Grignan.

[3] François Adhémar de Monteil, Archbishop of Arles, Commander of the King's Orders, uncle of M. de Grignan.

pleasure and satisfaction that ought at least to make me better; whenever I hear anything fine, I wish for you: you share in all my thoughts, and I admire in myself the effects of a sincere friendship. I embrace you most affectionately; do the same to me on your part. A small remembrance to my Coadjutor: as for M. de Grignan, he, I suppose, is so proud of having you with him, that he no longer cares for anyone else.

LETTER 70

From Madame DE SÉVIGNÉ *to Madame* DE GRIGNAN.

Paris, Tuesday, March 3, 1671.

If you were here, my dear child, you would certainly laugh at me. I am sat down to write beforehand; but from a very different reason from that which I once gave you for writing to a person two days before I could send my letter: it was a matter of indifference to me, when I wrote, as I knew I should have no more to say to him at the two days' end, than I had then. But here the case is otherwise. I do it now from the regard I have for you, and to satisfy the pleasure I take in writing to you every moment, which is the sole comfort I have now left. To-day I am shut up by myself in my room, through excess of ill humour. I am weary of everything. I took a pleasure in dining here, and still a greater one in writing to you out of season. Alas! you have none of these leisure moments! I write quite at my ease, but can hardly suppose you will be able to read what I write in the same manner. I do not see how it is possible for you to be a minute by yourself. On one side I behold a husband who adores you, who is never tired of being with you, and who scarcely knows the end of his happiness: on the other side, harangues, compliments, visits, and honours paid you without end; all these need to be responded to by you. Indeed, you have enough upon your hands. I could not bear it myself in my little circle. But what becomes of your favourite Indolence amidst all this noise and bustle? It suffers now; it retires into a corner, just dead with apprehension of losing its place in your heart for ever; it seeks some vacant moment to put you in remembrance, and just drop a word to you by the by. "Alas!" it says, "and have you then forgotten me? Remember I am your oldest acquaintance; the friend who has never abandoned you; the faithful companion of your happy hours, who made you amends for the want of every pleasure, and for whose sake you have sometimes hated them. It was I who prevented your dying of the vapours, while you were in Brittany, and during your pregnancy. Sometimes, indeed, your mother would break in upon our joys, but then I knew where to have you again. Now I know not what will become of me. These shows, all this pageantry, will be my death, unless you take some care of me." Methinks I hear you speak a kind word to it as you go by; you give it some hopes of possessing you when at Grignan; but you are gone in an instant, and cannot find time to say more. Duty and reason are with you, and allow you not a moment's repose: I who have always so highly honoured these personages, am now quite out with them, and they with me. How then will they permit you to waste your time in reading such trifles as these? I assure you, my dear child, I am continually thinking of you; and I experience every day the truth of what you once told me, that there are certain thoughts which are not to be dwelt upon, but passed over as lightly as possible, unless we would be for ever in tears: that is my case; for there is not a place in the house which does not give a stab to my heart when I see it: but your room especially deals a deadly blow from every part of it. I have placed a screen in the middle of it, that I may at least take something from the prospect. As for the window from which I saw you get into d'Hacqueville's coach, and then called you back again, I shudder every time I think how near I was throwing myself out of it after you. I was likely enough to have done it; for at times I am not in my senses. The private room where I held you last in my arms, without knowing what I did; the Capuchins, where I used to go to mass; the tears that fell so fast from my eyes that they wetted the ground, as if water had been thrown on it; Sainte-Marie's, Madame de La Fayette, my return to the house, your room, that night, the next morning, your first letter, and everyone since, and still every day, and every conversation of those who feel with me, are so many remembrances of my loss. Poor d'Hacqueville holds the first rank: I shall never forget the compassion he showed me. These are the thoughts incessantly uppermost; yet these are to be passed over, it seems; we are not to abandon ourselves to our thoughts, and the emotions of our heart. I had rather however continue my reveries on the kind of life you are leading. It occasions a sort of diversion, without making me abandon my principal, my beloved object. I do then think of you. I am always wishing for letters from you. One wish of this nature, when gratified, is followed by another continually. I am in this state of expectation now, and shall go on with my letter, when I have received one from you. My dearest child, I really abuse your patience, but I was willing to indulge myself for once beforehand: my heart stood in need of it; but I will not make a practice of this.

LETTER 71

From Madame DE SÉVIGNÉ *to Madame* DE GRIGNAN.

Paris, Wednesday, March 4, 1671.

Ah! my dear child, what a letter! What a description of the condition you have been in! how sadly should I have kept my word with you, had I made you a promise of not being terrified at so much danger! I know it is over now; but it is impossible to think of your life having been so near to its end, and not shudder with horror: and

Monsieur de Grignan to let you steer the boat; and when you were rash and venturous, to take a pleasure in being still more so himself, instead of staying till the storm was over! one would think he wished to expose you. Oh, heavens! how much better would it have been to have had a little less courage, and to have told you plainly, that, if you were not afraid, he was; and not have suffered you to have passed the Rhône in such weather! I cannot think what became of all his tenderness for you at that moment. The Rhône, a river that strikes everyone with dread! the bridge of Avignon, which it would be wrong to pass, even with the most wary precaution! and behold a violent squall of wind throws you on a sudden under one of the arches! What a miracle that you had not been dashed to pieces, and every creature drowned in an instant! I tremble whenever I think of it; I have waked in such fright and distress, that I have been scarcely mistress of myself since. Do you still look upon the Rhône as no more than a common river? Were you not, tell me truly, greatly terrified at the prospect of death, so near, and seemingly so inevitable? Will you not another time be less daring? Has not this adventure exhibited the dangers of the scene in their true light? Tell me how you felt. I hope at least you returned thanks to heaven on your knees for your deliverance. I shall come upon M. de Grignan for this. The Coadjutor too shall have his share: he was scolded even about the mountain of Tarare; but that appears like the plains of Nemours to me now. Monsieur Busche has been to see me; I thought I should have thrown my arms around the man's neck, when I considered how safely he had conveyed you: I held him a long while in discourse; asked him how you looked, how you were; and then dismissed him with something to drink my health. This letter will appear very ridiculous to you; for you will receive it at a time when the bridge of Avignon will be quite out of your head. And must I still think of it? This is one of the misfortunes that attend a distant correspondence: but we must reconcile ourselves to it; there is no resisting this inconvenience; it is natural, and it would be too great a constraint to endeavour to stifle such thoughts. We should always enter into the state of mind a person is supposed to be in at the time he is replying to anything that interests the heart. If you observe this maxim, you will make frequent excuses for me. I am expecting your account of what passed during your stay at Arles. I know you must have seen a great many people there. Do you not love me now, for making you learn Italian? What service it must have been to you with the Vice-Legate! Your description of that scene is excellent. But how little was I pleased with the rest of your letter! However, I will spare you the renewal of that eternal theme, the bridge of Avignon. But while I live I shall never forget it.

LETTER 72

From Madame DE SÉVIGNÉ *to Madame* DE GRIGNAN.

Paris, Friday, March 6, 1671.

It is to-day the sixth of March, I entreat you to let me know how you are. If you are well, you are ill; if you are ill, you are well. Indeed, my dear child, I wish you to be ill, that you might be well, at least for some time. Here is a riddle, very difficult to be solved; I hope however that you will explain it to me. You have given me a most delightful account of your entry into Arles; but methinks you must stand greatly in need of rest: you have the fatigues of the whole journey to get over; and how will you find time to do it? You are there like the Queen; she never takes rest, but is always as you have been lately: you must endeavour then to acquire her spirit, and bear with patience the load of ceremonies you have to undergo. I am persuaded that M. de Grignan is delighted with the reception you met with. You never say anything about him now; and yet it is a subject respecting which I am a little curious. As for the Coadjutor, I suppose he was drowned under the bridge of Avignon. Heavens, how that hideous place still runs in my head! Tell me once more, will not this make you a little less venturesome? You will always suffer by such rashness: witness your first pregnancy, and how it had nearly cost me very dear, as well as you. The Rhône is passed, that is certain; but I am in continual apprehension lest you should be for climbing some precipice, and nobody to hinder you from doing it. My dear child, have some compassion on me, if you have none on yourself. Madame de Caderousse's coachman puts me often in mind of the Cardinal de Retz's. Ah! M. Busche, what a charming man are you! I told you how well I received him. I am persuaded poor Caderousse will die soon: it is hardly known here whether she is living or dead. I shall tell all about her, if it be worth telling. Corbinelli writes me wonders about you: but what gives him the greatest pleasure is, that he thinks he can perceive that you love me; and he has so great a regard for me, that he is charmed to find others of the same way of thinking with himself. But how happy does he appear to me, to have seen you, touched you, to have sat and written by the side of you! It was some satisfaction to you likewise, I flatter myself, to see a person, who is so much my friend, and who, I assure you, is no less yours.

Monsieur DE SÉVIGNÉ *writes a few lines to his Sister in his Mother's letter.*

I take the opportunity of stealing out between the Acts, to let you know that I have just come from a most delightful concert, composed of the two Camus's and Ytier. You are sensible that the usual effect of music is that of softening the soul; though I have no occasion for that with respect to you, yet has it renewed a thousand little circumstances of tenderness, that one would have thought extinguished by so long a separation as ours has been. But do you know what company I have been in? There were Mademoiselle de Lenclos, Madame de La

Sablière, Madame de Salinis, Mademoiselle de Fiennes, and Madame de Montsoreau, all met together at Mademoiselle de Raymond's. After this, if you do not think me a fine fellow, you are to blame; for you have not the same reason on your side as they have, since you cannot see my black wig where you are, which makes me look frightful; but I shall have another to-morrow, which will make amends for all, and set me off like a *Cavaliero Garbato.* Adieu. I give you joy of your escape from the Rhône, and of your reception in your Kingdom of Arles. I made Monsieur de Condom [1] shudder, by telling him your adventure; he has a sincere regard for you.

Madame DE SÉVIGNÉ *continues and concludes her letter.*

We are in pain here to know if you can keep from laughing when you are harangued. I am under some apprehensions for you upon that score. If your actions are of a piece with your words, the good folks do well to worship you. The number of those who compliment you by me, and desire me to let you know it, and beg to hear from you, is infinite: I should have my face as much ruffled as yours, were I to embrace them all. I shall communicate your accounts to Brancas. Father Bourdaloue's sermon this morning was beyond any he ever preached before. The Court is going continually to and from Versailles: the Dauphin and M. d'Anjou are better. There is rare news for you! Madame de La Fayette, and the company that are generally at her house, beg to have their friendship for you remembered, and desire that you will have a little for them. Madame de La Fayette says she should be highly pleased to act for a while the part you are acting, if for the sake of change only; you know she is apt to be weary of the same thing. M. d'Usèz [2] is charmed with the honours that are paid you; and is sure, that, since

[1] Bossuet, afterwards Bishop of Meaux.

[2] Jacques Adhémar de Monteil, Bishop of Usèz, uncle of M. de Grignan.

the days of Saint Trophime [1], there never was such a niece as you. Madame de Tourville is dead; Gouville weeps much. The Princess [2] is at Châteauroux *ad multos annos.* Your daughter is a handsome little dear; I love her, and take great care of her. I embrace M. de Grignan in spite of the bridge of Avignon.

LETTER 73

From Madame DE SÉVIGNÉ *to Madame* DE GRIGNAN.

Paris, Wednesday, March 11, 1671.

I am still without a letter; I may perhaps receive one before I seal this; think, my dear child, that it is upwards of a week since I have heard the least tidings of you, and that to me a week is an age. You have been at Arles, but I have not heard of your arrival at Aix from yourself. A gentleman [3] of that country called upon me yesterday, who was present when you arrived there, and saw you playing at *primero,* with Vardes, Bandol, and another person. I wish I could tell you in what manner I received him, and how he appeared to me, after having seen you no longer ago than last Thursday. You very much wondered at the Abbé de Vins leaving M. de Grignan; I wondered much more at this man being able to leave you: he found me with Father Mascaron, whom I had invited to dinner; as he preaches in my parish, and came to see me the other day, I thought it would be right to act the *devotee* a little by showing him this civility. He comes from Marseilles, and was quite pleased to hear us talk of Provence. I have learned too, by other hands, that you have had two or three little disputes since you have been there. My dear child, there is no possibility of being in Provence, without meeting with some unlucky accident.

[1] The first Bishop of Arles.

[2] Claire-Clémence de Maillé-Brézé, wife of Louis de Bourbon, Prince de Condé.

[3] Monsieur de Julianis.

But perhaps there may be no truth in what has been told me; so I will wait till it is confirmed by yourself, before I give my advice on the subject. I asked this gentleman if you were not very much fatigued, and he answered that you looked extremely handsome; but you know I am more clear-sighted than others, with respect to you, and I could plainly perceive, through their praises, that you are weak and dejected. I have had a cold for some days, for which I have kept my room: almost all your friends took the opportunity of coming to see me: the Abbé Têtu [1] desired me to make particular mention of him when I wrote to you. I never knew an absent person so truly present in the hearts of others; it is a miracle reserved for yourself. You know, we used to find we could do very well without our friends when they were gone; but there is no doing without you: my whole life is employed in talking of you: and I seek the company of those most who listen to me most. But do not imagine that I make myself ridiculous by it; for, in the first place, the subject is not so in itself; and then I know perfectly well my time, place, and persons, and what is proper to be said, and what not. You see I can speak pretty well of myself now and then: I beg pardon for it of Bourdaloue and Mascaron, for I go to hear one or the other every morning: and the tenth part of the glorious things they say, is more than sufficient to make a saint.

I have just received your letter, my dearest child, which I shall answer with all imaginable speed, for it is very late; this is the advantage of writing beforehand. I plainly perceive that what was told me respecting the affair at your first arrival was not all true: these little disputes in the towns of Provence, where the people think of nothing else, must necessarily bring on a multitude of explanations that are extremely tiresome. But, Madame la

[1] Jacques Têtu, Abbé of Belval, author of a book entitled, *Christian Stanzas on several Passages of the Scriptures and Fathers.* He was a Member of the French Academy: we must not confound him with another Abbé Têtu, who was of the same Academy, but of whom there is not the slightest mention in any of Madame de Sévigné's Letters.

Comtesse, are you not a very extraordinary personage to show my letters as you do? where is your principle of secrecy for those you love? Do you remember what trouble we used to have, to get a sight of the date only of one of M. de Grignan's to you? You think to appease me by the praises you bestow upon me; and at the same time hand me about like the *Holland Gazette*; but I will have my revenge! You conceal all the kind things I write to you, you little baggage; but I show those I receive from you, now and then, to particular friends: I do not intend that people shall think I have been very near death, and am daily in tears, *for whom? for a base ingrate*! I would have it seen that you love me, and that if you possess my whole heart, I have at least a part of yours. I shall deliver all your compliments; everyone asks me, "Am not I mentioned?" I answer, "Not yet, but you will be by and by." There are Monsieur d'Ormesson, for instance, and many others of the same stamp, who crowd around me to get a remembrance from you; so that all you send me are presently disposed of; and no wonder, my dear child, for you are truly amiable; there is no one like you. This however you may conceal, for surely, since Niobe [1], never mother talked as I do. As for M. de Grignan, he may assure himself, should I ever lay hold of his wife, I shall not readily give her back again. What! not even to thank me for such a present! nor to tell me that he is transported with it! He writes to beg an inestimable favour of me; and then when I have granted it, never once acknowledges it! However, I can easily suppose him overwhelmed with business as well as yourself: my anger weighs but little with me, but my love for you both a great deal. Your letter is very entertaining; it is a pity you had not time to say more. Good heavens! how do I long for your letters! it is now more than half an hour since I received one. I have no news for you: the King is in good health; he goes from Versailles to St.-Germain, and from St.-Germain to Versailles: everything remains as it did. The

[1] See her story, in Ovid, *Metam.* Book 6.

Queen performs her devotions very frequently, and goes to the elevation of the host. Father Bourdaloue continues to preach; no praises are adequate to his merit. Our Abbé had a little dispute the other day, before sermon, with Monsieur de Noyon [1], who gave him to understand that he ought to cede his place to a person of the house of Clermont. We laughed very heartily at this title taking precedence of an Abbé, at church. We reckoned how many keys [2] had been in the house of Tonnerre, and canvassed the good Prelate's knowledge in point of Peerage. I dine every Friday at Le Mans' [3], with M. de La Rochefoucauld, Madame de Brissac, and Benserade, who is always the life of the company. If Provence loves me, I am its most obedient humble servant; pray continue me in its good graces. I shall pay my respects to it whenever you think proper. I say nothing to M. de Vardes, nor to my friend Corbinelli, for I fancy they are returned to Languedoc. I love your daughter for your sake; for I do not yet find the bowels of grandmotherly affection yearn within me.

LETTER 74

From Madame DE SÉVIGNÉ *to Madame* DE GRIGNAN.

Paris, Friday, March 13, 1671.

To the joy of my heart, I am alone in my own apartment, and writing quietly to you—nothing is more agreeable to me than this. I dined to-day at Madame de Lavardin's after having been to Bourdaloue, where I saw the Mothers of the Church, for so I call the Princesses de Conti and de Longueville. All the world was at the sermon, and the sermon was worthy of the audience. I thought

[1] François de Clermont-Tonnerre, Bishop and Comte de Noyon, Peer of France, and Commander of the King's Orders.

[2] The cross keys are the proper symbol of the episcopal function, as well as the crosier.

[3] Philibert-Emmanuel de Beaumanoir, Bishop of Mans, Commander of the King's Orders.

of you twenty times, and wished as often that you were with me: you would have been delighted to hear it, and I should have been still more delighted to have seen you listening to it. Monsieur de La Rochefoucauld was at Madame de Lavardin's, and received with pleasantry the compliment you sent him: we talked a great deal about you. Monsieur d'Ambres was there with his cousin de Brissac: he appeared greatly interested in your supposed shipwreck; and but one opinion prevailed respecting your temerity. Monsieur de La Rochefoucauld said that you wished to appear courageous in the hope that some compassionate person would hinder you from going; and that finding no such person, you must have been precisely in the situation of poor Scaramouche. We have been to the fair to see a monster of a woman; she is taller than Riberpré by a whole head: she was brought to bed the other day, of two enormous children, who came into the world abreast, with their arms a-kimbo. She is a perfect giantess. I have given your compliments to the de Rambouillets, who send you a thousand in return. I have been to Madame du Pui-du-Fou's, and, for the third time to Madame de Maillanes': I often smile to myself at the pleasure I take in these little things. And now, should you suppose that the Queen's women are all run mad, you would not suppose amiss: for about a week since, Mesdames de Ludres, Coëtlogon, and little Rouvroi, were bitten by a little dog belonging to Théobon, which has since died mad; so that de Ludres, Coëtlogon, and Rouvroi, are gone this morning to Dieppe, for the purpose of bathing in the salt water: it is a melancholy journey for them, Benserade was quite in despair; Théobon would not go, though she was slightly bitten; but the Queen will not let her be in waiting, till it is seen how this adventure terminates. Can you fancy de Ludres an Andromeda? For my part, I think I see her bound to a rock, and Tréville on a flying horse, slaying the monster. *Ah! my Cot, Matame der Grignan, vat a ting it is to pe trown naket into der zea*[1]!

[1] Madame de Ludres' way of speaking.

Here is a budget full of nonsense, but not a syllable yet from you: you may suppose that I can guess at what you are doing; but the state of your health and your mind is too precious for me to rest satisfied with mere conjecture. The most trifling circumstances that relate to those we love are as dear to us as the concerns of others about whom we are indifferent are troublesome. In this truth we have often agreed. La Vauvineux sends you a thousand compliments; her daughter has been very ill, and so has Madame d'Arpajon: take notice of all this, and of Madame de Verneuil likewise, when you have leisure. I send you a letter from M. de Condom, which I received enclosed in a very pretty note. Your brother wears the chains of Ninon [1]; I wish they may do him no harm. There are minds that shudder at such ties. This same Ninon corrupted the morals of his father. Let us commend him to God. A Christian, or at least one who wishes to be a Christian, cannot see these irregularities without concern. Ah, Bourdaloue! what divine truths did you tell us to-day on the subject of death! Madame de La Fayette was there for the first time in her life, and was overcome with admiration: she is highly delighted with your remembrance of her. I have made her a present of a fine copy of your portrait; it ornaments a room in which you are never forgotten. If you are still in the same humour you were in at Sainte-Marie's, and preserve my letters, see if you have not received one dated the eighteenth of February.

A circumstance took place yesterday at Mademoiselle's which gave me no small pleasure. Who should come in but Madame de Gêvres, with all her airs and graces! I fancy she expected I should have offered her my place; but, to say the truth, I have owed her a little grudge for her conduct the other day, and now I paid her with interest, for I did not stir. Mademoiselle was in bed; Madame de Gêvres was therefore obliged to place herself at the lower end of the room, a provoking thing to be sure. The Princess called for drink; somebody must present the

[1] Mademoiselle Ninon de Lenclos.

napkin. I perceived Madame de Gêvres drawing the glove from her withered hand, upon which I gave Madame d'Arpajon, who was above me, a push, which she understood; and pulling off her glove, with the best grace in the world, advanced a step, got before the Duchess, took the napkin, and presented it. The Duchess was thoroughly embarrassed; for she had reached the upper end of the room, and had pulled off her gloves, only to have the mortification of being a nearer witness of Madame d'Arpajon's presenting the napkin before her. My dear child, I am very wicked; this pleased me infinitely: it was uncommonly well done. Would anyone have thought of depriving Madame d'Arpajon of a little piece of honour, which is naturally her due, as being one of the bed-chamber? Madame de Puisieux was very much diverted by it As for Mademoiselle, she did not dare look up, and my countenance was not the most settled. After this, a thousand kind things were said to me about you; and Mademoiselle was pleased to order me to tell you, that she is very glad you escaped drowning, and are in good health.

I shall give you the two volumes of La Fontaine; and be as angry as you please, I insist upon it that they have some entertaining passages, and some very dull ones. We are never satisfied with having done well, and in endeavouring to do better, we do much worse.

LETTER 75

From Madame DE SÉVIGNÉ *to Madame* DE GRIGNAN.

Paris, Sunday, March 15, 1671.

Monsieur de La Brosse wishes me to give him a letter of introduction to you. Is not this an excellent jest? You know the esteem and friendship I have for him; you know his father is one of my oldest friends; you know the merits of them both, and have all the esteem for them that I could wish to inspire you with: of what use then can my letters be to him? It is to me only that it can be of service, for it furnishes me with an opportunity of writing to you. It is amusing enough to observe what pleasure we take in conversing with a person we love, though at a distance; and how tiresome it is to be obliged to write to others. I think myself happy in having begun my day with you. Little Pecquet has attended me for a horrible cold I have had, and which will be gone by the time you receive this. We talked of you, and afterwards I set about writing to you. I do not understand why the post should be so irregular, and why the people who are so obliging as to set out at midnight with my letters to you, should be so very remiss in bringing back your answers. The Abbé and I are continually talking about your affairs; but as he gives you an account of all that passes, I shall say no more. Your health, your ease, your affairs, are the three principal subjects that occupy my thoughts, from which I draw an inference that I leave you to reflect upon.

LETTER 76

From Madame DE SÉVIGNÉ *to Madame* DE GRIGNAN.

Paris, Wednesday, March 18, 1671.

I have received two packets at once, which have been delayed for a considerable time. By these I am at length informed from yourself, of your entry into Aix, but you do not mention whether your husband was with you, or in what manner Vardes honoured your triumph; but you describe the triumph itself very humorously, as well as the embarrassment you were under, and your many misplaced civilities. I wish to God that I had been with you; not that I should have done better than yourself, for I have not so good a gift of fixing names upon faces; on the contrary, I daily commit a thousand blunders in that way;

but I think I could have been of some assistance to you, at least I should have done the honours: it is true, that such a multiplicity of ceremonies and attentions are very tiresome. You should, nevertheless, endeavour not to be deficient in any of these points, but accommodate yourself, as much as possible, to the customs and the manners of those amongst whom you are to live.

An event has just taken place, which engrosses the whole conversation of Paris. The King has ordered Monsieur de S**** to resign his post, and to quit Paris, immediately. Can you guess the reason? For having cheated at play, and won upwards of five hundred thousand crowns with false cards! The man who made these cards was examined by the King himself: he denied the fact at first; but, upon His Majesty promising him a pardon, he confessed that he had followed the trade for a long time: it is said, that the affair will not stop here, for that there are several houses which he used to furnish with these cards. It was some time before the King could prevail upon himself to disgrace a man of Monsieur de S****'s quality; but as, for several months past, everybody who had played with him had been in a manner ruined, he thought he could not in conscience do less than bring such a scene of villiany to light. S**** was so perfectly master of his adversaries' game, that he always made *sept et le va* upon the Queen of Spades, because he knew the Spades lay all in the other packs. The King as constantly lost at *trente-un* upon Clubs, and used to say, "Clubs never win against Spades in this country." This man had given thirty pistoles to Madame de La Vallière's *valets de chambre* to throw all the cards they had in the house into the river, under the pretence that they were not good, and had introduced his own card-maker. He was first led into this fine way of life by one Pradier, who has since disappeared. Had S**** known himself innocent, he would immediately have delivered himself up, and insisted upon taking his trial; but instead of this, he took the road to Languedoc, as the surest way of the two: many, however, strongly advised him to take a journey to La Trappe [1], after such a disgrace.

Madame d'Humières has charged me with a thousand good wishes for you: she is going to Lille, where she will receive as many honours as you did at Aix. Maréchal de Bellefonds, through a pure motive of piety, has settled with his creditors: he has given up to them the principal part of his property, besides half the profits of his post [2], to complete the payment of the arrears. This is a noble action, and shows that his visits to La Trappe have not been without effect. I went the other day to see the Duchess de Ventadour, she was as handsome as an angel. The Duchess de Nevers came in with her hair dressed very ridiculously. You may believe me, for you know I am an admirer of fashion. La Martin had cropped her to the very extremity of the mode.

Your brother is at St.-Germain; he divides his time with Ninon, a young actress [3], and, to crown the whole, Despréaux. We lead him a sad life.

LETTER 77

From Madame de Sévigné *to Madame* de Grignan.

The same day, 18th March, 1671.

Before I send away my packet, I shall reply to your letter of the eleventh, which I have just received. You cannot possibly feel so keenly as I do, the delays of the post.

[1] *La Trappe* is a society of religious monks, remarkable for the austerity of their lives, and the severe discipline practised amongst them.

[2] That of Chief Maître d'hôtel, or Master of the Household, to the King.

[3] Called La Champmêlé.

Monsieur DE BARILLON [1] *writes to Madame* DE GRIGNAN *in her Mother's letter.*

I interrupt your amiable mother to write two or three words to you, which if not very elegant will at least have the merit of being true. Know then, Madame, that I have always loved you more than I have ever ventured to express, and that if ever I am King, Provence shall no longer have a *Governante*. In the meantime govern well, and reign with mildness over the people whom heaven has subjected to your law. Adieu, Madame; I quit Paris without regret.

Madame DE SÉVIGNÉ *continues and concludes her letter.*

Poor Barillon has interrupted me: he finds me still unable to receive your letters without tears. I cannot help it, my dear child; wish me not to suppress them. Love me for my affection, love me even for my weakness; I am satisfied myself. I prefer my feelings to all the fine sentiments of Seneca or Epictetus. I am tender and affectionate even to folly, you are everything to me, my dear child, I know nothing but you. Alas! I am precisely in the condition you suppose; fond of those who love and think of you. I feel this every day more and more. When I met *Mellusine,* my heart beat with anger and emotion; she came up to me in her usual way: "Well, Madame," said she, "are you very much grieved?"—"Yes, Madame," I replied, "as much as it is possible to be!"—"Ah, I believe it; well, I must come and comfort you."—"You may spare yourself the trouble, Madame, for it will be to no purpose."—"Why, are you not at home then?" said she.—"No, Madame, I am never to be met with." Thus ended our dialogue. I assure you she is quite *debellated,* as M. de Coulanges says; she seems at present to have no tongue left. But to return to my letters, which have not been

[1] Counsellor of State, and Ambassador to the Court of England.

sent to you; I am very much mortified about it. Do you think they will be opened or detained? Alas! I conjure those who give themselves all this trouble, to consider how little pleasure they will reap from the perusal, and how much vexation they will occasion to us both. Be careful at least, gentlemen, to seal them up again, that they may come to hand one time or another. You talk of painting in description; the picture you draw of the dress of the ladies of your Province, is certainly as excellent as it is possible for description to be. You say you wish you could see me enter your room, and hear me speak. Alas! it is my greatest delight to see you, to converse with you, to listen to you; I destroy myself with vain longings, and with vexation for not having gazed and listened to you more; though I lost few of the precious moments that were left me, I am still discontented. I am a fool; that is beyond dispute; but you are bound to love my folly. I cannot conceive how one can be always thinking of the same person. Shall I never cease to think of you? No! not till thought is no more.

LETTER 78

From Madame DE SÉVIGNÉ *to Madame* DE GRIGNAN.

Paris, Friday, March 20, 1671.

The Coadjutor of Rheims was with us the other day at Madame de Coulanges'. I complained to him of the irregularity of the post; and he told me he too had been served in the same way; for he had written twice to you, and had received no answer. He is going to Rheims, and Madame de Coulanges said to him, "Rheims! what folly to think of going there! what are you to do there? you will be as weary as a dog. Pray stay here, and we will take a jaunt now and then together." We could not help laughing at this speech to an Archbishop, nor could she herself; but though we did not think it very canonical, yet we were persuaded, that, were the ladies to address many of our reverend prelates in the same manner, they might not altogether lose their labour. Monsieur de La Rochefoucauld has asked me twenty times, whether you had received his sugar-plums, and I told him all the sweet things you said upon the occasion. Instead of sugar-plums, he now sends you a story. He was told by the Comte d'Estrées [1], that in his voyage to Guinea he happened to fall in with some of the inhabitants who had been converted to Christianity, and that going one day into one of their churches, he saw twenty negro Canons, quite naked, with square caps upon their heads, and the *aumusse* [2] upon their left arms, chanting the service. He begs you will make some reflections upon this singular experience, and says you must not suppose they had anything like a surplice on them, but were as naked as they were born, and as black as so many devils. There, my commission is executed.

Madame de Guise has made a *faux pas* at Versailles, which she endeavoured to conceal: she was brought to bed at the four months' end of a poor little infant, who was not baptised. This is a warning to us to take care of ourselves, and not hide our faults when we have committed them. D'Hacqueville has sent you a very droll song, that has been made on Monsieur de Longueville; it is in imitation of a recitative in an entertainment that you are not acquainted with, but which you have heard me extol highly. I know it, and can sing it very well. You have written a very pretty letter to Guitaud. I am passionately fond of your letters. If I possess the art of painting in words, and you that of seeing what I describe, you will certainly not forget the Canons of Guinea. The other day, as Father Desmares [3] was going into the pulpit, a *billet*

[1] Charles-Maurice Le Tellier.

[2] An ornament which Canons wear on the left arm when they go to their office.

[3] Priest of the Oratory.

was slipped into his hand; and putting on his spectacles, he began to read it aloud; it was as follows:

> De par Monseigneur de Paris,
> On déclare à tous les maris
> Que leurs femmes on baisera.
> Alleluia. [1]

He read about half of it before he discovered his mistake; everyone was ready to die with laughing. You see we have wits among us. I suppose you know that MADEMOISELLE has turned off Guilloire; and poor Segrais is not very highly in favour: it seems they had both expressed their sentiments too freely on the affair of Monsieur de Lauzun. Say something respecting Madame de Lavardin in one of your letters; she always speaks with enthusiasm of your merit, and I feel with enthusiasm a mother's fondness; if I do not tell you so as often as I would like to, it is from discretion; but you occupy me incessantly; and without establishing a rendezvous for the mind, like Mademoiselle de Scuderi, you may be assured that you can never think of me when I am not thinking of you. Fix your eye upon the moon, which I behold also, and we shall both see the same object, though at the distance of two hundred leagues from each other.

LETTER 79

From Madame DE SÉVIGNÉ *to Madame* DE GRIGNAN.

Paris, Monday, March 23, 1671.

Is it not hard that your letters should still be delayed? Monsieur de Coulanges has received his, and has just been here to insult me with them. He has shown me your answer to the *extempore,* which I thought so pretty that

[1] His Grace of Paris gives to know
To every husband, high and low,
That we their wives will kiss.
Hallelujah. [Translation.]

I read it twice over, with pleasure. How exactly you express my idea! This *extempore* was made at one end of the table on which I was writing to you; it pleased me extremely, and put me in mind of that in which I failed so dreadfully. Do you remember how cruel you were to me on that day? You condemned me without mercy, and not all the entreaties of d'Hacqueville could prevail on you to grant me a second hearing. I had committed a great fault to be sure, but to be condemned as I was, without judge or jury, was really very hard. Monsieur de Coulanges' song was also a good one. It is a pleasure to send you these trifles, you answer them so charmingly. What can be more provoking, than, after having written something that we imagine will please and amuse, to have it passed by unnoticed, or at least received with indifference? You are not so cruel; you are amiable in every respect and everywhere. How much too are you beloved! in how many hearts do you hold the first place! There are few who can say so much. Monsieur de Coulanges is writing you the most ridiculous letter in the world, but quite natural; it has diverted me extremely. I was yesterday at Monsieur de La Rochefoucauld's. I found him screaming violently; his pain was so acute that it quite overcame his fortitude. He was sitting in his chair, in a violent fever, and delirious from the excess of pain: I was greatly concerned for him; I never saw him in such a condition before. He desired I would inform you of it, and assure you that the tortures of those who are breaking upon the wheel, do not exceed what he endures half his life; and that he wishes as earnestly for death as they for the *coup de grâce*. His night was not any better.

I have just received your letter, and have retired to my room, to answer it. After coming from any place where I have dined, I fly here, and if I find a letter from you, I immediately sit down, and write. No pleasure is equal to this; so that I long with impatience for the days when the post comes in. Ah! my dear child, what a difference there is between my manner of receiving letters from you, and letters from persons I do not love! You desire me to read calmly the account of your danger: I have been more alarmed, if possible, from the letters I have seen from Avignon and other places, than from those I received from yourself. I enter fully into M. de Grignan's feeling when he cried out, *Vogue la galère* [1]! You are really sometimes enough to drive me mad! If you had concealed this adventure from me, I should have heard of it from others, and then I should have taken it very unkindly of you. I shall be very much displeased with M. de Marseilles, if he does not grant our request. Notwithstanding all his fine speeches, I have no great opinion of the love he pretends to have for Provence, when he neither does nor says anything to put a stop to those four hundred and fifty thousand francs, and makes such a fuss about trifles. I am his most humble servant. I am extremely impatient to know the result of this. Madame d'Angoulême tells us she has heard you are the most polite person in the world; she sends you a thousand compliments. I dread my journey to Brittany more than you do. Methinks it will be a second separation, grief upon grief, parting upon parting, absence upon absence. In short, I begin to be seriously uneasy about it; it will be towards the beginning of May. As to my other journey, for which you tell me the road is free, you are sensible it depends wholly upon yourself; I have left it to you, and you have only to inform d'Hacqueville when it is to take place. Monsieur de Vivonne has an excellent memory, to pay me so hackneyed a compliment; pray make my respects to him, I shall write to him two years hence. Are you not delighted with Bandol? Say a great many civil things to him for me. He has written a letter to M. de Coulanges, a letter that is like himself, perfectly amiable. Let me now desire you to take care, not to lose your money at play, through indolence; these losses, trifling as they may appear, if often repeated, are like small showers, which, by frequently falling, spoil the roads. I embrace you, my dear child, and conjure you

[1] Happy, go lucky, let the world go how it will. [Translation.]

to continue to love me; that being the only thing upon earth that I am solicitous about with respect to myself. I have many wishes with regard to you: in short, everything turns on you, of you, or by you.

LETTER 80

From Madame DE SÉVIGNÉ *to Madame* DE GRIGNAN.

Livry, Tuesday in Passion-week, March 24, 1671.

I have been here these three hours, my dear child: I set out from Paris with the Abbé, Hélène, Hébert, and *Marphise*[1], in order to retire from the noise and bustle of the world till Thursday night. I purpose to remain in strict retirement; I shall make this a little La Trappe, and pass my time in prayer and reflection. I am resolved to observe a strict fast while I am here, for many reasons; to walk now, for all the time I have hitherto kept my room, and, above all, to humble myself before God. But what I shall observe more strictly than all this, is to think of you, my child. This I have not ceased to do since the moment of my arrival; insomuch that, being no longer able to contain the sentiments that fill my heart, I am set down to give vent to them on paper, at the end of the little shady alley you are so fond of; I sit upon the bank of moss on which I have so often formerly seen you lie. But, good God, what place is there here where I have not seen you? and how do all these thoughts crowd upon my heart! There is not a place, not a spot, in the house, in the church, in the country round, or in the garden, where I have not seen you; and which does not furnish me with some fresh subject for remembrance, and present you in a manner to my eyes. I think of the same things again and again; my head, my heart, my mind, are all at work;

[1] Hélène, Madame de Sévigné's *femme-de-chambre,* Hébert, her *valet-de-chambre,* and Marphise, the name of a favourite dog.

but in vain I turn my eyes, in vain I look around: the dear child that I adore, is two hundred leagues from me—she is no longer with me: then I cannot forbear bursting into tears. This is a great weakness, but I have not the power to resist a feeling so just and so natural. I know not what disposition you may be in when you read this; chance may direct it to your hand in an unlucky moment, and then perhaps, it will not be read with the same spirit in which it is written; if so, I cannot help it; however, it serves at present to relieve me, and that is all I expect from it. The state into which this place has thrown me is scarcely conceivable. I beseech you to conceal my foibles from others; but you ought to love them yourself, and to respect the tears which flow from a heart that is wholly your own.

LETTER 81

From Madame DE SÉVIGNÉ *to Madame* DE GRIGNAN.

Livry, Holy-Thursday, March 26, 1671.

Had I shed as many tears for my sins as I have on your account, since I have been here, I should be in an excellent disposition to observe my Easter and jubilee. I should have passed my time here in the manner I proposed, had not the remembrance of you haunted me more than I thought it would. How strange is the force of imagination! it represents things as if they were actually present to us; we consider them so, and to a heart like mine, this is death. I know not where to hide myself from you. When in Paris, the house there renews my grief daily, and Livry overwhelms me. On your part, it is from an effort of memory that you think of me. Provence cannot set me before your eyes, as every place here presents you to mine. I have experienced something like pleasure here, even in the midst of my grief. The deep solitude, the awful silence, the melancholy office of the day, the devout singing of the *tenebræ* [1], and the solemn fast, added to the beauty of the gardens, which would charm you, all these have afforded me great pleasure. I never passed a Passion-week here before: how often have I wished for you here! but I am obliged to return to Paris; there I shall find some letters from you. I intend going to-morrow to hear Bourdaloue, or Mascaron, on *The Passion*: I always had a great veneration for those devotional seasons. Adieu, my dear love, you will hear no more from me from Livry: could I have had resolution enough to forbear writing to you from here, and to have made a sacrifice to God of the emotions of my heart, it would have been of more value than all the penances that could be imposed: but, instead of making a good use of this retirement, I have amused myself with nothing but writing to you about it. Ah! my child, how weak, how wretched is this in me!

LETTER 82

From Madame DE SÉVIGNÉ *to Madame* DE GRIGNAN.

Paris, Good-Friday, March 27, 1671.

I found a large packet of letters from you, on my arrival here. I shall answer the gentlemen when I am less employed in my devotions: in the meantime, embrace your dear husband for me; I am sensibly affected with his friendship and his letter. I am very glad that the bridge of Avignon falls upon the back of the Coadjutor; for I find it was he that made you pass it. As for poor Grignan, he was resolved to be drowned with you, out of spite; choosing rather to die, than live with such unreasonable people; it is all over with the Coadjutor, now he has this fault to answer for along with the rest. I am extremely obliged to Bandol, for his agreeable narrative. But what reason, my dear, have you to fear that any other

[1] A service in the Romish church.

letter should set aside yours? you certainly could not have read it over a second time. To me, who have perused it with the greatest attention, it gave real pleasure, a pleasure that nothing can exceed; a pleasure too great to be indulged in on a day like this: you have satisfied my curiosity in a thousand things I wanted to know. I doubted whether the predictions relating to Vardes were all false; I doubted whether you had not been guilty of some omission in point of ceremony; I doubted whether the life you led was so dull as you represented: but what will surprise you most is, that with all the aversion which I know you have for relating little stories, I believed that you had too much good sense not to see, that it is sometimes both agreeable and necessary.

I am of opinion, that no subject should be absolutely prohibited in conversation; and that a proper discernment, and proper occasions, may introduce by turns everything that is proper to compose it. I cannot conceive why you should say you do not tell a story well; I am sure I know few that command more attention than yourself: this is not the only necessary qualification, I grant; but when that supplies the place of wit, and makes it impossible for you to say anything disagreeable, I think you ought to be satisfied with acquitting yourself as you do.

I heard Mascaron on *The Passion,* and he made a very fine and affecting discourse: I had a great inclination to go afterwards to Bourdaloue, but it was impossible: places had been kept ever since Wednesday, and the crowd was terrific. I knew it was to be the same sermon that Monsieur de Grignan and I heard him preach last year at the Jesuits, and it was that which gave me so strong a desire to go: it was extremely fine, but it was only like a dream to me. How I pity you in having such a wretched preacher! but was that a reason for laughing? I shall be apt to say to you, as I did once before, "What tired! oh for shame!" I never suspected your being happy with M. de Grignan; nor, to my knowledge, did I ever express the least doubt of it; only I should be glad to hear that you were so from you or from him, not by way of information, but as a pleasing confirmation of what I so ardently desire. Without that, Provence would be indeed insupportable; but I readily believe, Monsieur de Grignan takes no small pains to make you pass your time there as agreeably as possible. He and I have the same feelings at heart.

Maréchal d'Albret has gained a suit on which depended forty thousand livres a year, and is put into the possession of all that belonged to his ancestors. He has ruined all Béarn: there are twenty families that had bought and sold for considerable sums, who are now obliged to restore the whole with interest for a hundred years past. This affair will be attended with dreadful consequences. But farewell, thou little demon! who divertest my thoughts from everything else; I ought to have been an hour ago at the *tenebræ*.

LETTER 83

From Madame DE SÉVIGNÉ *to Madame* DE GRIGNAN.

Paris, Wednesday, April 1, 1671.

I returned yesterday from St.-Germain with Madame d'Arpajon. Everyone at Court inquired after you; among the rest, it will not be amiss, I think, to distinguish the Queen, who accosted me, and asked how my daughter was after her affair upon the Rhône: I returned Her Majesty thanks for the honour she did you in remembering you. She then desired me to tell her in what manner you had like to have been lost: I accordingly gave her an account of your crossing the river in a storm of wind, and that a sudden gust had thrown you under an arch, within an inch of one of the piles, which if you had once touched, all the world could not have saved you. "But," says the Queen, "Was her husband with her?" "Yes, Madame, and the Coadjutor too." "Really," said she, "they were greatly to blame." She gave two or three Alases! while I was talking to her, and said many obliging things of you. Afterwards a number of ladies came in, and among the rest, the young Duchess de Ventadour, very fine and very handsome; it was some time before they brought her the divine tabouret [1]; "Ah," said I, turning to the Grand Master [2], "why do they not give it her, she has purchased it dearly enough?" [3] He was of my opinion. In the midst of a silence in the circle, the Queen turned to me, and asked me who my grand-daughter was like? "M. de Grignan, Madame," replied I; upon which Her Majesty exclaimed, "Indeed! I am sorry for it;" and added, in a low tone of voice, "She had better have resembled her mother or grandmother:" so you see how much I am indebted to you in making my Court. Maréchal de Bellefonds made me promise to distinguish him from the crowd: I made your compliments to Monsieur and Madame de Duras, and to Messieurs de Charost and de Montausier, and *tutti quanti,* not to forget the Dauphin and Mademoiselle, who both talked a great deal to me about you. I likewise saw Madame de Ludres, she accosted me with an excess of civility and kindness that surprised me, and talked in the most affectionate manner of you; when all on a sudden, as I was going to make her a suitable answer, I found she was not attending to me, and saw her fine eyes wandering round the room; I presently perceived it, and those who saw I took notice of it, were pleased with me, and could not help laughing. She has been dipped in the sea [4]: the sea beheld all her naked beauties, and is grown, if possible, more proud than ever; the sea I mean, for the pride of the fair one was rather humbled.

I have been extremely diverted with our hurly-burly head-dresses; some of them looked as if you could have

[1] The tabouret was a stool to sit on in presence of the Queen, a privilege never enjoyed but by ladies of the first quality.

[2] The Comte du Lude, Grand Master of the Artillery.

[3] Monsieur de Ventadour was not only very ugly and deformed, but, at the same time, a great debauchee.

[4] See Letter 74, of the 13th March, 1671, in this volume.

blown them off their shoulders. Ninon[1] said that La Choiseul was as like the flaunting hostess of an inn, as one drop of water to another; a most excellent simile! But that Ninon is a dangerous creature; if you only knew how she argues upon religion, it would make you shudder. Her zeal to pervert the minds of young people is much the same as that of a certain gentleman of St.-Germain that we saw once at Livry. She says, your brother has all the simplicity of the dove, that he is just like his mother; but that Madame de Grignan has all the fire of the family, and has more sense than to be so docile. A certain person would have taken your part, and put her out of conceit with you on that head; but she bid him hold his tongue, and told him, that she knew more of the matter than he did. What a depravity of taste! because she knows you to be handsome and witty, she must needs saddle you with the other qualification, without which, according to her rule, there is no being perfect. I am greatly concerned for the harm she does my son on this point; but do not mention or allude to it with him. Madame de La Fayette and I use all our endeavours to disengage him from so dangerous an attachment: besides her, he has a little actress[2], and all the players of the town upon his hands, to whom he gives suppers; in short, he is perfectly infatuated. You know what a joke he makes of Mascaron. I fancy your Minim[3] would suit him. I never read anything more diverting than what you wrote to me about that man; I read it to Monsieur de La Rochefoucauld, who laughed heartily at it. He desires me to tell you, that there is a certain apostle who is running up and down after his rib, which he would fain appropriate to himself, as a part of his goods and chattels; but unluckily for him, he is not clever at enterprise. I fancy *Mellusine* is fallen into some pit, we do not hear a single word about her. M. de La

[1] Ninon de Lenclos, notorious for her wit and free-thinking, and for other things too.

[2] La Champmêlé.

[3] The Priest who preached at Grignan.

Rochefoucauld says besides, that if he was only thirty years younger, he should certainly have a great inclination for M. de Grignan's third rib [1]. That part of your letter, where you say he has already had two of his ribs broken, made him laugh heartily: we always wish for some oddity or other to divert you, but we very much doubt whether this has not turned out rather more to your satisfaction than ours. After all, we pity you extremely, in not having the word of God preached in a suitable manner. Ah, that Bourdaloue! his sermon on *The Passion* was, they say, the most perfect thing of the kind that can be imagined; it was the same he preached last year, but revised and altered with the assistance of some of his friends, that it might be wholly inimitable: how can one love God, if one never hears him properly spoken of? you must really possess a greater portion of grace than others. We went the other day to hear the Abbé Montmort [2]; I never heard a prettier sermon for so young a beginner: I wish you had such a one in the place of your Minim. He made the sign of the cross, and gave out his text; he did not anathematise his audience, he did not load us with abuse; he told us not to be under any apprehensions concerning death, since it was the only passage we had to a glorious resurrection with Jesus Christ. We agreed with him in this, and everyone went away contented: he has nothing offensive in his manner; he imitates Monsieur d'Agen without copying him; he has a modest confidence, is learned, and pious; in short, I was highly pleased with him.

Madame de Vauvineux desires me to send you a thousand thanks: her daughter has been very ill. Madame d' Arpajon embraces you, and M. Le Camus professes to adore you; and I, my dear child, what do you think I do?—love you, think of you incessantly, melt into tears much oftener than I wish, busy myself in your affairs, make myself unhappy about your thoughts of me, feel all your dis-

[1] That is, to Madame de Grignan, who was M. de Grignan's third wife.

[2] Afterwards Bishop of Perpignan.

quiets and chagrins, wish to suffer them for you, and, if it were possible, to remove everything unpleasing from your heart, as I used to remove whatever I found superfluous or disagreeable in your apartment; in a word, think what it is to love another infinitely beyond yourself, and this is what I do. These are often words of course, and the expression is much abused; but I repeat it again, without profanation, and I feel it truly in its full force.

LETTER 84

From Madame DE SÉVIGNÉ *to Madame* DE GRIGNAN.

Paris, Friday, April 3, 1671.

I send you a number of letters, which I beg you to distribute for me. I hope the two which are unsealed will please you; they were written off hand; for you know I never attempt to mend but I spoil. If we were nearer to each other I might alter them to your fancy, for you know I always had a great opinion of your judgment. But what can be done at such a distance? You have charmed me by writing to M. Le Camus. Your own good sense has made you act as if *Castor* and *Pollux* had conveyed my thoughts to you. I send you his answer. We laughed very heartily yesterday, at M. de La Rochefoucauld's, at the letter your brother sent you. I saw the Duc at Madame de La Fayette's; he enquired very kindly after you, and desired me to tell you, that he is going to the States of Burgundy, and that he shall judge, by the fatigue of his own entry, what you must have suffered in yours. Madame de Brissac came in; there is an air of warfare, or at least, of ill-conditioned peace, between them, which enlivened us. We found they were playing at cross-purposes, as you and he formerly did. There was a keenness in all this that highly amused those who observed it. Just then came in La Marans [1], she smelt a rat. I must tell you

[1] Mellusine.

what Madame de La Fayette and I said to her, without having concerted it beforehand, when she desired us to take her with us to spend the evening with her son [1]. "You will be kind enough, Madame, to bring me back in your carriage," said she to me. "Pardon me, Madame, I am obliged to stop at Madame du Pui-du-Fou's;" a great lie, for I had been there before. Well, away she goes to Madame de La Fayette; "Madame," says she, "I suppose my son can send me back in his carriage." "Indeed, Madame, I do not think he can, for he sold his horses yesterday to the Marquis de Ragni." This was another lie; the sale was an invention of her own. Soon after, Madame de Schomberg called for her; and she was obliged to go, and leave both this show of love, and the hope of seeing her son with us. She went off with her heart ready to burst with rage; and then Madame de La Fayette and I consecrated our two answers to you, unwilling to omit any occasion of offering a just sacrifice to your revenge. I took upon myself to give you this account, and we join in wishing it may delight you, as much as it did us. I am going to dine *en Lavardin*. I shall finish my letter this evening; I will not make it a long one; I am afraid it will fatigue you.

Friday night.

I have dined *en Lavardinage* [2], or rather *en bavardinage*. I have never seen anything like it; but though Madame de Brissac was in one of her best humours, yet she could not supply the want of Monsieur de La Rochefoucauld and Benserade.

The King has insisted upon a reconciliation between Madame de Longueville and Mademoiselle. They met at the Carmelites, and there it was effected. Mademoi-

[1] So she used to call M. de La Rochefoucauld.

[2] With Madame de Lavardin. The joke here lies in the similitude of sounds in the two words *Lavardinage* and *Bavardinage*, which it is impossible to preserve in English, and means no more than that the afternoon was spent in mere tittle-tattle, or what we call tea-table chat. *Bavarder*, to *talk idly*, to *babble* or *rattle*.

selle has given Guilloire fifty thousand francs: we all wish she had done as much for Segrais. The Marquis d'Ambres is at length acknowledged as the King's other Lieutenant of Guinea, on paying two hundred thousand francs. I do not know whether his regiment [1] is yet taken into pay; when I do, I will inform you. Adieu, my dearest love, I will not fatigue you, there is reason in all things.

LETTER 85

From Madame DE SÉVIGNÉ *to Madame* DE GRIGNAN.

Paris, Saturday, April 4, 1671.

[This Letter, which is written partly by Madame de Sévigné, and partly by her friend Madame de La Troche, is wholly taken up with describing the new fashion of cutting and curling the hair, which then prevailed among the ladies of the Court; a subject which, however entertaining it might have been at that time, between the persons concerned in the correspondence, does not appear of consequence enough to merit a translation.]

LETTER 86

From Madame DE SÉVIGNÉ *to Madame* DE GRIGNAN.

Paris, Wednesday, April 8, 1671.

Good God! my dear child, how charming are your letters! there are passages in them worthy of the press: you will certainly find, some day or other, you will have a treacherous friend who will print them. You have been, it seems, to your devotions, where you found our poor sisters of St. Marie. You have got a cell among them; but take care you do not fatigue your mind too much; gloomy reveries indulged in too much are sometimes dangerous. We should pass over lightly painful images: you will find great satisfaction in being at a house where you were mistress.

[1] The regiment of Champagne.

I cannot but admire the customs of your ladies in Provence; the description you give me of their ceremoniousness, is a finished piece of its kind: but it would drive me mad, and I cannot conceive how you bear it. You imagine that I should do admirably well in Provence; far from it, I assure you I should be quite rude; everything unreasonable vexes me, and want of sincerity offends me. I should say to them, "Ladies, let us understand one another; am I to conduct you back again? If I am, I desire you will not prevent me, nor let us stand wasting our time and breath to no purpose: if you do not wish this, pray spare me the ceremony of making the offer." I am not in the least surprised, that their farcical mode of proceeding puts you out of patience; I should have still less patience than you have.

But a word or two concerning your brother: Ninon has dismissed him. She is weary of loving without being loved in return; she has insisted upon his returning her letters, which he has accordingly done. I was not a little pleased at this separation. I gave him a hint of the duty he owed to God, reminded him of his former good sentiments, and entreated him not to stifle all notions of religion in his breast: had it not been for his allowing me this liberty of throwing in a word or two now and then, I should not have permitted a confidence with which I had nothing to do. But this is not all; when one side gives way, we think to repair it with the other, and are deceived. The young *Merveille* has not broken as yet, but she will soon, I believe. I know now why your brother came yesterday from the farther end of Paris to see me. He wanted to acquaint me with an accident that had befallen him: he found a favourable opportunity; but when he came to the point —— it was a strange thing! the poor damsel never had been so entertained in her life: the disconcerted Cavalier retired, thinking himself bewitched, and what is better still, he could not be easy till he had acquainted me with his disaster: we laughed very heartily at him: I told him I was overjoyed to find him punished in the sinful part; he laid the blame upon me, and told me he fancied I had given him some of the ice that was in my composition; that he did not desire to resemble me in that particular, and that I had better have conferred it on my daughter. He was resolved to apply to Pecquet to put him to rights again; said the most extravagant things in the world, and so did I too; in short, it was a scene worthy of Molière. But the truth of the matter is, this affair has given such a check to the gentleman's imagination, that he will not come to himself again very soon. In vain I assure him, that the empire of love abounds in tragic stories; he is deaf to all reasoning on this head. The poor *Chimenè* says, she sees plainly, that he no longer loves her, and has applied herself elsewhere for comfort. In short, this affair makes me laugh, and I wish sincerely it may be the means of weaning him from a state so offensive to God, and dangerous to his own soul. Ninon told him, that he was *a mere pumpkin fricasseed in snow.* See what it is to keep good company! one learns such pretty expressions!

Your brother told me the other day of a player, who being resolved to marry, though he laboured under a certain dangerous disorder, one of his companions said to him, "Zounds, cannot you stay till you are cured? you will be the ruin of us all." I thought there was something very epigrammatical in this turn.

A few days ago, Madame de Marans was at Madame de La Fayette's; "Lord bless me," says she, "I must have my hair cut!" "Dear Madame," says Madame de La Fayette, pointedly to her, "I would not advise you to have that done upon any account; it is a fashion that becomes none but young people." If that stroke does not please you, let us hear something better of your own.

I send you a letter I received from Monsieur de Marseilles. I fancy my answer will be such as you will approve, since you would have it frank and sincere, "and agreeable to that friendship you have sworn to yourself, which is built on interest, and cemented by dissimulation." This last phrase is in Tacitus: I think I never read anything more beautiful: I approve the sentiment, and shall adopt it, since it must be so. Adieu, my love, I think of nothing but you; and if by a miracle, which I neither desire nor wish, you should for a moment be absent from my mind, I should fancy myself as void of soul as one of Benoît's figures [1].

Monsieur d'Ambres has resigned his regiment to the King for eighty thousand francs, and one hundred and eighty thousand livres, which makes the two hundred thousand francs [2]. He thinks himself very happy in being out of the infantry, that is, the hospital.

LETTER 87

From Madame DE SÉVIGNÉ *to Madame* DE GRIGNAN.

Paris, Thursday, April 9, 1671.

Monsieur Magalotti is going to set out for Provence: how I should like to accompany him! I do not know what pleasure he may take in seeing you, but I am sure it would be a sensible one to me. He is now at play with my little grand-daughter: he thought you must be very handsome when he saw the child. I too, who think all the Grignans beauties, am very well pleased with her. I dare say you will be glad to see a man of worth, a man of the world, a man who, if you choose it, will talk French and Italian with you, a man whose accomplishments are acknowledged by all the Court, a man, in short, who brings you two pairs of Georget's shoes; what more can I say in his praise? He is going to visit Madame de Monaco, and I will lay any wager that you will write to her by him: he says, that without a letter from me, he should not be received by you as he could wish; in short, he makes a jest

[1] An artist very famous for his figures in wax.

[2] The price that was given for the post of Lieutenant-General of Upper Guyenne.

of me. I envy him, and embrace you most sincerely, but not in order to make an end of my letter.

LETTER 88

From Madame DE SÉVIGNÉ *to Madame* DE GRIGNAN.

Paris, Friday, April 10, 1671.

I wrote to you on Wednesday by the post, yesterday by Magalotti, and to-day again by the post; but last night I lost a charming opportunity. I went to walk at Vincennes, *en Troche* [1], and by the way met with a string of galley-slaves; they were going to Marseilles, and will be there in about a month. Nothing could have been surer than this mode of conveyance, but another thought came into my head, which was to go with them myself. There was one Duval among them, who appeared to be a man of good conversational powers: you will see them when they come in, and I suppose you would have been agreeably surprised to have seen me in the midst of the crowd of women who accompany them. I wish you knew of what importance the words Provence, Marseilles, Aix, are become to me; even the Rhône, that devilish Rhône, and Lyons, are something to me. Brittany and Burgundy appear like places under the pole, in which I take no sort of interest: I may say, with Coulanges, "O the surprising power of my orvietan!" Really, my child, it was admirable of you to desire the Abbé [2] to prevent my sending you any more presents! What nonsense! Do I in reality make you any? You call the newspapers I send you by that name. You never can divest me of the desire of thus giving; it is the most sensible pleasure I can enjoy. You should rather rejoice with me, if I indulged myself more frequently in it. The method you took of thanking me was highly pleasing to me.

[1] With her friend Madame de La Troche.

[2] The Abbé de Coulanges, who lived with his niece Madame de Sévigné.

Your letters are excellent; one might venture to swear they were not dictated by the good ladies of the country where you reside. I find that M. de Grignan, to his other connections with you, adds that of being your companion; he seems to me the only one who understands you: be careful to preserve the happiness of his heart by the tenderness of yours, and consider that if you do not both love me, each according to your proper degree of estimation, you will be the most ungrateful of beings. The new opinion, that there is no such thing as ingratitude in the world, appears to me, for the reasons which we have so frequently discussed, like the philosophy of Descartes, and the contrary one, like that of Aristotle: you know the deference I always paid to the authority of the latter; it is the same with respect to my opinion of ingratitude. I should pronounce you then, my child, to be a little ungrateful wretch; but, happily, and the idea constitutes all my comfort, I know you to be incapable of such conduct, and I therefore yield without reserve to the feelings of my heart. Adieu, my dearest love, I am going to close this letter; I shall write you another to-night, in which I shall give you an account of the occurrences of the day. We are every day in hopes of letting your house; you may suppose I can forget nothing that relates to you; I am as interested in your affairs as the most selfish being ever was in his own.

LETTER 89

From Madame DE SÉVIGNÉ *to Madame* DE GRIGNAN.

Friday night, April 10, 1671.

I make up my packet at Monsieur de La Rochefoucauld's, who embraces you very heartily; he is delighted with your answer about the Canons and Father Desmares; there is some pleasure in sending you these trifles [1], you answer them so prettily. He begs you to be assured that

[1] See Letter 78, of the 20th of March, 1671, in this volume.

you still live strongly in his remembrance, and that if he hears anything worth your notice he will certainly communicate it to you. He is at his home, having no longer any hopes of recovering the use of his feet; he talks of going to the waters; I am for sending him to Digne, others to Bourbon. I dined *en Bavardin*[1], and in so complete a style, that I thought we should have died. We did not talk merely, as we used to do; we did nothing but chatter.

Brancas was overturned the other day into a ditch, where he found himself so much at his ease, that he asked those who came to help him out, if they had any occasion for his services. His glasses were all broken, and his head would have been so too, if he had not been more lucky than wise: but all this did not seem to have destroyed his reverie in the least. I wrote this morning to let him know he had been overturned, and was very near breaking his neck, as I supposed he was the only person in Paris who was ignorant of it; and that I took the opportunity of expressing the concern it gave me. I expect his answer. The Comtesse de Fiesque, and Briole, send you their compliments. Adieu, my very dear child, I am going to seal my packet. As I am persuaded you have no doubt of my love and friendship for you, I shall say nothing to you upon that subject to-night.

Madame DE FIESQUE *writes to Madame* DE GRIGNAN *in her Mother's letter.*

The Comtesse[2] cannot see a letter going to you, without putting in something of her own, if it is only to congratulate you on the addition of the five thousand francs. By what you know of her disposition, you will easily judge that she looks upon five thousand francs as a much better

[1] That is, at Madame de Lavardin's, who was extremely fond of news.

[2] Madame de Fiesque was known in the polite world by the name of *the Comtesse: Madame la Comtesse.*

subject for congratulations than five hundred thousand admirers, and as many orations, which your perfections and honours have procured you.

LETTER 90

From Madame DE SÉVIGNÉ *to Madame* DE GRIGNAN.

Paris, Sunday, April 12, 1671.

The pleasure I take in writing to you daily, makes me very accommodating to those who request letters of me, without which they do not choose to appear before you; I desire nothing better. This will be delivered to you by Monsieur de ***; let me die if I know his name; but, however, he is a very worthy man, and seems to me to have some understanding: we have seen him here; his face is known to you; for my part, I have not been able to affix a name to it. Do not take pattern by my letters, they are infinite; they are my only pleasure; but yours are of a length that surprise me, I should never be weary of reading them. If Monsieur de Grignan, who says, no one can like long letters, could once have a thought of that kind when he received yours, I would petition to have you divorced, and come myself and fetch you away, instead of going into Brittany. Brancas and I had a quarrel last night: he pretended I had made use of an indecorous expression relating to friendship; nobody heard it, not even I myself; this was crowning the fault; he flung out of the room in a violent passion. These over-niceties are troublesome; I have them not for him, but I have them too much for a certain beautiful love who is dearer to me than my life, and whom I embrace with all the affection of my heart.

LETTER 91

From Madame DE SÉVIGNÉ *to Madame* DE GRIGNAN.

Paris, Wednesday, April 15, 1671.

I have just received the letter you sent me by Gacé [1]. You speak of Provence, as if it were Norway; I always thought it had been warm there; and I had persuaded myself of it so strongly, that the other day, which was remarkably sultry, made me feel quite melancholy; the company thought it was from my apprehension that you were still more incommoded with heat than myself; and indeed I could not imagine that to be the case without being uncomfortable. And now, my dear child, I must tell you that chocolate no longer holds the place in my esteem that it used to do; fashion has influenced me, as it always does; those who used to praise chocolate, now speak ill of it, revile it, and accuse it of all the disorders to which we are subject. It occasions the vapours, and palpitation of the heart; it flatters you for a time indeed, but presently lights up a fever that continues, and at length carries you to the grave. In short, my dear, the Grand Master [2], who used to live upon it, has become its declared enemy: judge then, if I can be its friend [3]. Let me entreat you no longer to be an advocate for it, for it is no longer in fashion with the genteel part of the world.

I have not seen Gacé; I believe I shall kiss him. Good heavens! a man who has seen you, who has but just quitted you, who has even spoken to you! with what pleasure shall I behold him! Your description of Cardinal Grimaldi [4] is

[1] Afterwards Maréchal de Matignon.

[2] The Comte du Lude.

[3] It was said that the Comte du Lude was in love with Madame de Sévigné, but as he was a man whose attachment could never be of prejudice to the character of any lady, Madame de Sévigné was the first to laugh at it. See the *Amours des Gaules,* by the Comte de Bussy.

[4] Archbishop of Aix.

excellent; the words, "Does it sting?" are exquisite, and made me laugh heartily; I wish you could oftener do the same. Montgobert diverts me; she understands your language; how happy she is in having good sense, and in being so near you! I have no patience with fools! they make my blood boil. I thank you for remembering the game of *reversis*, and for playing at mall. The latter is admirably adapted to persons who are well-made and skillful, like yourself. I shall play at it in my desert. Apropos of deserts. Did not Adhémar send you word that the Coadjutor's servant, who had been at La Trappe, had returned almost beside himself, not having been able to undergo the austerities of that place? They are looking out for a convent of cotton for him, in order to recover him a little from his present wretched condition. I hope that La Trappe, in aiming at more than is consistent with human nature, may not, by that means, become a mad-house.

I wept bitterly when I wrote to you from Livry, and I weep anew at the affectionate manner in which you received my letter, and the effects it produced in your heart. Our souls were very communicative, and passed faithfully from Livry into Provence; if you feel the same sentiments everytime I afflict myself about you, I pity you, and advise you to renounce so unpleasant a sympathy. Never, surely, was anything so easily awakened as my affection for you; a thousand circumstances, a thousand thoughts, a thousand remembrances, occupy my heart; but always in the manner you could wish; my memory presents me with nothing but pleasing images of your amiable qualities; I hope yours does the same. The letter you have written to your brother is an excellent one; you guessed rightly, he has quite the fashionable air about the eyes; but no Easter, no jubilee. The only good thing I know in him is, that he avoids sacrilege; indeed, I endeavoured to persuade him from it: but the disease of his soul is fallen upon his body, and his mistresses are not inclined to bear with patience this inconvenience. God directs all for the best; I hope the journey to Lorraine will break up these vile connections. He is very facetious upon his disaster; he says he is like old Æson, and is resolved to be boiled in a caldron of herbs, to recover his youth. He relates all his follies to me; I scold him, insist upon hearing no more, and yet I still listen to him. He enlivens me, and does all in his power to amuse me. I know he has a regard for me; he professes to be charmed with the affection you show me; he gives me many rubs upon my own attachment, which I confess is greatest when I would most conceal it. And I will confess, my dear, yet another thing, that I believe you love me likewise; you appear to be steady, and I think your word is to be depended upon, which is one reason among others of my esteeming you so much. So your gentlemen begin to be used to you, but the ladies have as yet no taste for you! Poor souls!

LETTER 92

From Madame DE SÉVIGNÉ *to Madame* DE GRIGNAN.

Paris, Friday, April 17, 1671.

This Friday's letter will be a pin's point, a mere nothing; for, in the first place, I have nothing to answer; and, in the next place, nothing to send. D'Hacqueville was telling me the other day, the sort of things he has sent you, and which he calls news. I laughed at him, and assured him I should never load my paper with any such trash. For instance, he sends you word, that it is reported that Monsieur de Verneuil resigns his government to Monsieur de Lauzun, and takes that of Berry, with the reversion to Monsieur de Sully; this is a false and idle report, that is not so much as mentioned in any place of credit. He informs you likewise, that the King is to leave Paris the twenty-fifth: very pretty truly! Be assured, my child, I shall send you nothing but what is absolutely true; and when I can get no better intelligence than this, I shall even let it pass unnoticed, and entertain you with something else. I am very much pleased with d'Hacqueville, as well as with you. He takes great care of your mother, in your absence; and whenever the least dispute arises between the Abbé and me, we choose him arbitrator. It is a great satisfaction to reflect that we have such a friend, who is deficient in no one good or valuable qualification, and consequently can never be wanting in any respect. If you had forbidden us to talk of you, when together, as a thing disagreeable to you, we should be greatly embarrassed: for a conversation of that kind is so natural to us, and the propensity so agreeable, that we fall into it as it were insensibly; so that if by chance, after much discourse on this topic, we turn to another for a while, I presently relapse into the old strain, and say, "Come, one word about my poor girl! we are very ungrateful to forget her so long;" and then we begin anew. If I was to swear a thousand times over to him, that I did not love you, I do not think he would believe me. I value him as a confidant who enters into my sentiments; what can I say better of him?

Hélène and Marphise [1] are very much obliged to you; but as for Hébert, poor fellow, he is no longer with me. I took it into my head the other day, in a jesting mood, to offer him to Gourville, telling him that he must get him a place in the Condé Mansion; that I was sure he would like him, and would thank me for the favour, and that I would answer for his integrity. Monsieur de La Rochefoucauld and Madame de La Fayette, said much in his praise; but there the affair rested for near three weeks; yesterday however I was greatly surprised by Gourville's sending for him. Hébert dressed himself genteelly, and waited on him. Gourville told him he had a place in view for him in the Condé Mansion, which would be worth two hundred and fifty livres a year, besides his board and lodging; but that at present he should send him to Chantilly, to take charge of the linen while the King remained there. He accordingly took ten chests of linen under his care, and set out for Chantilly. The King is to go there

[1] A favourite lap-dog of Madame de Sévigné's.

the twenty-fifth of this month, and stay a whole day: the expense will be as great as at the most magnificent triumphs: every curious fancy is received, cost what it will; and it is imagined that it will stand the Prince in no less a sum than forty thousand crowns. There will be twenty-five tables of five courses each, without reckoning an infinite number of others, for chance-comers. To entertain in this manner is in fact to board and lodge half the kingdom. Every place is furnished; little holes, which served only for watering-pots, are converted into apartments for courtiers. There is to be a thousand crowns' worth of jonquils alone; judge of the rest by that. See, what the mention of Hébert has led me into! thus have I made his fortune by a mere joke; for I look upon it as good as made, as I am persuaded he will acquit himself well in this first employ. We shall not dine *en Bavardin* to-day: they are all in a hurry, sending away the Marquis de Lavardin's equipage, so I shall take my eggs and sorrel at home. After dinner, I shall go for a while to the Faubourg [1], and if I hear anything worth your notice, I will add it to divert you.

I have read a very pretty letter from the Coadjutor: he is displeased at nothing but my styling him *my lord,* and will have me call him *Pierrot,* or *Seigneur Corbeau.* Let me urge you to preserve the good understanding that at present subsists between you and him. I find he is very sensible of your merit, interests himself greatly in your affairs, and possesses an application and solidity that may be of the greatest use to you. My son is not yet cured of that disorder of his, which excites in his precious mistresses such doubts of his love for them. He told me that during Passion-week he had led so abandoned a life, that he was absolutely disgusted; he felt a nausea, his very heart sickened at it, insomuch that he could scarcely bear a woman in his presence. This disorder has not been a thing of yesterday: I took my opportunity to read him a little lecture upon the subject, and we both entered into a train of

[1] To Madame de La Fayette, who lived there.

moralising. He seems to approve my sentiments [1], particularly now, that his distaste is at its height. He showed me some letters which he had got out of his actress's hands. I never read anything so warm, so passionate; he wept, he sighed, he died; he believed it all while he was writing it, and laughed at it the moment afterwards. I assure you he is worth his weight in gold. Adieu, my dear child: how have you been since the sixth of this month? I hope you love me still; for it is my life, my vital air. I will not say that I am yours, it is an expression too poor for a love like mine. You would have me embrace the poor Comte; but do we not love each other too well already?

Friday night, April 17.

I am making up my packet at Madame de La Fayette's, to whom I have given your letter; we read it together with pleasure, and agreed that no one could write better. You flatter her very agreeably, and I found a short passage in it relating to myself, which went directly to my heart; a place that you keep possession of in a very strange manner. Madame de La Fayette was yesterday at Versailles; Madame de Thianges having sent for her there; she was received extremely well, extremely well indeed! for the King made her get into his own carriage with the rest of the ladies, and took great pleasure in showing her all the beauties of Versailles, as a private gentleman would show his country seat to any one who visited him. He directed all his discourse to her, and received with great satisfaction and politeness the praises she bestowed on the amazing beauties he pointed out to her. You may think

[1] The Marquis de Sévigné, after he was married, passed his life in the strictest devotion. He was a very amiable man, and had a great share of wit. He was, moreover, versed in many things which young men of quality do not always pique themselves upon knowing. The Letters of his which are remaining, are so charming, that it is to be regretted they are so few in number. He is known in the literary world by a dissertation relating to a passage in Horace, which gave rise to a dispute between him and M. Dacier; in which he had the good fortune to get authority and the critics on his side.

how agreeable a jaunt of this kind must have been. Monsieur de La Rochefoucauld embraces you, and begs you to believe, that he is as likely to forget you as he is to dance a rigadoon; he has a touch of the gout in his hand, which hinders him from writing you a line in this. Madame de La Fayette both esteems and loves you, and does not think you so void of virtue, as the day you lay by her fire-side, which you remember so well.

LETTER 93

From Madame DE SÉVIGNÉ *to Madame* DE GRIGNAN.

Paris, Wednesday, April 22, 1671.

Can you really be afraid that I should love Madame de Brissac better than you? Are you apprehensive, knowing me as you do, that her manner should please me more than yours? Do you believe that her wit is more agreeable to me? that her beauty can eclipse your charms? In a word, can you suppose that there is a person in the world who can surpass Madame de Grignan in my opinion, setting wholly out of the question the interest I have in her? Consider all this at your leisure, and you may rest assured that your conclusion will be a just one.

But now, my child, a word or two respecting your brother; his folly is really disgusting; he is at every creature's disposal. It pleased some of his friends yesterday to carry him with them to sup at a certain honourable house. Those gallants were too knowing to run any risk themselves, and so told Sévigné to pay; [1] I mean, pay with his person; and notwithstanding the miserable condition he is in at present, he complied, and then came and related the whole affair to me, declaring that he was sick at heart of his own conduct. I told him he made me sick at heart too. I made him ashamed of himself, told him that the life he leads is far from being that of a gentleman, and

[1] He was at this time 24 years of age.

that I had not the least doubt but he would one day or other smart severely for thus exposing himself. Then I throw in one of my little sermons. He agrees to the truth of all I say while I am talking to him, and then goes on exactly as before. He has left his actress [1] at last, after having for a long time followed her everywhere. While he saw her, or was writing to her, he was in earnest; the next moment he would make the greatest jest of her. Ninon has completely discarded him; he was miserable while she loved him, and now he knows she loves him no longer, he is in perfect despair; especially as he hears that she does not speak very favourably of him. "It is the merest water-gruel creature!" says she: "His body is no better than a sheet of wet paper; and his heart is as cold as a pumpkin fricasseed in snow." But I have told you this speech of hers before. She wished him the other day to give her the letters he had received from his actress, which he did. You must know she was jealous of that Princess, and wanted to show them to a gallant of hers, in hopes of procuring her a small bastinado. When your brother told me what he had done, I represented to him how base it was of him to treat the poor girl so ill, merely for having loved him; that I was sure she had never exposed his letters, as some would have him believe; but, on the contrary, had returned them all to him again; that such treacherous conduct was mean, and unworthy a man of quality: and that there was a degree of honour to be observed even in things dishonourable in themselves. He acquiesced in the justice of my remarks, and ran directly to Ninon's lodging; and, partly by cunning, partly by force, got the poor girl's letters out of her hands, which I made him burn the instant he came home. You see by this what a regard I have for the name of an actress. It is a little like the visionary in the play; she would have done just so. My son has related all his follies to Monsieur de La Rochefoucauld, who, you know, is very fond of originals. I told him the other day that Sévigné was not a fool in head, but

[1] La Champmêlé.

a fool in heart; his sentiments are all just, and all false; all cold, and all warm; all deceitful, and all sincere; in short, it is his heart that should wear the cap. This remark occasioned a general laugh, and my son joined in it, for he is very good company; he always says as the rest do. We are upon very good terms; I am his confidante, and bear with the disagreeable office, which often subjects me to such disagreeable confessions, merely to have an opportunity of telling him my sentiments freely. He attends to me as well as he can, and begs me to give him my advice, which I do as from friend to friend. He is very desirous to accompany me to Brittany for five or six weeks; and if there is no camp in Lorraine, I shall take him. What a deal of nonsense I have written! but as this is all interesting to you, I am in hopes you will not be fatigued by reading it.

What you write about La Marans, and the punishments that will be inflicted on her in hell, is altogether incomparable; but do you know that you will certainly bear her company there, if you persist in your hatred of her. Think of being condemned to her society throughout eternity, and that surely will be more than sufficient, of itself, to put you upon making your peace with God, by forgiving her. This is a happy thought of mine; it is certainly an inspiration from heaven. She came to Madame de La Fayette's the other day, while Monsieur de La Rochefoucauld and I were there. In she bounced without a cap on; she had just had her hair cut, and was curled and powdered like a girl of fourteen: she seemed out of countenance, when she saw us, as she knew she was not likely to escape. Accordingly Madame de La Fayette began with her first: "Well," said she, "you are certainly beside yourself, Madame: why, do you know, you look completely ridiculous." "Ah!" said Monsieur de La Rochefoucauld, "my dear *mother* [1], upon my soul you must not stay there; pray come a little nearer, that I may see if you are like

[1] So M. de La Rochefoucauld used to call this lady; and she used to call him her *son*.

your sister, whom I saw just now." Her sister had just been having her hair cut too. "Indeed, *mother,* you look vastly well." Cannot you fancy you hear him speaking in his dry way? As for me, I laughed heartily in my sleeve; she was so much embarrassed that she could not stand the attack, but put on her hood, and sat in the pouts till Madame de Schomberg came to take her up; for there is no other carriage for her but that. I think this story will afford you some amusement.

Some days ago we passed an afternoon very agreeably at the Arsenal. There were men of all ranks there: the women were Madame de La Fayette, Madame de Coulanges, Madame de La Troche, Mademoiselle de Méri, and myself. We took our walk; talked of you every now and then, and in tolerably high terms. We go sometimes to the Luxembourg Mansion. Monsieur de Longueville was there yesterday; he desired me to assure you of his best wishes. As for Monsieur de La Rochefoucauld, he loves you tenderly. I am overjoyed that you approved my letters. I have more pleasure in your approbation and praise, than in all I meet with from others; and why should not such daughters as you be at liberty to praise a mother like me? Such an odd respect! You know what an opinion I have of your taste. I much approve your lottery: you will let me know what success you have in it. The plays likewise will doubtless afford you some diversion. Amuse yourself as much as possible, I mean as much as Provence can possibly amuse you: I applaud you highly for not conducting your ladies to the door; there would have been no end to it; let them take their revenge, and not see you to the door in their turn, and there will be a vile custom abolished. Adieu, my dearest child, it grows late. I prose on with a facility that wearies you to death.

LETTER 94

From Madame DE SÉVIGNÉ *to Madame* DE GRIGNAN.

Paris, Friday, April 24, 1671.

We have now the finest weather in the world; it set in yesterday, after a long continuance of tremendous rains: this is lucky for the King, whose good fortune has been often remarked: it is a lucky circumstance for the Prince too; for he had ordered everything for a spring and summer season, and such rains as we had the day before yesterday would have overthrown all his measures, and rendered the vast expense he has been at ridiculous. His Majesty arrived at Chantilly last night, and is there to-day. D'Hacqueville is gone there too, and, on his return, will give you a true account of everything that passed. I expect to hear a little about it myself this evening, which I will send you with the letter I am now writing, before I go a gossiping[1]; I shall make up my packet at Madame de Lavardin's; and if they should say that we make mere barometers of our letters, to tell when it rains, and when it shines, they will not be much in the wrong; for I think I have expatiated pretty largely on the subject. You do not tell me enough respecting yourself; this is an entertainment I am as much in want of, as you are of a good story now and then. I heartily wish you partaker of all that I hear; as for my own, they are no longer good for anything, since I have lost your assistance. You used to inspire me, and I sometimes inspired you. It is a painful idea, and one that too often intrudes, that I am at such a distance from you. I have been taking leave of my friends these three or four days past; the truth of the matter is, that when I set out for Brittany, it will seem to me another separation from you. If I were deceitfully inclined, I might impose upon my friends here; but they would soon see through the shallow pretence; besides, I

[1] To Madame de Lavardin's.

would not, even in appearance, give anyone the preference to you in my sentiments. It will therefore be a real grief to me, to find, that it is not sufficient to be already at the distance of two hundred leagues from you, but that I must be removed still further, and that every step I take will be one towards making up the third hundred. This is too much; it strikes to my heart.

Yesterday, while I was at Madame de Richelieu's, the Abbé Têtu called there: he was in so frisky a humour, that his most indifferent friends blushed for him. I told him of the journey I was about to take: *"Well,"* said he, with a smile upon his face, and in the same tone, *"we shall see one another again."* There is not much wit in this as described, but it was impossible to hear him without laughing. I could get nothing more out of him; as for my absence, that he seemed to pass over as a matter of indifference. We have made it a by-word now, whenever we take leave of one another; and I say the same in my mind when I think of you, but not quite so gaily, for the length of our separation is a circumstance not easily to be forgotten.

I have bought for myself a stuff like your last petticoat, to make me a morning gown; it is very beautiful. There is a shade of green in it, but violet predominates: in short, I could not resist the purchase. They would have had me line it with flame-colour, but this appeared to me inconsistent, for, while the outside is expressive of frailty, the inside would have been emblematical of impenitence: that might be termed obduracy; so I fixed on a white taffeta. I have put myself to very little expense, as I hate Brittany, and shall be saving till I come to Provence, that I may support the dignity of a middle-aged wonder, to which you have raised me.

Madame de Ludres astonished me the other day at St.-Germain: there was no want of attention in her manner; she also expressed herself as being quite in love with you. *"As to Matame te Grignan, she is perfectly atorаple."* Brancas related to me a dispute between M. Le

Premier and M. de Grignan: "I have seen the letters that passed between them; I am for Grignan." Brancas has written you a very humorous letter; but it is illegible: he has repeated passages out of it; it will take us a whole day to read it through. M. de Salins has discharged a porter. I do not know the particulars, but they talk of a gray cloak, of four o'clock in the morning, and of drawn swords: *they are silent respecting the rest.* They talk too of a certain apostle who makes converts: however, I say no more; they shall not accuse me of blabbing. I know when to hold my tongue. If this conclusion appears to you a little nonsensical, you will only like it the better. Adieu, my dear child; I shall send you some news this evening, when I seal my packet.

LETTER 95

From Madame DE SÉVIGNÉ *to Madame* DE GRIGNAN.

Friday evening, April 24, 1671.
From Monsieur de La Rochefoucauld's.

Here then I make up my packet. I had intended to tell you that the King arrived yesterday evening at Chantilly: he hunted a stag by moon-light; the lamps did wonders; the fire-works were a little eclipsed by the brightness of our serene friend, the moon; but the evening, the supper, and the entertainment, went off admirably well. The weather we had yesterday gave us hopes of an end worthy of so fine a beginning. But what do you think I learned when I came here? I am not yet recovered, and hardly know what I write. Vatel, the great Vatel, late *maître-d'hôtel* to M. Fouquet, and in that capacity with the Prince, a man so eminently distinguished for taste, and whose abilities were equal to the government of a State,—this man, whom I knew so well, finding, at eight o'clock this morning, that the fish he had sent for did not come at the time he expected it, and unable to bear the disgrace that he thought would inevitably attach to him, ran himself through with his own sword. Guess what confusion so shocking an accident must have occasioned. Think too, that perhaps the fish might come in just as he was expiring. I know no more of the affair at present; and I suppose you think this enough. I make no doubt, the consternation was general; it must be very disagreeable to have so fatal an event break in upon an entertainment that cost fifty thousand crowns.

Monsieur de Menars is to be married to Mademoiselle de La Grange-Neuville; but I do not know how I can have the heart to speak to you about anything but Vatel.

LETTER 96

From Madame DE SÉVIGNÉ *to Madame* DE GRIGNAN.

Paris, Sunday, April 26, 1671.

This is Sunday, April twenty-sixth; and this letter will not go out till Wednesday, but it is not so much a letter as a narrative that I have just learned from Moreuil, of what passed at Chantilly with regard to poor Vatel. I wrote to you last Friday, that he had stabbed himself; these are the particulars of the affair. The King arrived there on Thursday night; the walk, and the collation, which was served in a place set apart for the purpose, and strewed with jonquils, were just as they should be. Supper was served, but there was no roast meat at one or two of the tables, on account of Vatel's having been obliged to provide several dinners more than were expected. This affected his spirits, and he was heard to say several times, "I have lost my fame! I cannot bear this disgrace!" "My head is quite bewildered," said he to Gourville. "I have not had a wink of sleep these twelve nights, I wish you would assist me in giving orders." Gourville did all he could to comfort and assist him; but the failure of the roast meat (which however did not happen at the King's table, but at some of the other twenty-five) was always uppermost with him. Gourville mentioned it to the Prince, who went directly to Vatel's apartment, and said to him, "Everything is extremely well conducted, Vatel; nothing could be more admirable than His Majesty's supper." "Your Highness's goodness," replied he, "overwhelms me; I am sensible that there was a deficiency of roast meat at two tables." "Not at all," said the Prince; "do not perplex yourself, and all will go well." Midnight came: the fire-works did not succeed, they were covered with a thick cloud; they cost sixteen thousand francs. At four o'clock in the morning Vatel went round, and found everybody asleep; he met one of the under-purveyors, who was just come in with only two loads of fish. "What!" said he, "is this all?" "Yes, sir," said the man, not knowing that Vatel had dispatched other men to all the sea-ports round. Vatel waited for some time; the other purveyors did not arrive; his head grew distracted; he thought there was no more fish to be had; he flew to Gourville: "Sir," said he, "I cannot outlive this disgrace." Gourville laughed at him; Vatel, however, went to his apartment, and setting the hilt of his sword against the door, after two ineffectual attempts, succeeded in the third, in forcing the sword through his heart. At that instant the carriers arrived with the fish; Vatel was inquired for to distribute it; they ran to his apartment, knocked at the door, but received no answer; upon which they broke it open, and found him weltering in his blood. A messenger was immediately dispatched to acquaint the Prince with what had happened, who was like a man in despair. The Duc wept, for his Burgundy journey depended upon Vatel. The Prince related the whole affair to His Majesty with an expression of great concern: it was considered as the consequence of too nice a sense of honour; some blamed, others praised him for his courage. The King said he had put off this excursion for more than five years, because he was aware that it would be attended with infinite trouble, and told the Prince that he ought to have had but two tables, and not have been at the expense of so many, and declared he would never suffer him to do so again; but all this was too late for poor Vatel. However, Gourville endeavoured to supply the loss of Vatel; which he did in great measure. The dinner was elegant, the collation was the same. They supped, they walked, they hunted; all was perfumed with jonquils, all was enchantment. Yesterday, which was Saturday, the same entertainments were renewed; and in the evening the King set out for Liancourt, where he had ordered a *media-noche* [1]; he is to stay there three days. This is what Moreuil has told me, hoping I should acquaint you with it. I wash my hands of the rest, for I know nothing about it. M. d'Hacqueville, who was present at the scene, will no doubt give you a faithful account of all that passed; but, because his hand-writing is not quite so legible as mine, I write too; if I am circumstantial, it is because, on such an occasion, I should like circumstantiality myself.

LETTER 97

From Madame DE SÉVIGNÉ *to Madame* DE GRIGNAN.

Begun at Paris, Monday, April 27, 1671.

I have a very bad opinion of the languor you complain of. I am one of those vile prognosticators who always think the worst of things. This is what I feared. But, my dear child, if it continues, be careful of yourself in these early days, and do not stir about too much, nor fatigue yourself by your journey to Marseilles; let things be settled a little first; think of the natural delicacy of your constitution, and that it has been owing to the greatest care

[1] *Media-noche* is a flesh-meal just after midnight, among the Roman Catholics.

that you have been preserved till now. I begin to be very uneasy about the interruption our correspondence will meet with in this journey into Brittany. If you are in the family way, you may depend upon it I shall have no will but yours, and shall make it my first object to do as you desire, leaving business, and every other consideration, a thousand miles behind me. I fancy what I wrote you about your brother diverted you: he is now a little settled; he sees Ninon every day, but then it is merely as a friend: he went with her the other day to a place where there were five or six of his acquaintances, who, as soon as they saw him come in with her, showed by their countenances, that they looked upon him as sole possessor. Ninon presently discovered their thoughts, and told them, "Gentlemen, you are wrong if you suspect anything wicked between us, I assure you we live together like brother and sister." It is certain he is no longer the same man. I shall take him with me into Brittany, where I hope to restore him body and soul: La Mousse and I have at length prevailed on him to go to confession.

Monsieur and Madame de Villars are about to leave this place; they send you a thousand remembrances, and are very desirous to have a copy of your portrait which hangs over my chimney, to carry with them to Spain. My little girl is every day in my apartment, dressed in all her finery, and does the honours of the house; a house that puts me continually in mind of you, where you were a prisoner as it were for nearly a year; a house that everybody comes to see, that everybody admires, and that nobody will take.

I supped the other evening at the Marquise d'Uxelles', with the lady of Maréchal d'Humières, Madame d'Arpajon, de Beringhen, de Frontenac, d'Outrelaise, Raymond, and Martin: you were not forgotten. I entreat you, my dear child, to send me a faithful account of your health, of your plans, and what you would have me do. I am very uneasy at your condition, and I am afraid you are the same. I foresee a thousand vexations, and have a train of thoughts in my head, that are neither fit for night nor day.

Livry, Wednesday, April 29.

Since I began this letter I have made a pretty little excursion. I set out from Paris early yesterday morning, and went to dine at Pomponne, where I found our good old man[1], who expected me; I would not on any account have gone without bidding him adieu. I found him more pious than ever, and the nearer he approaches death, the more heavenly-minded he becomes. He reprimanded me very seriously; and, in the warmth of his zeal and friendship, told me I was very much to blame for not changing my course of life; that I was a heathen, and you were the idol I worshipped; that this species of idolatry was to the full as dangerous as any other, though I might perhaps consider it in a less criminal point of view; and then concluded with seriously admonishing me to look to myself. He spoke in such strong terms, that I had not a word to say. In short, after six hours of very serious but agreeable conversation, I took my leave of him, and came here, where I found May in all its glory; the nightingale, the cuckoo, and the linnet, have already introduced the melody of spring into our woods: I walked alone the whole evening, and found some melancholy thoughts I left behind me, but which I shall not now recall to you. I have destined a part of this afternoon to writing to you in the garden, where I am almost deafened by three or four nightingales that are perched just over my head. I shall return in the evening to Paris, where I shall make up my packet, and send it to you.

I own, my child, that I was deficient in warmth of friendship, when I met the galley-slaves: I ought to have set out with them, instead of contenting myself with barely writing to you. How agreeably you would have been surprised to have met me at Marseilles, in such good com-

[1] Monsieur Arnauld-d'Andilly, who was then 83 years of age.

pany! And so you propose going there in a litter? what a whim! I thought you were only fond of litters when they were standing still; you are greatly changed. I confess myself a slanderer; and all the credit I can allow you, is to believe that you never would have made use of that conveyance, if you had not left me, or if M. de Grignan had remained in Provence. How sorry I am for this misfortune! how plainly I foresaw it! For heaven's sake, then, my beloved child, take care of yourself; remember that poor *Guisarda* [1], by making too free after a favourable lying-in, injured herself so materially, that she was for three days at the point of death. Let that be a warning to you. Madame de La Fayette is in continual apprehensions for your life; she yields to you without murmuring the first place in my heart, on account of your perfections; and when she is more than commonly kind, she says it is not without pain; but all is settled and approved between us: the justice she does you entitles her to the second place in my love, and of that she is in full possession. La Troche is dying with envy; but I go on at the old rate, not forgetting the journey to Brittany. It is certain we shall lead very different lives; mine will be interrupted by the States, who are all coming to Vitré to torment me, towards the end of June. This is a disagreeable circumstance for me. Your brother will take his departure before that time. You tell me, my dear child, you wish Time would fly more rapidly: alas! you know not what you say. He will obey you but too implicitly; he will overtake you before you are aware, and when you would restrain his impetuous career, it will not be in your power. I was formerly guilty of the same fault, of which I now repent; and, though he has been more lenient with me than he has been to many others, yet I trace his depredating progress in the loss of a thousand little charms, of which he has robbed me.

So you find your comedians are able to repeat Corneille's lines tolerably well? he is sometimes sublime. I

[1] Madame de Guise.

amused myself very agreeably yesterday evening with a volume of his works, which I brought here with me.

But are you not pleased with some of the Fables in La Fontaine's works which I sent you a short time ago? We were quite delighted with them the other day at M. de La Rochefoucauld's, and learned that of the "Monkey and the Cat" by heart, and the "Pumpkin and the Nightingale" is worthy of a place in the first volume. But it is very foolish to write you so much nonsense: the leisure of Livry will certainly be the death of you. The note you have written to Brancas is admirable; he filled a whole quire of paper to you the other day; it was a rhapsody, but tolerably good: he read it to Madame de Coulanges and me, and I told him to finish it, and send it to me, on Wednesday. "Not I, indeed," said he; "she shall not see a line of it, it is such wretched stuff!" "Well but," said I, "what do you take us for? You have read it to us." "She shall not see it, for all that," said he. I could get no other reason out of him; he made himself quite a fool. What say you, my dear child, to this long letter? I could find in my heart to write till this time to-morrow. *Be careful of yourself!* this is the constant burden of my song; do not get a fall, keep your bed occasionally. Since I have given so good a nurse to the dear little one, such a nurse, in fact, there has not appeared since the reign of Francis I., you ought to pay great deference to my advice. Do you suppose I shall not come and see you this year? I had indeed arranged my plans differently, and on your account too; but this litter-affair has quite disconcerted my measures: how can I resist coming to you, if you desire it? Alas! I may well say, there is no fixed place of abode for me, but where you reside. Your portrait hangs in triumph over my chimney; you are now the object of general admiration in Provence, at Paris, at Court, and at Livry; in short, my child, you must certainly become ungrateful, for how can you return all this? I embrace and love you; I shall always tell you so, because my feelings will always be the same. I would embrace that rogue Grignan too, if I were not very, very angry with him.

Poor Paul [1] died about a week ago: our garden mourns for him.

LETTER 98

From Madame DE SÉVIGNÉ *to Madame* DE GRIGNAN.

Paris, Friday, May 1, 1671.

I kept your secret as faithfully as if you had made away with your child; but I am now no longer responsible, since Valcroissant has told it to Mademoiselle de Scuderi, priding himself upon the civilities you showed him, and telling her how much you are adored in Provence. How are you, after your Marseilles journey? Are you not resolved to take better care of yourself? Allow me, my dear child, to feel some concern for you; it is impossible I should do otherwise.

I dined yesterday at Madame de Villars's, in company with Monsieur de Vindisgras, two of his countrymen, Monsieur and Madame Schomberg and Monsieur and Madame de Béthune. *La plupart des amants sont des Allemands* [2], as you see. Monsieur de Schomberg seemed to me the most delightful husband in the world; exclusive of his being a hero, his cheerful manners and excellent understanding make him extremely agreeable; his wife perfectly adores him, but, as there is no happiness in this world without alloy, she scarcely enjoys a moment's health. You were very much talked of, and your merit was extolled to the skies; but what pleased me most, was Vindisgras's remembering a witticism of yours full six years ago, upon Comte de Dietrichstein [3], who, you said, was very

[1] The gardener at Livry.

[2] Alluding to a song of Sarasins', beginning: *Tircis, la plupart des amants sont des Allemands,* etc. *For the most part our favorites are Germans.* [Translation.]

[3] A German nobleman.

like Monsieur de Beaufort[1], only that he spoke better French: we thought it singular that he should remember it so long; this gave us an opportunity to talk of your wit: he saw you when you took leave of the Queen, and has a very high opinion of your person. Poor Madame de Béthune is in the family-way again. I really pity her exceedingly. It is feared that the Princess d'Harcourt is with child too. Not a day passes here without something to call forth my feelings. Madame de Coulanges came in the evening, and we went together to the Tuileries, where we saw all the men who remain in Paris, and who will not be there long; among the rest was Monsieur de Saint-Ruth[2]; good God! what a being! the disgusting ugliness of his face gives no very high opinion of the beauties of his mind. But how shall I describe to you the kindness, the friendship, the thanks, of M. de La Rochefoucauld, of de Segrais, and of Madame de La Fayette, to whom I showed your letter last night at supper? There were so many things in it that concerned them, that it would be doing you great injustice to have concealed it from them. I did not, however, say a word about your interesting condition; that I reserved for Madame de La Fayette's private ear, for the conversation yesterday turned upon subjects much more agreeable for you. Langlade came in, and, as he was going to Bourbon, we desired he would call on you. Segrais showed us a collection he has made of De Blot's songs; they are very impudent, but abound with wit and spirit. He told us too, that he had just come from seeing a Norman lady, who had been talking to him about her son, who is an Abbé, and told him, that his design was to preach till he could meet with something better. We all laughed heartily at this arrangement. You remember the witticism I sent you some time ago of a player[3]? Segrais has given it a place in a col-

[1] The Duc de Beaufort was remarkable for speaking his mother-tongue very badly.

[2] It was said that the Maréchale de la Meilleraie, though otherwise a very proud woman, had been secretly married to him.

[3] See Letter 86, of the 8th of April, 1671, in this volume.

lection he is making of all the good things that have been said. There is great news talked of from England, but nothing has yet transpired. There is no certainty of the King's arrival at Dunkirk. Madame de Richelieu has gained her cause against Madame d'Aiguillon. The Duc has set out for Burgundy; Maréchal d'Albret for his government; and the Prince has followed the King. You see by this, that there is nothing new stirring to-day. We did not dine *en Lavardin*; they are gone to Versailles.

Madame de Verneuil has been very ill at Verneuil; d'Escars has had a sort of apoplectic fit, which has greatly alarmed her, and all those who are a little too well in health. I gave your note to Brancas. "Well, well, I shall answer Grignan." Father Ytier salutes you with all due reverence. Were I not angry with M. de Grignan, I could find in my heart to love him. Ninon says, that your brother is a non-descript; it is certain that he does not understand himself, and others understand him still less. Farewell, my amiable child; never did there exist a stronger attachment than that I bear you.

LETTER 99

From Madame DE SÉVIGNÉ *to Madame* DE GRIGNAN.

Paris, Wednesday, May 6, 1671.

I beg, my dear child, that we may not henceforth give to absence all the credit of having established so perfect an understanding between us, nor of having confirmed me in the opinion of your love: but allowing absence to have had a share in the latter, since it has fixed your affection for ever beyond the possibility of change, let me at least regret the time when I saw you everyday; you, who are the delight of my eyes, and the only joy of my life; when I heard you everyday, you whose mind is more to my taste than that of any person I have ever met with; let me not separate your presence from your friendship: it would be cruel to divide them. No, I will rather believe the time is come when they shall go hand in hand, when I shall have the exquisite pleasure of seeing you, without a cloud of regret, and at once make reparation for all my past injustices, since you will term them so.

I saw Madame de Guise yesterday; she loaded me with a thousand expressions of friendship for you, and charged me to tell you of her having been at the point of death for near three days; Madame Robinette had lost all hopes of her, and all this by building too much upon her first lying-in, and taking too much exercise. Continual agitation, which does not give a child time to replace itself when it has been turned by violent exercise, brings on premature labour, which is often fatal. I promised to give you all these instructions in case you should have occasion for them, and to let you know what she herself suffered from the thought of having sacrificed her child, body and soul. I have now executed faithfully the commission, in the hope of its being useful to you. Let me conjure you, my child, to be very particular with regard to your health; you have nothing else to do.

That gentleman of yours, who so elaborately described my wit by line and rule, *wound up* his definition extremely well, as a certain little devil said. I laughed heartily at what you wrote me about him, and regretted that you had nobody present when he was passing on me such fine encomiums. I should very much like to have been behind the tapestry. I thank you, my child, for your attentions to La Brosse; what a sad thing is an old letter [1]! I have long thought it worse than an old person; everything it contains has an air of dotage.

It is very true that I love your daughter, but you are a wicked creature to talk to me of jealousy; there is neither in you nor in me the materials that compose it: it is an imperfection of which you are incapable, and I give you no more reason for jealousy than M. de Grignan

[1] The Letter 75, of the 15th of March, 1671, did not come to hand till six weeks after date.

does. Alas! when the heart is occupied with one object with which no other can enter into competition, how is it possible to give cause for jealousy, even to jealousy itself? But let us talk no more of a passion that I detest; though it springs from an amiable source, its effects are cruel and hateful. In the next place, let me beg of you not to entertain such frightful apprehensions respecting my health, it gives you too much concern and uneasiness. I am persuaded you are already too much alive, and too ready to take alarm, on that subject; you always were so, and therefore I once more entreat you to follow my example, and not care about it: the health I enjoy is above the reach of common fears; I shall live to love you; I give up my whole life to this single occupation, that is, to all the joy, the sorrow, the pleasures, the torments, in short, to every sentiment that affection for you can possibly inspire me with.

I shall set out between this and Whitsuntide: I shall pass the holidays either at Chartres or at Malicorne; but most assuredly not at Paris. You are too kind to enter, as you do, into all the dullness of my journey; you may easily imagine how often La Mousse[1] and I shall talk of you; exclusive of the never-dying thought of you, that makes so much a part of myself. It is certain I shall not have Hébert with me; I am sorry for it, but I must be content. He is come back from Chantilly, very disconsolate over the death of Vatel, which has been a considerable loss to him: Gourville has put him in possession of that small post in the Condé Mansion, which I was mentioning to you. Monsieur de La Rochefoucauld says, that Gourville is willing to form an acquaintance with the fellow, because he looks upon him as a rising man. I told him that my servants were not so fortunate as his[2]. This Duc of ours loves you sincerely, and has desired me to tell you, that he will not send your letters back unopened.

[1] A relation of the Coulanges' family.

[2] Gourville had formerly been a servant to Monsieur de La Rochefoucauld; and everyone knows the character he afterwards appeared in.

Madame de La Fayette always bids me say a thousand things to you on her part; I know not how well I acquit myself of my commission.

I desire you will not speak so slightingly of La Fontaine as you do. Some of his Fables will delight you, and some of his stories charm you; the conclusion of his *Oies de Frère Philippe, les Remois,* and *le petit Chien,* and everything in that way is very pretty; it is only when he quits that style he becomes insipid. I wish I could write a fable on the folly of forcing genius out of its proper sphere; and show him what discord is made, when a person attempts to strike all notes at once.

Monsieur de Marseilles has told the Abbé de Pontcarré of your being with child. I have done all in my power for a long time to conceal this misfortune: but it is now too late, everybody laughs at me. I embrace M. de Grignan a thousand times, notwithstanding all his wickedness, and beg, since he has been the cause of the evil, he will at least be at the pains of administering the remedy: I mean by taking all the care of your health that is in his power; allow him to be master in this, as you ought to be mistress in everything else. Farewell, my dear child; I embrace and kiss you. Continue to write to me no longer than is consistent with your health, and never forget the condition you are in. Reply less to my letters and tell me more of yourself. The longer I am in Brittany, the more I shall be in want of that consolation; when you are not able to write yourself, make little Deville do it; but do not let her run into her *do me the justice to believe,* and, *I am with the greatest respect*; let her talk of you; of what else? of you and you alone.

LETTER 100

From Madame DE SÉVIGNÉ *to Madame* DE GRIGNAN.

Paris, Friday, May 8, 1671.

Here I am still! and here I must remain another week. The uncertainty of a Camp in Lorraine, which is to determine whether my son goes with me or not, is the occasion of my uncertainty, and gives me a good deal of uneasiness, but I am under greater apprehension respecting your health, and your journey to Marseilles. The air, which is impregnated with the small-pox and the noise of the cannon, gives me but too serious cause for disquiet. You are more obliged to me for my forbearance in keeping away from you, than if I was to cross all France after you. The state I am now in, and that in which I shall shortly be, is difficult to bear; and nothing could detain me, but the reasons that are known to you and me, and our dear and confidential friend d'Hacqueville [1]. It is some consolation to me to have him for a witness of my sentiments: not that I stand in need of a witness with you but it is a great pleasure to deposit our dearest thoughts in the bosom of a friend such as he is.

I was a long time yesterday at Madame du Pui-du-Fou's; she has a great regard for you; and you are under obligations to her for the care and concern she expresses for you. The Abbé is rejoiced to find you apply yourself to the inspection of your household affairs. From the moment you begin to introduce regularity into your house, from that moment you become the immediate object of his care; add that perfection then to the many others you possess; and do not relax in it: we must not devote ourselves entirely to fine sentiments, but have a little consideration for ourselves as well as for others; in a word, continue what you have so well begun, and take pains to pre-

[1] Meaning the arranging of and the settling of the family affairs in Brittany on the most advantageous footing.

serve your health, and to regulate your affairs. I hope the Abbé's journey, whenever it happens, will be useful to you. Farewell, my beloved child. I am in the utmost impatience to hear how you are after your journey.

LETTER 101

From Madame DE SÉVIGNÉ *to Madame* DE GRIGNAN.

Paris, Wednesday, May 13, 1671.

I have received your letter from Marseilles; never was I so much entertained with any account in my life. I read it with the greatest pleasure and attention; I am sorry to tell you, as I know you do not like to hear it, but you have certainly a very happy mode of description. My impatience made me at first read your letter with avidity, but I soon stopped short, unwilling to devour it too fast; I grieved when I had no more to read, and I grieved for many reasons; for I see nothing but obstacles to your return, though it is what I so ardently desire. Ah, my dear child, do not rob me and yourself of all hope! for my part I shall certainly come to see you before you can fix any resolution upon that head; this journey is necessary to my existence. I tremble for your health: you say you were almost stunned with the noise of the cannon, and the shouts of the galley-slaves; you had all the honours of a Queen paid to you, and I had infinitely more than I am deserving of; never, surely, was anything more gallant than giving my name for the watch-word. I plainly perceive I am frequently in your thoughts, and that *dear little mamma,* as Monsieur de Vivonne says, passes current still. I fancy Marseilles must have appeared a fine place to you, by the extraordinary description you give me of it, which is in itself very agreeable. A novelty of this kind has not its equal; my curiosity is greatly roused, and I should be glad to see this new hell. Alas! that there should be men groaning night and day under the weight of their chains!

We see nothing of this kind here: it is true we hear frequently of such things, and now and then see a string of them going through our streets, but this is nothing to what passes at Marseilles: the image is very strong in my mind.

E' di mezzo l'orrore, esce il diletto.[1]

You say you looked well, but what then became of your shape? how did that agree with your beauty, and with so much fatigue? I have heard from several quarters, that you have so good, so just, so clear, and so solid an understanding, that you are sole arbiter in the most important affairs. It seems that you adjusted the quarrels between Monsieur de Monaco and another person, whose name I have forgotten. Your understanding is so clear, so much above the common level, that the beauty of your person is forgotten in the charms of your mind: all this is said of you here. If you should find a Prince Alamir, you have all the requisites in yourself to make the first volume of a romance, without my caring to set them forth to you; but I was unwilling to do Provence so great an injustice, as not to let you know how much you are honoured there, and in what manner they speak of you. I want to know if you are quite insensible yourself to all the honours you receive; for my part, I own to you, that they would not be displeasing to me. If you are still at Marseilles, I beg you will make my compliments to the General of the galleys[2]. But you will be gone before you receive this. I am here still; I am half distracted at the thought: I intended to have set out last Friday, but the Abbé was almost upon his knees to have it put off till Monday. There is no getting a priest out of Paris; none but the women are for leaving it. I will go however on Monday. I fancy you will be glad to know my travelling equipage, that you may see me pass by as I used to see Monsieur Busche. I shall have two coaches, seven coach-

[1] And from the midst of horror springs delight. [Translation.]

[2] Monsieur de Vivonne, brother of Madame de Montespan.

horses, a packhorse for my bed, and three or four men on horseback: I shall be in my own coach, drawn by my two beautiful horses: the Abbé will be sometimes with me. In the other, which will have four horses and a postillion, will be my son, La Mousse, and Hélène, sometimes the Abbé with his breviary will fall into the second rank, and give place to Sévigné and the breviary of Corneille. These are important details; but they please, when coming from those we love.

I shall take no notice of the preference you give to our ocean; this would only make it too proud, and it is but too much so already. Numbers leave Paris on Monday, as well as myself. I do not know whether it is true, that Brancas has already gone, for he has not taken leave of me; I suppose he thought he had. The other evening, at Madame de Coulanges's, when supper was brought in, and we were all sat down, he continued standing at one end of the table. "Sit down," said I to him: "you will take some supper I suppose." But still he continued standing. Madame de Coulanges too desired him to sit down: "Faith," says he, "Madame de Soubise makes us wait for her strangely; surely she does not know that supper is on the table:" so he was waiting all the while for Madame de Soubise; and she, you must know, has been at Autry these five weeks. This complaisance of his set us all a-laughing. Madame de Soubise [1] is with child: she has complained to her mother of it, poor thing! but to no purpose. You know how it is with Madame de Louvigny. I wish I knew some good widow or girl who was in the same situation; I would acquaint you with it for your comfort. The Abbé Têtu has gone; he says Paris grows insupportably dull to him; he is gone straight to Fontevrault; it is all in his way, which is fortunate; from thence he goes to Richelieu, which is not above five leagues

[1] Daughter of the Duchess de Rohan, so famous for the part she took in the intrigues of the minority: Madame de Soubise was secretly beloved by Louis XIV. This concealed amour made the fortunes of her family.

further, and there he will remain. This journey of his is laughed at by many people, as carrying him still farther from his Bishopric; but I say it is the nearest road he could take to it. You see he is not quite so easy about the absence of Madame de Fontevrault, as he was about yours. If I were a little nearer to you, I would adopt your way of telling things; it is a thousand times more clear and intelligible than mine: however, you have guessed my meaning extremely well; what is there too difficult for you? You think my son's company will console me for the amusements of Paris, and that the States will console me for the loss of my son. But what, my lovely child, is to console me for your absence? In the world I have hitherto found that nothing has the least pretensions to this.

LETTER 102

From Madame DE SÉVIGNÉ *to Madame* DE GRIGNAN.

Paris, Friday, May 15, 1671.

I am still here, my dear daughter, in all the vexation that attends delayed journeys, and journeys that carry us still further from a beloved object: what madness it is to take a road so opposite to that of the heart! If I should ever live to see all distance removed between Provence and me, I shall be transported with joy. The continual desire I have to receive your letters, and to know the state of your health, so preys upon my heart, that I wonder how I am able to support it. I expect to hear from you on Sunday, and on Monday I shall set out. I am busy giving all the necessary orders for having your letters conveyed to me as frequently and as speedily as possible, and I hope I shall succeed in my wish.

Madame de Crussol is with child, and a hundred others besides. I went yesterday to take my leave of her, and of the shadow of Madame de Montausier. Had I time, I would relate all the polite things she said to me: but my hands this morning are full of farewells and business; I am going to take leave of Lavardin. I shall make up my packet this evening; I shall then be more at leisure.

Friday evening, May 15, 1671.
At Monsieur de La Rochefoucauld's.

I am now with a man who loves you, and begs you to believe it. He was greatly delighted in hearing me read your description of the galleys at Marseilles. Madame de La Fayette is dictating a number of fine things to me, which I shall not tell you. We have been taking a walk to Faverole's at Issy, where the nightingales, the hawthorn, the lilacs, the fountains, and the fine weather, afforded us all the innocent pleasures our hearts were capable of enjoying. It is a place where I have seen you. Oh, what food for my affection! If you remember, we saw a cat there once that had like to have torn out Madame de La Fayette's eyes, no doubt with envy of their brilliancy. I have bid adieu to all the beauties of this country; I am bound for one far more rude: but there is no spot, my dear child, where you are not the sole object of my thoughts. I have recommended my dear little girl to Madame Amelot and Madame d'Ormesson, but particularly to Madame du Pui-du-Fou, with whom I spent two hours yesterday. She has promised to take as much care of her as if she were her own. I have taken my leave of the d'Usèz's and a hundred others. Monsieur de Rambures is dead: can you picture to yourself his afflicted widow [1] with her *bandeau de crêpe* [2]? The Abbé de Foix is dying: he has received all the sacraments, and is at his last gasp. I have received a letter from Corbinelli; he appears to be extremely pleased with Monsieur de Vardes, and his liberality. If you write sometimes to Vardes, I beg you will let him know this, that he may see his friend is not ungrate-

[1] Marie de Bautru, Marquise de Rambures, was anything but a respectable woman.

[2] In those days widows wore a broad band of black crêpe across their foreheads, like the cloth ones worn by the nuns.

ful. Good night, my little one; I am dull; I have nothing entertaining to send you. If you love to be perfectly beloved, love the love I bear you.

---

*LETTER 103

From Madame DE SÉVIGNÉ *to the Comte* DE BUSSY.

Paris, May 17, 1671.

I write to you from the cell of our little sister of St. Marie. I love this dear child; her understanding charms me, and her piety excites my envy; for after all, my poor cousin, there is nothing so beneficial and so wise, as the care of our eternal salvation. This good creature is occupied with no other thought; I should honour her therefore, if I were not in other respects inclined to esteem her. I now leave her, however, to tell you that I highly approve your present occupation. It is worthy of yourself; and I have pleasure in anticipating the interest our nephews will take in these *Mémoires.* I set out to-morrow for Brittany, where I shall remain till All-Saints. The sun of Provence shines upon my poor child. If the honours she receives could make her happy, she would be happy indeed; but I doubt that nothing can console her for our loss. Write to me, my dear Comte, in Brittany, and believe that you are scarcely less esteemed by me than you are by our little sister, except that she reverences you as a father, and I honour you as my cousin.

LETTER 104

From Madame DE SÉVIGNÉ *to Madame* DE GRIGNAN.

Monday morning, May 18, 1671.
Just going to start.

At last, my dear child, I am just ready to step into my carriage: there!—I am in:—adieu!—I never shall use that word to you without real grief. I am now on my way to Brittany; is it possible that anything can increase the distance between us, when we are already separated from each other more than two hundred leagues? But so it is; I have found a way to complete it; and as you thought your town of Aix not quite far enough from me, I, also, look upon Paris as too much in your neighbourhood. You went to Marseilles to fly me, and I, to pay you in your own coin, am going to Vitré. But to be serious, my dear, our correspondence will suffer by this; it used to be a great source of consolation and amusement to me. Alas! what shall I have to say to you from the midst of my woods? I shall have nothing to entertain you with but accounts of Mademoiselle du Plessis and Jaquine [1]; charming subjects these! I am very happy in what you tell me of your health, but, in the name of God, if you have any love for me, take care of yourself; do not dance, do not fall, take a good deal of rest; and, above all things, arrange your plans so as to lie-in at Aix, where you may have the best and most timely assistance. You know how expeditious you are on those occasions; be sure to have everything ready rather too soon than too late. Good heavens! what shall I not suffer at that period!

You relate the dispute you had with our friend Vivonne very agreeably. I think the fault lies entirely on his side: you laid a famous trap in which you caught him completely; his confusion made me sweat for him, and he did so himself, I dare say: but in the end you made it up and embraced him! a great [2] undertaking that, for one in your condition; if your quarrels must end thus, you ought to have no quarrels nor enemies upon your hands.

The poor Abbé de Foix is dead: what a melancholy event is this! who would have thought that a woman, who, but the other day, saw herself the mother of three sons, and the eldest of them married, should now be at the point

[1] A pretty servant girl of Madame de Sévigné's at her house in Brittany.

[2] Monsieur de Vivonne was remarkable for his great bulk.

of seeing her house extinct? But nothing is more true; for I would not give a penny for the life of the young Duc de Foix: he is at present at Bordeaux with his mother, carrying on a law-suit. What sad news this will be to them! It is said the fair Armentière tears her beautiful hair, and beats her breasts; I see this will comfort you. Do you know that our little Senneterre [1] was brought to bed at Grenoble? I do not know how many people are going away to-day. Yesterday we counted no less than twenty persons of quality who were all going to do like me. Monsieur de Coulanges gave a grand supper in compliment to me, to which everybody came to take leave of me. Adieu, my most lovely and best beloved child; I shall sleep at Bonnelle where I hope to find the same spirit of devotion that you left there some time ago; if so, I will make the most of it; for, alas! I shall stand in need of it to make me support with patience this separation from a child I so passionately love, and all the fears I have for her health: think then, what I must suffer, with nothing to divert me from giving full scope to my thoughts. I take your brother with me, and by that means take him from all the disgrace his foolish conduct had brought upon him. You may suppose his mistresses will not be inconsolable for his loss; I fancy I shall do very well with him. I am now fully persuaded of what M. de Grignan says. Ah, my dear Comte! I firmly believe you; there is no person but would have acted as you did, had they been in your place: you give good reasons for everything, and make your defence in so able a manner, that I must forgive you; but, however, you ought to reflect, that the youth, beauty, health, good spirits, and perhaps life, of the woman you love, may be destroyed by too frequent recurrence of the evils you are the author of. And now, my dear child, having taken leave of your husband, I return to you. I have heard you are both unsuccessful at play. Bless me! whence arises this ill luck? What can be the

[1] She was a Longueval, and mother of Madame de Florensac, who left behind her M. de Crussol and the Duchess d'Aiguillon.

reason of these continual drizzling rains that I have always found so injurious? but I am as incessant as the rain I am speaking of, and never know when to have done. Farewell then, for the hundredth time, farewell, my dearest child: give d'Hacqueville a thousand thanks for the daily acts of friendship I receive from him: he enters into my feelings; that is a thing of the greatest consequence to me in the world. Do not forget to acquaint Vardes how highly Corbinelli speaks of him.

LETTER 105

From Madame DE SÉVIGNÉ *to Madame* DE GRIGNAN.

Malicorne, Saturday, May 23, 1671.

I have just arrived here, where I found a letter from you; such care have I taken to keep our correspondence uninterrupted. I wrote to you last Monday, just as I was going to start; since then, I have been continually going farther and farther from you, with so much grief of heart, and so lively a remembrance of you, as sometimes made thought wholly insupportable. I set out with your portrait in my pocket, which I am every moment gazing upon. It would be no easy matter to steal it from me without my perceiving it; it is a charming portrait! my mind is full of your dear idea, and my heart of the most unbounded tenderness; this is my travelling-equipage, and thus attended am I going three hundred leagues from you. We have been greatly incommoded by the heat. One of my fine horses has had to be left behind at Palaiseaux; the other six have held out very well so far.

We set out before two o'clock in the morning, to avoid the extreme heat. To-day again we were in these woods before dawn, in order to see Silvie, I mean Malicorne, where I shall stay to-morrow. Here I found the two little girls.

> Rechignées, un air triste, une voix de Mégère. [1]

Said I,

> Ces petits sont sans doute à nôtre ami:
> Fuyons les . . . . . [2]

But however,

> Nos repas ne sont point repas à la légère. [3]

For I never met with better cheer anywhere, nor a more agreeable house: I stood in need of all the water the place afforded, to refresh me after the dreadful heat I have suffered the past week. Our Abbé is very well; my son and La Mousse are great comforts to me. We have read over Corneille again and again, and repeated with the same pleasure our former admiration of him. We have likewise a new book of Nicole's with us. The subject is much the same as Pascal's, "The Education of a Prince;" but it is of that sort that there is no being weary of. We shall arrive at "The Rocks" the twenty-seventh, where I shall find the greatest pleasure I can have, a letter from you. For the future you need not write to me more than once a week, for the letters will be sent from Paris only on Wednesdays, and I should have two at once. Methinks I am robbing myself of half my treasure; I am, however, content to do it, since it is so much trouble saved to you in your present condition. I must be in very good humour to allow this. For heaven's sake, my child, take care of yourself, if you have the least regard for me. Oh! what concern am I in about your dear person! Will you

[1] With phizzes grim and air demure,
And screaming voices . . . . . [Translation.]

[2] These are the children of our friend!
Let us avoid them . . . . . [Translation.]

[3] Our meals are not of airy kind. [Translation.] See La Fontaine's Fable: "The Eagle and the Owl" (l'Aigle et l'Hibou).

never have a moment's rest? must your whole life be thus worn out with continual fatigue? I perfectly understand M. de Grignan's reasons; but, in truth, if a man loves his wife, it is natural to sometimes have a little compassion for her.

My fan, then, came very opportunely. Did you not think it very pretty? But what a trifle! do not deprive me of this little pleasure when I have an opportunity of enjoying it; rather thank me for indulging myself in these mere nothings. Let me hear a good deal about you, that is the main point. Remember I am to have a letter from you every Friday, but remember at the same time, that I cannot see you now; that you are as it were a thousand leagues from me; that you are with child; that you are in a bad state of health. Think,—but no; think of nothing, leave the business of thought to me, in my long shady alleys, whose dreary melancholy will add to mine; I may walk there long enough before I shall find the treasure I had with me the last time I was in them. Adieu, my dearest child! you do not mention yourself often enough to me: be always exact in observing the dates of my letters. Alas! what amusement can they now afford you? My son embraces you a thousand times; he helps greatly to amuse me; he does all in his power to please me; sometimes we read, sometimes we chat, you know how. La Mousse contributes his share, and our Abbé as much as the best of them; we all adore him, because he adores you. He has at last left me his whole fortune [1]; he had not a moment's rest till that was done; do not mention this to anyone; the family would be all upon his back if they heard it: but love him dearly upon my recommendation, and love me also upon my own. I embrace that rogue Grignan, notwithstanding all his crimes and misdemeanors.

---

[1] Madame de Sévigné was the favourite niece of the Abbé de Coulanges, and as he passed the greatest part of his life with her, nothing could be more natural than his leaving her his whole fortune at his death.

LETTER 106

From Madame DE SÉVIGNÉ *to Madame* DE GRIGNAN.

From The Rocks,[1]
Sunday, May 31, 1671.

At last, my child, I am at "The Rocks." Can I behold these walks; can I view these ornaments, this little secluded room, these books, this chamber, and not die with grief? Some recollections are agreeable; but there are others again so real and so tender that they are hardly supportable; such are mine with respect to you. And you may easily guess the effect this is likely to produce in a heart like mine.

If you continue pretty well, my dear child, I believe I shall not come to you till next year. Brittany and Provence are not very compatible; long journeys are strange things: if we were always to continue in the same mind we are in at the end of a journey, we should never stir from the place we were then in: but Providence, in kindness to us, causes us to forget it. It is much the same with lying-in women. Heaven permits this forgetfulness that the world may be peopled, and that folks may take journeys to Provence. Mine therefore will afford me the greatest joy I ever received in my life, but how cruel a thought is it to see no end to your stay there! I more and more admire and applaud your prudence; though, to tell you the truth, I am greatly affected with this impossibility; but I hope time will make us see things in a different light. We must always live in hope; without that consolation there would be no living. I sometimes pass such melancholy moments in the woods, that I return as changed as one just out of a fever. I fancy you pass your time pretty agreeably at Marseilles. Do not fail to tell me how you were received at Grignan. The people here had designed to make a kind of triumphal entry for

[1] The name of Madame de Sévigné's château and estate in Brittany.

Dessiné sur les Lieux en 1813 par Mr. le Cte. Joseph d'Estourmel. *Gravé par Lorieux*

"THE ROCKS", BRITTANY.

my son; Vaillant had drawn out near fifteen hundred men under arms, very well dressed, with new ribbons round their necks, and had marched them within a league of "The Rocks." But guess what happened! our Abbé had written word that we should be there on Tuesday, and afterwards forgot to mention it to us. Accordingly these poor people were waiting under arms the whole day till ten o'clock at night, when they returned home very much chagrined at their disappointment; and behold the next day, which was Wednesday, we came in as quiet and peaceably as lambs, without dreaming that a little army had been drawn out to receive us! We were a good deal vexed at this mistake, but there was no remedy; so much for our first setting out. Mademoiselle du Plessis is just as you left her; she has formed a new acquaintance at Vitré that she plumes herself mightily upon, because she is a great genius, has read all the romances, and, more than that, has had two letters from the Princess de Tarente. I was wicked enough to set Vaillant upon telling her that I was jealous of this new friend of hers, and that, when I heard of their intimacy, it had given me the greatest uneasiness, though I had taken no notice of it to her. It requires the pen of a Molière to describe all she says upon the occasion; and it is highly amusing to see how artfully she manages me, and with what care she avoids speaking of my supposed rival before my face; I too, also play my part very well.

My little trees are grown surprisingly; Pilois [1] is raising their stately heads to the clouds. In short, nothing can be more beautiful than these walks, which you first saw planted. You may remember I once gave you a little device which was thought very suitable. Here is a motto I wrote the other day upon a tree which I intend for my son who is just returned from Candie. *Vago di fama* [2]. Is it not pretty, notwithstanding its conciseness? Yesterday I had another inscribed in honour of the idlers, *Bella*

[1] The gardener at "The Rocks."

[2] Anxious for fame. [Translation.]

cosa far niente[1]! Ah! my dear child, what a wild romantic tone my letters have! What is become of the time when I used to talk of Paris like other people? now you will hear of nothing but myself; and to show you what confidence I have in your affection, I am persuaded this will be the most agreeable intelligence I can give you. I am highly pleased with my company here. Our Abbé is at all times an excellent companion. La Mousse and my son are satisfied with me, and I with them. We always seek one another; and if business at any time takes me from them, they are at their wit's end, and think it very odd in me to prefer a farmer's account to a tale of La Fontaine's. They are all passionately in love with you. I fancy you will hear from them soon. I choose however to be beforehand with them, for I do not love talking to you in a crowd. My dearest child, will you always love me? my life depends upon your affection! that, as I told you the other day, constitutes all my joy and all my sorrow. Let me add, that my prospects are embittered with the cruel thought that I must necessarily pass so much of my life at a distance from you.

LETTER 107

From Madame DE SÉVIGNÉ *to Madame* DE GRIGNAN.

The Rocks, Sunday, June 7, 1671.

I received your two letters with a joy that no tongue can express. That which you wrote to my son is not fricasseed in snow; but rather in salt, and that in large quantities; it is a finished piece: I leave him to answer it, and to acquaint you how he has succeeded in his parish, and at the ball at Vitré. We read "Bertrand du Guesclin" through in four days, and were very much amused. But you did not see clearly, my child; my carriage did not break down on the road; its springs were forged by the

[1] What a fine thing it is to do nothing! [Translation.]

hands of Vulcan himself, or they could never have held out a third journey into Brittany. You mean, that one of my horses, the finest creature in the whole kingdom, was left behind at Nogent, and, as I have since been informed, died there: this is what deceived you. I had indeed a fit of the colic some time ago; but I admire d'Hacqueville's telling you, that I did not acquaint him with it. The jest is, that he was himself to blame upon the occasion; and as he had engaged to be quite perfect, he would not push his justification with me, but endeavours to acquit himself to you, by laying the blame upon me: but I never can be wanting in any point of friendship to him; I have a great regard for him, and his friendship is an inestimable treasure to me. I will tell you how it happened. I went to mass in the coach with my aunt, and on the way found myself very ill; I was apprehensive of what would follow, and so drove back immediately: when I got home, I vomited excessively; a violent pain seized me in the left side, the vomiting continued during the night, and the pain grew worse and worse, attended with a great oppression. The alarm was presently given: Pecquet was sent for directly, who took very great care of me; an apothecary was sent for likewise, he ordered me into the slipper-bath; people were dispatched for the herbs to make it with: if I had had twenty servants, they would have been all busy. I never once thought of Madame de La Fayette. Our little tapestry-maker, who was then gone to work for her, told her how ill I was: she came in while I was in the bath; she told me what had brought her, and that she had met a footman of d'Hacqueville's, and had informed him of my illness, in the certainty that his master would come to see me the moment he heard of it. Well, the day passed over in this manner, without my colic being at all abated: the next night I was very ill: no news however of d'Hacqueville: I felt his neglect very sensibly; it gave me uneasiness, and I could not help speaking of it. The next morning I was somewhat better; and in these cases, to be better and to be cured, is much the same thing. Then Monsieur d'Ormesson came in a great fright, having been told at the Palace, he said, by d'Hacqueville, that I was very ill; so he knew it. In the evening I sent him a little tender complaining note, which embarrassed him a good deal. He made, when he came, a great many trifling excuses. I told him I had not sent to Madame de La Fayette. He took no notice of what he had said to Monsieur d'Ormesson, which was what made most against him; and I, observing this, took no notice of it myself, but admitted his excuse, that he did not know of my illness till he received my note. This is a mighty entertaining story, and an extremely necessary one: but, however, it is all truth. My dear child, if you are not fatigued with this recital, you must be in excellent health. Well! I vow I will never plague you with so long a one again.

And so you saw a poor old man who was going to be broken upon the wheel. He behaved better, it is to be hoped, than a certain Comte Frangipani, who was executed about two months ago at Vienna, for a conspiracy against the Emperor. This Frangipani found himself so unable to undergo the shame and horror of a public death, that they were forced to draw him to the place of execution, and hold his legs and arms till the executioner did his office. This is just as I should behave upon the same occasion. Now we are talking of punishments, I must tell you of one that will make you shudder. Monsieur du Plessis had a complaint in both his feet, similar to what you once had in yours: instead of treating it in the same manner as Charon treated you, he met with a very skillful personage, *a wonderful man*! as Madame du Plessis called him, who proposed a little anodyne of his own; and what do you think it was? Why to tear out the nails of his two great toes by the roots, in order, as he very sagely observed, to prevent the disorder from returning again. The poor man was confined to his bed with this gentle operation, when we came here; he walks about a little now, but in a very tottering manner. I think he will always hear from somebody or other during his whole life: "Take care you do not fall, you are not very firm on your feet." As for Mademoiselle du Plessis, she is the same adorable personage as ever; she had heard, it seems, that Monsieur de Grignan was the handsomest youth in the world: think you hear her say this in her peculiar tone, and you will be ready to give her another box on the ear [1]. I am sometimes unfortunate enough to say a thing that pleases her: I wish you could hear her praise and imitate me: she has retained some good things of yours too, when you were last here; these she gives us over and over again with the same grace. Ah me! if I had nothing stronger to put me in mind of you, how happy should I be!

Pomenars [2] has constantly some action or other against him, and of so serious a nature, that his life is at stake. He was soliciting his judges the other day at Rennes, with a very long beard, and was asked by somebody, why he did not get himself shaved: "Who, I?" said he, "I think I should be a very great fool to give myself any trouble about my face, till I know to whom my head belongs: the King disputes it with me at present; when the affair is decided, if it belongs to me, I will take care of it." This is the pathetic style in which he endeavours to engage the compassion of his judges.

You will see by the Bishop of Marseilles' letter, that we are still upon a friendly footing: it seems to me as if I had received the very same letter ten times: he does not run into *the justice to believe,* but desires me to be persuaded *that he is, with extraordinary veneration, the Bishop of Marseilles,* and I take him at his word. Keep up the friendship that is between you; do not take off the mask, nor be at the trouble of having an enmity upon your hands; it is a greater burden than you are aware of. What

[1] See Letter 120, of the 26th of July, 1671, in this volume.

[2] A gentleman of Brittany, of whom it is said, that having had an action brought against him for uttering false money, and being cleared on his trial, he paid his fees and charges in the same coin. See the Letters 120, 121 and 150, of the 26th and 29th of July, 1671, and the 11th November, 1671, in this volume: also the article "Bouille" in the "Memoirs of Amelot de La Houssaie.

impudence, for you to paint: I am glad of it however; it is a sign you are feeling well. Your brother is a composition of oddities, but he does very well here. We have now and then a little serious conversation which might be of advantage to him, but his mind is rather too much like whipped syllabub: were it not for that, he would be amiable enough. How progresses your Italian? have you forgotten it? I read a little now and then, by way of keeping it up. You say that M. de Grignan embraces me. You have laid aside your respect then, my dear Grignan; but come and play a little at mall with me; it is at present such charming weather, I so long to see you play, you play with such a grace, and make such pretty strokes; indeed it is very cruel of you to refuse me an hour's walk only. Come then, my dear child, and let us have a little chat together.

LETTER 108

From Madame DE SÉVIGNÉ *to Madame* DE GRIGNAN.

The Rocks, Wednesday, June 10, 1671.

I am going to entertain you to-day, my dear child, with what is called rain and fine weather. I did not receive your letters till Friday, and I answered them the Sunday following. I begin then with the rain, for fair weather is out of the question. For this week past it has rained incessantly: I say incessantly; for the rain has only been interrupted by storms. I cannot stir abroad, my workmen are all dispersed, and I am devoured with melancholy: La Mousse too is very low-spirited: we read indeed, and that just keeps us alive. My son has gone to Rennes, whither we thought it necessary to send him, to pay a visit to the first President, and several other friends that I have there; if he has time, I shall prevail on him to go and see Monsieur de Coëtquen; he is old enough now for these things. There was a ball at Vitré again on Sunday. I very much fear that my son will become too fond of the company of ten or a dozen men who supped with him the other night at the Sévigné Tower; they may be endured, but he should be very cautious of forming too great an intimacy with them. A dispute arose between two of the party, about some trifle or other: the lie was given; to it they went; the company endeavoured to part them; there was a great deal of talk, and very little sense: however, Monsieur le Marquis [1] had the honour of making up the difference, and afterwards set out for Rennes. There have been great cabals at Vitré: Mademoiselle de Croqueoison complains, that at a ball the other day, Mademoiselle du Cernet did not offer her part of some oranges she had. We must hear what Mademoiselle du Plessis and the Launays have to say on this subject, as they know all the circumstances relating to it. As to Mademoiselle du Plessis, she lets all her affairs at Vitré run to ruin, because she will not stir in them, from the fear of making me jealous on account of her new friend: and it was but the other day, that, to make me quite easy, she said as many ill-natured things of her as she could. When it is fine weather, this nonsense makes me laugh; but when it is bad and gloomy, I could give her a box on the ear, as you once did. Madame de Coulanges writes me word, that she has heard nothing of Brancas, except that, out of his six coach-horses, he has only one left, and that he was the last person who discovered it. I hear no news: our little Alègre is at her mother's, and it is thought that M. de Seignelai is to be married to her. I suppose you are in no want of persons to furnish you with intelligence; for my part, I despise trivial occurrences; I am only for those that surprise and astonish: such a one I met with this very morning, while the Abbé and I were in his study together. We found, in reckoning with those counters of his, which are so good, that with all that has fallen to me, I ought to be worth five hundred and thirty thousand livres [2]: do you know, that what our dear Abbé has left me, will not amount to less than eighty thousand francs? And

[1] Meaning her son the Marquis of Sévigné.

[2] About £25,000 or $125,000 in round figures.

do you think I am not impatient to be in possession? And one hundred thousand francs from Burgundy; this has come since you were married, the rest, namely, one hundred thousand crowns, by my marriage; one hundred thousand crowns since from M. de Châlons, and twenty thousand francs, in little legacies, from one or two of my uncles; but do you not wonder whither my pen is running with me? I should do much better to tell you what I suffer every day, when I reflect in what places Providence has destined us to pass our lives. This is a continual source of uneasiness to me, but let it not be so to you; you have not the same reason; you are with a husband who adores you, and in the midst of honours and splendour; but endeavour, if possible, to work some miracle in your affairs, so that your return to Paris may be retarded only by the duties of your post, and not from necessity. It is very easy to talk thus; I wish it was as easily carried into execution; and wishes are not forbidden us. They write me word, that Madame de Valavoire is in Paris, and that she is for ever talking of your beauty, politeness, wit, talents, and, in short, of the new head-dress you have invented, which it seems you have executed in as good a style as if you had been in the midst of the Court: Madame de La Troche and I have at least the honour of having described it so well, as to put you in the way of performing these wonders. She is in Paris still, that La Troche: she is going to her own house about the latter end of this month. As for me, I do not know what the States intend doing; but I fancy I shall run away for fear of being ruined: it is a mighty pretty thing to put myself to the expense of near a thousand crowns in dinners and suppers, and all for the honour of keeping a summer-house for M. and Madame de Chaulnes, Madame de Rohan, M. de Lavardin, and half Brittany; who, without knowing anything of me, will, to be in the fashion, honour me with their company. Well, we shall see how it will turn out. I shall only regret leaving M. d'Harouïs and this house, before I have half finished by business. But, my dear child, the greatest inclination I have at present is, to be a little religious. I plague La Mousse about it every day: I belong neither to God nor to the devil: I am quite weary of such a situation; though, between you and me, I look upon it as the most natural one in the world: I am not the devil's, because I fear God, and have at the bottom a principle of religion; then, on the other hand, I am not properly God's, because his law appears hard and irksome to me, and I cannot bring myself to acts of self-denial; so that altogether I am one of those called lukewarm Christians, the great number of whom does not in the least surprise me, for I perfectly understand their sentiments, and the reasons that influence them. However, we are told, that this is a state highly displeasing to God; if so, we must get out of it; alas! this is the difficulty. Was ever anything so mad as I am, to be thus eternally pestering you with my rhapsodies? My dear child, *I ask excuse*, as they say here: but I must chat with you; it is so truly delightful to me; be sure however not to return me an answer, only let me hear of your health, with a little spice of your sentiments, that I may see that you are happy, and that you like Grignan; that is all. Love me; though we have turned the world into ridicule, it is natural, it is good.

LETTER 109

From Madame DE SÉVIGNÉ *to Madame* DE GRIGNAN.

The Rocks, Sunday, June 14, 1671.

I counted on receiving two letters from you last Friday, and instead of two I have not received one! Ah! my dear child, whatever may be the cause of this delay, it is impossible to express the anxiety it has given me. I have not been able to sleep these two nights. I sent twice to Vitré, in order to amuse myself with hopes, but in vain. I now perceive, that my peace depends wholly upon the pleasure of hearing from you. Here am I insensibly fallen into all the extravagances of Chesières; I can now enter into his griefs; they are like mine; I now know what he must have felt in not receiving that letter of the twenty-seventh; it is impossible to be happy if one is to resemble him; God forbid that I should be in his situation; it is you, my dear child, who must preserve me from it. Farewell, I am out of humour, and am very bad company: when I receive another letter from you, I shall find my tongue again. When we go to bed, our thoughts are only of a dark gray, as M. de La Rochefoucauld says, but in the night, they become quite black: I know but too well what he means.

LETTER 110

From Madame DE SÉVIGNÉ *to Madame* DE GRIGNAN.

The Rocks, Sunday, June 21, 1671.

Now, my dear child, I once more breathe at my ease. I have supped like Monsieur de La Souche [1]; my heart is freed from a load that would not suffer me to rest a moment: I had been two posts without receiving a letter from you, and was in such anxiety about your health, that I was reduced almost to wish that you had written to everybody except myself. I could better have borne to have been a little behindhand in your remembrance, than to have undergone the dreadful uncertainty I was in. But, good heavens! how much do I repent communicating all my uneasinesses to you! I know they will give pain to you when they are at an end with me. This is the misfortune of being at such a distance. Alas! it is not the only one.

You tell me marvellous stories of your ceremonies on *Corpus Christi* day; they are so dreadfully profane, that I am surprised how your good Archbishop [2] could suffer them. It is true indeed, he is an Italian, and this fashion comes from his country. And so, my dear child, you still preserve your good looks; what! you are not pale, thin, cast

[1] See Molière's "School for Women" (*l'Ecole des Femmes*). Act II., *Scene VI.*

[2] Cardinal Grimaldy.

down, like the Princess Olympia[1]! Oh! I am too happy; for heaven's sake amuse yourself in every possible way, and do everything in your power to preserve yourself. I am glad to hear you are attentive to your dress: the negligence we so much reproached you for, may have pleased your husband, but it was very much commented on by others. We have had incessant rains here, and, instead of saying, after rain comes sunshine, we say, after rain comes wet weather. Our workmen are all dispersed; and, instead of addressing your letter to me at the foot of a tree, you might have directed it to the chimney-corner. We have had a great deal of business upon our hands since we came here: we have not yet determined whether we shall fly the States, or shall face them. This is certain, that we are very far from forgetting you; we talk of you very frequently; but I think of you more, insomuch that I sometimes will not talk of you at all, there are certain excesses that require correction, both in regard to good manners and policy. I think how we ought to act to avoid being troublesome to others, and study my old lessons. We read a great deal here: La Mousse has desired that we may read Tasso together; I understand that author well, as being perfect mistress of Italian; it is an amusement to me. La Mousse's Latin and good sense together, render him an apt scholar, and my practice, and the good masters I have had, make me a good mistress. My son is always reading some trifle or other; comedies, which he repeats like Molière himself; verses, romances, histories, etc.; in short, he is a very entertaining companion, has wit, good understanding, and has found the way to allure us from reading serious subjects as we at first intended; when he has left us, we shall begin again with some of Nicole's moral pieces. We must endeavour to pass life as agreeably as possible, and how can that be done at a hundred thousand leagues' distance from you? You observe very justly, that we see and speak to each other through a thick crêpe. You know *The Rocks*, and your imagination can easily direct you to

[1] An allusion to a heroine of Ariosto's.

me. For my part, I cannot manage so well in this respect. I have formed to myself a Provence of my own, a house at Aix, perhaps more splendid than yours really is, and there I find you. I see Grignan too, but you have no trees there, which vexes me, for I cannot see distinctly where you walk: I am afraid the wind might blow you off your terrace. Oh! could I but think some sudden gust would transport you here, I would always keep my window open to receive you. God knows, I am carrying this folly of mine to a great length. But to return: I think the Castle of Grignan a very fine one, it has a great deal of the ancient Adhémars about it. I am delighted to find how much our good Abbé loves you; his heart seems as warm towards you, as if I had fashioned it with my own hands: for this very reason I almost adore him. It is droll that your little girl, finding she durst not aspire to the perfection of her mother's nose, would not . . . but I say no more: however, she has taken the third way, and thought proper to have a little flat nose[1]. My dear, are you not angry with her for it? But let not that trouble you at present. Look in your glass, that is all you have now to do, in order to finish happily what you have so well begun.

LETTER 111

From Madame DE SÉVIGNÉ *to Madame* DE GRIGNAN.

The Rocks, Wednesday, June 24, 1671.
From my fire-side.

Well! I will say no more about the weather, lest I should grow as insupportable as the rain; so

> Qu'il soit beau, qu'il soit laid, je n'en veux plus rien dire;
> J'en ai fait vœu, etc.[2]

I have had no letter from you this week; but that has given me no uneasiness, as you told me in your last you

[1] That is, much the same kind of nose as Madame de Sévigné's.

[2] Be it foul, or be it fair,
I'll say no more on't, I declare. [Translation.]

should not write. However, I expect one from Grignan with impatience. But for last week, as I was not prepared for it, I own to you, the mistake that was the occasion of detaining your letters, gave me great disquietude. I was very troublesome to poor d'Hacqueville on that subject, and to you also, my child; I am heartily sorry for it now, and wish I had not done so; but I cannot disguise my feelings; and if my heart is oppressed I cannot help complaining to those I love; they must overlook and forgive these foibles in me: for, as Madame de La Fayette said one day, "Have we laid a wager to be perfect? No, surely; I am certain, if I had, I should have lost my money." Monsieur de Coëtquen has been here twice within these three days; he was going to let some lands upon lease at about three leagues from hence, and has laid out one hundred pistoles on his journey, to raise the rent of them about fifty francs. He inquired particularly after you and M. de Grignan, whom he took occasion to mention in the handsomest manner possible, in speaking of elegant and manly figures. Pray let me know in your next, whether he still merits the being placed in the first rank of worthies. We cannot sufficiently admire your procession; I do not think it can be equalled in France [1]. My walks are extremely fine; I sometimes wish you had them with you, for the use of the inhabitants of your great Castle. My son is here still, and does not seem at all weary or bored: I have several things to say to you about him, but shall reserve them for another opportunity. We have had a set of vile Bohemians [2] here, that were enough to make one sick, *and they danced no better, Madame, no offence to your Ladyship's honour, and with all respect to your greatness, no better than so many blind kittens.* This is what one of their own women told me, who was angry with half her com-

[1] The procession that is made at Aix, on *Corpus Christi* day, is the most extravagant and ridiculous thing that ever was seen.

[2] A set of people like gypsies, who travel up and down the country in France, and get their living by dancing, and fortune-telling; but chiefly by stealing everything they can lay their hands on.

pany. I found here the conversation you had one day with Pomenars, which made us laugh till the tears ran down our cheeks. He may now shave at least half his face, for he is cleared of his rape affair; nothing is now depending but that of the false money, which he makes himself very easy about. What more shall I say to you, my darling? There are very few things that one can discourse freely upon at three hundred leagues' distance. I find a conversation in my mall would do me most good: it is a delightful place for talking in, when the heart is in the same condition as mine is. I shall say nothing to you about the lively and well-grounded affection I have for you; it is a subject that will grow tiresome to you. Farewell then my dearest love! Kindest remembrances to M. de Grignan.

LETTER 112

From Madame DE SÉVIGNÉ *to Madame* DE GRIGNAN.

The Rocks, Sunday, June 28, 1671.

You have amply made up to me my late losses: I have received two letters from you, which have filled me with transports of joy. The pleasure I take in reading them is beyond all imagination. If I have in any way contributed to the improvement of your style, I did it in the thought I was labouring for the pleasure of others, not for my own. But Providence, who has seen fit to separate us so often, and to place us at such immense distances from each other, has repaid me a little for the privations in the charms of your correspondence, and still more in the satisfaction you express at your environment, and the beauty of your Castle: you represent it to me with an air of grandeur and magnificence that enchants me. I once saw a similar account of it by the first Madame de Grignan; but I little thought at that time, that all these beauties were one day to be at your command. I am very much obliged to you for having given me so particular an account of it. If I could be tired with reading your letters, it would not only betray a very bad taste in me, but would likewise show that I could have very little love or friendship for you. Divest yourself of the dislike you have taken to circumstantial details; I have often told you, and you ought yourself to feel the truth of this remark, that they are as dear to us from those we love, as they are tedious and disagreeable from others. If they are displeasing to us, it is only from the indifference we feel for those who write them. Admitting this observation to be true, I leave you to judge what pleasure yours afford me. It is a fine thing, truly, to play the great lady, as you do at present. I perfectly comprehend Monsieur de Grignan's feelings in seeing you so much admire his Castle: had you appeared insensible, or even indifferent, on the occasion, it would have given him a chagrin, that I can conceive better perhaps than any other, and I share in the pleasure he has in seeing you pleased. There are some hearts which sympathise for each other so truly, that they judge by themselves what others feel. You do not mention Vardes[1] often enough to me, nor poor Corbinelli. Was it not very agreeable to you to be able to speak their language? How goes on Vardes's love for the fair T. . . .[2]? Tell me whether he is much hurt at the infinite length of his banishment, or whether his philosophy, and a little dash of misanthropy, can support his heart against these vicissitudes of love and fortune. The books you read are very well chosen. Petrarch must certainly give you a good deal of pleasure, especially with the notes you have. Those of Mademoiselle de Scuderi on some of his sonnets rendered them very agreeable. As for Tacitus, you know how much I was charmed with it, when we read it together here; and how often I used to interrupt

[1] The Marquis de Vardes was banished to Provence in 1665, for having been concerned in some Court intrigues, and remained in exile till the year 1682. He was a man of amiable manners.

[2] Believed and thought to be Mademoiselle de Toiras, daughter of the Marquis de Toiras.

you, to make you observe the periods, where I thought the harmony particularly striking; but if you stop half way, I shall scold you: it will be doing great injustice to the dignity of the subject, and I shall say to you, as a certain prelate did to the Queen-Mother, "This is history, you know what stories are already." A reluctance, in this respect, is only pardonable in romances, which I know you do not like. We read Tasso with pleasure, and I am a pretty good proficient in the language, from the excellent masters I have had. My son makes La Mousse read "Cleopatra" [1], and I listen to him, whether I will or not, and am amused. My son is going to Lorraine; we shall be very dull in his absence. You know how it vexes me to see the breaking up of an agreeable party, and how transported I am when I see a train of carriages driving off, that have wearied me to death for a whole day; upon which we made this just observation, that bad company is more desirable than good. I recollect all the odd things we used to say when you were here, and all you said yourself, and all you did: your idea never leaves me; and then again, on a sudden, I think where you are; my imagination represents to me an immense space, and a great distance; on a sudden your Castle bounds the prospect, and I am displeased at the walls that enclose your mall. Ours is surprisingly beautiful, and the young nursery is delightful. I take pleasure in rearing their little heads to the clouds, and frequently, without considering consequences or my own interest, cut down large trees, because their shade incommodes my young ones. My son views all these proceedings, but I do not allow him to interfere. Pilois [2] continues to be a very great favourite with me, and I prefer his conversation to that of many who have the title of Chevalier in the Parliament of Rennes. I am grown rather more negligent than you: for the other day I let a coachful of the Fouesnel family go home through a tremendous rain for want of pressing them with a good grace to stay;

[1] A famous romance of La Calprenède's.

[2] The gardener.

but I could not get the words of invitation to pass my lips. It was not the two young women, but the mother and an old woman from Rennes, and the two sons. Mademoiselle du Plessis is exactly as you represent her, only, if possible, more impertinent. What she says and does every day to keep me from being jealous, is perfectly original, and I am quite provoked, sometimes, that I have nobody to laugh at it with me. Her sister-in-law is very pretty, without being ridiculous, and speaks Gascon in the midst of Brittany. I think you are very happy in having Madame de Simiane[1] with you; she has a fund of knowledge that will relieve you from all kinds of restraint; this is a great deal. You will have, too, a very agreeable companion in her. Since she has been so kind as to remember me, pray make my compliments to her in return, and likewise to our dear Coadjutor: we do not write to one another now, but we can assign no reason for it. I fancy we are at too great a distance; I admire however the expedition of the post. The comparison of Chilly enchanted me, and I was no less pleased to find that my apartment is already marked out: I wish for nothing so much as to occupy it, which will be early next year; the joy this hope gives me you may partly conceive by that you will yourself experience in receiving me. I am surprised at Cateau; I believe she is married, but her conduct has been very disgraceful and very shocking. I can less forgive her intending to kill her child, as it was her husband's, than if it had been another's: she must have a very wicked heart. Her husband, as they tell me from Paris, is one Droguet, who was once a footman to Chesières. Love must have little to do, I think, to amuse himself with such sort of people; I would have him confine his power, and its effects, to the select few, which is now dispensed in too general a manner. If you take upon you to blush for all your female neighbours, and have your imagination as lively as it was with regard to B. . . ., you will always leave company, as handsome as

[1] Madeleine Hai-du-Châtelet, wife of Charles Louis, Marquis de Simiane; she was afterwards mother-in-law to Pauline de Grignan.

an angel. You want me to load my conscience with the story of this woman; I will comply with your desire, but upon this condition, that I am not to answer for the truth of it; on the contrary, I am rather inclined to believe it false. I never give credit to evil reports; I renounce therefore my agreement. It was reported, then, that this M...... had been a little premature in the business, which made him in such a hurry to marry her. The grand point was, to make the best labour in the world pass for a miscarriage; and a fine healthy child, an abortion. This trial of skill cost an infinite deal of pains to those concerned in it, and might serve for the subject of a romance. I know the whole affair, but it would be a tedious narration. This is enough, however, to make you blush in talking of a miscarriage at five months. The child died very opportunely.

I now return to you, that is, to the divine fountain of Vaucluse! How beautiful! Well might Petrarch make such frequent mention of it! But, remember, I shall some day see all these wonders with my own eyes; I, who have such a veneration for antiquities. I shall certainly be transported with them, and the magnificence of Grignan. The Abbé will find employment enough there: after the Doric orders and splendid titles of your house, nothing is wanting but the order you are going to establish there; for let me tell you, without something substantial at the bottom, all is bitterness and anxiety. I have great pity for those who ruin themselves; it is the only affliction in life that is felt alike by all, and which is increased, instead of being diminished, by time. I have frequent conversations on this subject with a certain friend of ours. If he has a mind to benefit by them, he has had opportunity enough to lay in a good stock, and of such a nature he need not forget them. I am glad that you are to have two of your brothers-in-law with you this autumn. I think you have planned your journey well. We can travel a great way without being fatigued, provided we have something to amuse us by the way, and do not lose our courage. The return of fine weather has brought all my workmen back again, which is a great amusement to me. When I have company, I work at that fine altar-piece you saw me drawing when you were in Paris; when I am alone, I read, I write, or am with the Abbé in his private room upon business: I wish him with you sometimes, but it is for two or three days only.

I consent to the commerce of wit which you propose. The other day I made a maxim off-hand without once thinking of it; and I liked it so well that I fancied I had taken it out of M. de La Rochefoucauld's: pray tell me whether it is so or not, for in that case my memory is more to be praised than my judgment. I said, with all the ease in the world, that "ingratitude begets reproach, as acknowledgment begets new favours." Pray where did this come from? have I read it? or did I dream it? or is it my own idea? Nothing can be truer than the thing itself, nor than that I am totally ignorant how I came by it. I found it properly arranged in my brain, and at the end of my tongue.

As for that sentence, *bella cosa, far niente,* you will not think it so dull, when I tell you it is intended for your brother: remember last winter's disaster. Adieu, my dearest child; take care of yourself, continue handsome, dress well, amuse yourself, and take proper exercise. I have just been writing to Vivonne [1], about a Captain of a troop of Bohemians, whose confinement I have begged him to render as easy as possible, without detriment to the King's service. You must know there was among the troop of Bohemians that I was mentioning to you the other day [2] a young girl who danced extremely well, and put me very much in mind of your manner: I was pleased with her; she begged me to write to Provence in favour of her grandfather. "Where is he?" said I. "He is at Marseilles," said she, with as much composure and unconcern as if she had said, "He is at Vincennes." He was

[1] General of the galleys.

[2] See Letter 111, of the 24th June, 1671, in this volume.

a man of singular merit, it seems, in his way[1]; in short, I promised her to write about him; I immediately thought of Vivonne: I send you my letter: if you are not sufficiently upon terms with him, to allow of my jesting with him, you may burn it; if it is an ill-written letter, you may burn it; but if you are friendly with his corpulency, and my letter will save you the trouble of writing one, seal it, and send it to him. I could not refuse this request to the poor girl, and to the best-danced minuet that I have seen since the days of Mademoiselle de Sévigné; she had just your air, was about your height, has good teeth, and fine eyes. Here is a letter of so enormous a length, that I can easily forgive your not reading it through. Monsieur de Grignan cannot conceive how one can possibly read such long letters: but, in good earnest, can you read them in a day?

LETTER 113

From Madame DE SÉVIGNÉ *to Madame* DE GRIGNAN.

The Rocks, Wednesday, July 1, 1671.

At length the month of June has departed! I am really surprised at it, for I thought it never would have had an end. Do you not recollect a September that you thought had no inclination to give way to October? This month has gone on in the same way; but now I think it is finished: yes, I am sure it is.

Fouesnel[2] is a delightful place; my son and I went there yesterday, in a coach and six; nothing can be more delightful: we seemed to fly. We made some little songs as we went along, which I send you. The esteem we have for your prose does not hinder us from making you partaker of our verse. Madame de La Fayette is very much

[1] And had been condemned to the galleys, for having distinguished himself rather too much in his Bohemian faculty.

[2] This is a Château in the neighbourhood of "The Rocks."

pleased with the letter you wrote her. Well, my dear, it is all settled, your brother is going to leave us; La Mousse and I shall now apply ourselves to good reading. Tasso amuses us much at present; we read before all the trifles we could lay our hands on, in compliance with my son's humour, who is then in his glory. I shall now take long walks *tête-à-tête* by myself, as Tonquedec said. Do you imagine I think of you? But I have my *little friend* here, whom I also tenderly love. There is certainly nothing so charming as a portrait, when well done: say what you will, yours does you great justice. Your letters from Grignan are my support and comfort under all my vexations: I wait for them with impatience; but to say the truth, those I write are of an insufferable length; I am resolved to be more reasonable in future. It is not fair to judge of you by myself; it would be rash; you have not so much time upon your hands as I have.

Mademoiselle du Plessis came in, an hour ago, and smacked me on the cheek in her boisterous way, and then teased me to show her that part of your letter to me in which you mention her. My son had the insolence to tell her, before my face, that you remembered her in a very kind manner; and turning to me, "Show her the passage, Madame," says he, "that she may be convinced of it." I coloured up, as you do when you think of other people's faults; and was obliged to tell a thousand lies, and protest I had burnt your letter. Could anything be more malicious? I have received a very complimentary and civil letter from Guitaud: he tells me he has discovered a thousand good qualities in me, that he had not perceived before; and I, not choosing to answer humbly that I was afraid I should destroy his good opinion of me, replied, that I hoped the longer he knew me, the better he would like me. I had much rather answer all the extravagances that are said to me, thus, than make use of the common-place replies, that you and I have so often laughed at.

I am persuaded that you will meet with great assistance from Madame de Simiane; we should lay aside all form and ceremony with such people as soon as possible, and make them a party in our pleasures and whims, otherwise we should soon die, and it would be dying a villainous death too. I said I would put an end to this letter, I am now resolved to do it. I do myself great violence, however, in quitting you so soon, my dear; our correspondence is the sole pleasure of my life: I am persuaded you believe me.

LETTER 114

From Madame DE SÉVIGNÉ *to Madame* DE GRIGNAN.

The Rocks, Sunday, July 5, 1671.

It is a great proof of your love, my dear child, that you can bear with all the nonsense I send you from here; you defend Mademoiselle de Croqueoison extremely well; in return, I assure you there is not a single word in your letters that is not dear to me. I am afraid to read them, for fear of ending them, and if it were not for the consolation that I can read them over as often as I please, I should make them last much longer; but then on the other hand, my impatience makes me ready to devour them. What should I do if your writing was as illegible as d'Hacqueville's? would the greatness of my affection help me to decipher it? really I am afraid not; but I have heard of such instances. In short, I greatly esteem d'Hacqueville, and yet I cannot accustom myself to his hand-writing; I never can read his letters; I hunt out word by word; I puzzle myself with guessing at them; I say one word for another, and at last, when I can make neither head nor tail of it, away I fling the letter in a rage. But I tell you this as a secret, for I would not have him know that his letters give me all this trouble. He thinks, poor man, his hand is like print; but you, who know the contrary, tell me how you manage. My son set out yesterday, sorry and sad and dejected at parting from us; I endeavoured to inspire him with every good, just, and noble sentiment that I was mistress of, and to confirm all the good qualities I had remarked in him; he received my advice with all imaginable sweetness and marks of approbation; but you know the weakness of human nature; I leave him therefore in the hands of Providence, reserving to myself the comfort of having nothing to reproach myself with, in regard to him: as he has a fund of wit and humour, we shall necessarily miss him extremely. We are going to begin a "Moral Treatise" of Nicole's. If I were in Paris I would send it you: I am sure you would admire it. We continue to read Tasso with pleasure. I am almost afraid to tell you that I have returned to "Cleopatra;" and by good fortune, the short memory I have makes it still pleasing to me: I have a bad taste, you will say; but you know I cannot affect a prudery which is not natural to me; and as I am not yet arrived at a time of life that forbids the reading of such works, I suffer myself to be amused with them, under the pretence that my son brought me into it. He used to read us some chapters too out of Rabelais, which were enough to make us die with laughing; in return he seemed to take a good deal of pleasure in talking with me; and, if he is to be believed, he will remember what I have said to him: I know him well, and can often discern good sentiments through all the levity of his conversation. If he is dismissed this autumn, we shall have him again. I am very much perplexed about the States; my first intention was to avoid them, and save myself the expense. But you must know that while Monsieur de Chaulnes is making the circuit of Brittany, his wife intends to remain at Vitré, where she is expected in ten or twelve days, which will be a fortnight before M. de Chaulnes arrives, and she has requested me not to set out till she has seen me. There is no getting off this, without breaking with them at once. I might indeed go to Vitré, to avoid being plagued with them here, but then I cannot bear the thoughts of passing a whole month in such noise and confusion. When I am not in Paris I would be wholly in the country. But I declare to you I have not yet determined upon anything; let me have your advice, and tell me what you do with Cateau; is she married? If so, she may make a good nurse; only I am afraid, after her late fine machinations [1], her blood may be rather overheated. I desire you will temper yours, my dear, with good wholesome soups, as you did last year.

I have mentioned Launay to you; she was bedaubed the other day like a twelfth-day taper: we thought she resembled the second volume of a sorry romance, or the "Romance of the Rose," exactly. Mademoiselle du Plessis is always at my elbow: when I read the kind things you say of her, I am as red as fire. The other day La Biglesse played "Tartuffe" to the life. Being at table, she happened to tell a fib about some trifle or other, which I noticed, and told her of it; she cast her eyes to the ground, and with a very demure air, "Yes, indeed, Madame," said she, "I am the greatest liar in the world; I am very much obliged to you for telling me of it." We all burst out a-laughing, for it was exactly the tone of "Tartuffe:" "Yes, brother, I am a wretch, a vessel of iniquity." She attempts sometimes to be sententious, and gives herself airs of understanding, which sit still worse upon her than her own natural way. There! I think you know everything about *The Rocks*. I wish I could describe the cries and sobs of Jaquine and Turquesne [2], when they saw your brother get on horseback; it was such a scene! For my part, though I was ready to weep at parting with my poor boy, yet upon seeing their ridiculous grimaces, I could not, for the life of me, forbear bursting out a-laughing, and everyone else laughed with me:

. . . . . Mais les voyant ainsi,
Je me suis mise à rire, et tout le monde aussi.

I fancy you have no great amusement in the news you get from Paris, for there is none stirring there: what I

[1] See Letter 112, of the 28th of June, 1671, in this volume.

[2] Two servant girls at "The Rocks."

have from there tires me to death; they have told me nothing for this month past, but that the King was to be at St.-Germain on the tenth. They are reduced to the necessity of sending me the merest trash to amuse me; they tell me, among other things, that a young girl dropped her bundle in a chaise that brought her from the Marais to the Faubourg, which the porters took for a little dog. For my part, I had rather by half read "Cleopatra," and the wondrous feats of the sword of the invincible Artaban. Next winter, when I am out of pain about your lying-in, I shall endeavour to amuse you better than they amuse me. God knows what comparisons I make, between their letters, and those I receive from Provence.

Madame DE SÉVIGNÉ *writes also to Monsieur* DE GRIGNAN.

(*Enclosed with her Letter to her Daughter.*)

Come hither, son-in-law of mine. So then, you are resolved to send my daughter back to me by the first coach; you are displeased with her, and quite angry that she admires your Castle, and think that she takes too great a liberty in pretending to reside there, and command in everything. As you say you hate everything that is worthy of hatred, you certainly must hate her: I enter into all your displeasure; you could not have addressed yourself to one who feels the force of it better than myself. But do you know, after what you have said, that you make me tremble to hear you talk of wishing me at Grignan, and I am quite inconsolable for that reason, for there is nothing in futurity so dear to me as the hope of seeing you there; and whatever I may say, I am persuaded that you will be very glad of it too, and that you love me: it is impossible it should be otherwise; I love you so well, that the same sentiments must necessarily pass from me to you, and from you to me. I commend the care of my daughter's health to you, above all earthly things; watch over it, be absolute master in all that regards it; do not behave as you did at the bridge of Avignon; keep your authority in this one point, and in everything else leave her to her own way; she is more skillful than you. Ah, how I pity you for having lost the pleasure of receiving her letters! you were much happier a year ago; would to God you had that pleasure now, and I had the mortification of seeing and embracing her! Adieu, my dearest Comte, though I believe you are as much beloved as any man in the world, yet I do not think that any of your step-mothers[1] ever loved you so well as I do.

LETTER 115

From Madame DE SÉVIGNÉ *to Madame* DE GRIGNAN.

The Rocks, Wednesday, July 8, 1671.

I long to know how you are after your bleeding: I have taken it into my head, that, out of respect to you, they did not make the orifice sufficiently large; that your blood came only drop by drop; that it was neither so well cooled, nor so properly purified, as it ought to have been, and, consequently, was not of much service to you: this may be a mistake, I wish it may prove so; but we must have much less bile in our composition, to imagine nothing but what is agreeable; be it as it may, I assure you that your health is infinitely dear to me; and therefore, if you have too much writing upon your hands, I desire you would write to me less frequently: can I, after this, give you a stronger proof of my concern for your health? Madame de La Troche, in a letter I had from her a few days ago, tells me, that if Cateau's fine intentions during her pregnancy had not greatly altered her temper of mind and body, she would make a most excellent nurse; I thought it odd enough that we should both have thought alike; for, if you remember, I mentioned the very same thing to you. Our Chapel goes on very fast: it employs the Abbé, and amuses me. But my poor park is destitute of life and

[1] Madame de Sévigné was the third.

soul, that is of workmen, on account of the hay-making. Were you not greatly concerned for the death of M. de Montlouet[1], and for his poor wife? there is something very shocking in a man's falling from his horse and being dashed to pieces upon the spot. One may contrive to read such circumstances as these in a letter; but, till now, I could not take the trouble of reading what they have lately sent me. Here lies the difference. I am not solicitous about public affairs. I am only alive to extraordinary events; but from persons I love, the most trifling circumstances affect me, and interest my heart. Madame de La Fayette sends me word that she thinks herself obliged to write to you in my absence, which she intends to do frequently. I thought it very obliging of her; but since I find you answer her letters, I no longer consider myself under an obligation to her; can you solve this paradox? But methinks I wrong you, my child, in doubting your skill in unravelling mysteries; I fancy I am speaking to myself.

I was deeply affected, even at this distance, with the service performed for the soul of MADAME[2]. I thought on the emotion you felt, and what an illness it threw you into: I remember too in what a strange manner you passed the whole summer, confined to your room; how the heat used to make you faint, and affect your spirits. I know not what brings all these thoughts into my head; they do me good, and they do me harm. I think of everything, because my thoughts are continually employed on you; and I pass much more of my time at Grignan than I do at *The Rocks.* I hope you do not suffer yourself to be under restraint with your visitors. You must take these things easily, or it would be worse than death to you.

I have so thoroughly convinced the little du Plessis that the fashion at Court is to be free and easy, that I in-

[1] Monsieur de Montlouet fell dead from his horse as he was reading a letter from his mistress. He was of the Bullion family.

[2] The Princess Henriette-Anne of England, who died at St. Cloud the 29th of June, 1670.

dulge myself with an hour or two of Italian with La Mousse, notwithstanding her being present. She seems quite happy with this freedom, and so am I too, I promise you. Could you be so cruel as to leave Germanicus [1] in the midst of his conquests, and among the swamps of Germany, without lending him a hand to help him out? at least you might have conducted him to the feast where he was poisoned by Piso and his wife. I think he seems rather too prudent and politic; and to be in too much fear of Tiberius. I see many heroes who have not all his prudence, and whose great success gives a sanction to rashness. My son, as I told you, left me in the very midst of "Cleopatra;" I have finished it since he has been gone: but I beg you will let this folly of mine remain a secret. I have finished my books, and you are beginning yours: this would furnish us with excellent matter for conversation were we together. Ah, my child! what a pity it is we cannot be so at least sometimes, by help of some magic art, but must wait till next spring!

I am here with my three priests, who each of them play their parts admirably well, and, at mass excepted, I am never absent from them. I walk a good deal; the weather is now very fine and warm; we do not feel the least inconvenience from the heat in this house; when the sun comes into my room I leave it, and return to the wood, where I meet with delightful coolness. Let me know how it fares with you, in this respect, at your Castle.

You know what a favourite I am with Brancas, and yet it is above three months since I have heard from him: this conduct does not seem very consistent, but however he is not consistent himself [2].

---

[1] In Tacitus.

[2] On account of his singular characteristic—absence of mind.

LETTER 116

From Madame DE SÉVIGNÉ *to Madame* DE GRIGNAN.

The Rocks, Sunday, July 12, 1671.

I have received but one letter from you, my dear daughter, which vexes me; I used generally to have two: it is a bad thing to use one's self to such dear and tender cares as yours; there is no being happy without them. If M. de Grignan's brothers come to you this summer, they will be good company for you. The Coadjutor has been a little indisposed, but is now perfectly recovered; he is incredibly lazy, and is the more to blame, as he can write extremely well when he sets about it. He has a great regard for you, and intends visiting you about the middle of August; he cannot before. He protests, but I believe it is false, that he has no branch to rest upon; which hinders him from writing, and makes his eyes ache. This is all I know about *Seigneur Corbeau*: how odd it is of me, to tell you all this, when I do not know myself how I stand with him! If you should know anything of the matter, pray inform me. I reflect every hour of the day upon the times when I used to see you always about me, and am perpetually regretting the loss of those happy moments: not that I can reproach my heart with having been insensible of the pleasure of your company; for I solemnly protest to you, I never looked on you with the indifference or coolness that grows upon long acquaintance: no, I cannot reproach myself with that; what I regret is, that I did not see you so constantly as I could now wish I had; but suffered cruel business sometimes to tear me from you. It would be a fine thing to fill my letters with what fills my heart: alas! as you say, we should glide over many thoughts, without seeming to regard them. Here then I rest; and conjure you, if I am at all dear to you, to be particularly careful of your health: amuse yourself, do not study too much, carry yourself safely through your pregnancy; after that, if M. de Grignan really loves you, and is resolved not to kill you outright, I know what he will do, or rather what he will not do.

Have you cruelty enough not to finish Tacitus? Can you leave Germanicus in the midst of his conquests? If you really intend to serve him so paltry a trick, let me know where you leave off, and I will finish for you, which is all I can do to serve you at present. We have gone through Tasso, and with a great deal of pleasure; we found beauties in him, that are unknown to those who are only half-read in the language. We have begun our *Morality* [1], it is of much the same nature as Pascal's. Talking of Pascal, I have taken into my head to almost adore the reliableness of those men, the postillions, who are incessantly carrying our letters backwards and forwards. There is not a day in the week, but they bring one either to you or to me; there is one every day, and every hour of the day, upon the road. Kindhearted men, how obliging it is of them! What a charming invention is the post, and what a happy effect of Providence is the desire of gain! I sometimes think of writing to them, to show my gratitude; and I believe I should have done it before, had I not remembered that chapter in Pascal, and been afraid that they might perhaps have thought proper to thank me for writing to them, as I thanked them for carrying my letters. Here is a fine digression for you! But to return to our reading. It was without prejudice to Cleopatra, that I laid a wager I would read it through; you know how I stand by my wagers. I often wonder how I could like such ridiculous stuff; I can hardly comprehend it. You may perhaps remember enough of me to know how much bad style in writing displeases me; that I have some taste for a good one; and that no person is more sensible to the charms of eloquence. I well know how wretched La Calprenède's style is in many places, on account of its long-winded periods, and bad choice of words. I wrote a letter to your brother in that style the other day, which was

[1] M. Nicole's *Moral Essays.*

pleasant enough. However, though I find such glaring faults in Calprenède, though I know how destestable that way of writing is, yet I cannot leave it. The beauty of the sentiments, the violence of the passions, and the miraculous success of their redoubtable swords, entices me away like a child; I become a party in all their designs, and if I had not the example of M. de La Rochefoucauld and d' Hacqueville to comfort me, I should be ready to hang myself for being guilty of such a weakness: you appear before me, and cry Shame! yet still I go on. I shall have great honour in being intrusted by you with the care of preserving you in the Abbé's friendship. He loves you tenderly; you are often the subject of our conversation, with your state, your grandeur, and so forth. He would not willingly die without having first taken a trip to Provence, and rendered you some service. I am told, that poor Madame de Montlouet is on the point of losing her senses; she has been raving hitherto, without once shedding a tear; but now she has a violent fever, and begins to cry: she says she will be damned, since her dear husband is inevitably so. We go on with our Chapel: the weather is very hot; but the mornings and evenings are delightful in the woods, and under the shade of the trees before the house. My rooms are extremely cool: I am afraid you suffer from the heat in Provence.

LETTER 117

From Madame DE SÉVIGNÉ *to Madame* DE GRIGNAN.

The Rocks, Wednesday, July 15, 1671.

Were I to tell you all the fancies that come into my brain about you, my letters would always be of an unreasonable length; but that is not very easy to do; so I content myself with writing all that is *writeable,* and with thinking all that is *thinkable*: I have time and opportunities enough for both. La Mousse has a little inflammation of his gums, and the Abbé a little swelling of one of his knees, which leaves me my mall to myself to do what I please in; and I please to walk in it every evening till eight o'clock. My son is no longer with us, so that here is a silence and tranquillity that is scarcely to be met with anywhere else. I do not tell you on whom I think, or how affectionately; when things are easily to be guessed there is no occasion for speaking. If you were not pregnant, and the hippogriff was still in the world, it would be one of the most gallant and memorable actions that could be performed, to have the courage to mount its back, and take a ride to visit me sometimes. It would be no great undertaking, for he used to traverse the earth in two days; so you might come sometimes and dine with me, and be at home to supper with M. de Grignan; or you might sup here for the sake of the evening walk, and be at home in time enough the next morning to be at mass in your seat.

Your brother is in Paris; but he will not stay there long: the Court is expected back, and he must not show himself. I consider the death of the Duc d'Anjou[1] as a very considerable loss to the nation. Madame de Villars writes to me very frequently, and always remembers you in her letters: she has a tender heart, and knows how to love; which gives me a strong feeling of friendship for her; she begs me to say a thousand kind things to you in her name. Little St. Géran writes me such scrawls that I cannot read them, and I, in return, abuse her, and call her names, which diverts her mightily. This kind of pleasantry has not grown stale yet; when it does, you shall hear no more of it; for I should be terribly bored to be obliged to use any other style to her.

We continue to read Tasso still: I am sure you would like it, if you were to make up the trio; there is a wide difference between reading a book alone, and with those who can point out the beautiful passages as they occur, and excite the attention. This *Morality* of Nicole's is ad-

[1] Philippe, second son of Louis XIV., died the 10th July, 1671, at the age of 3 years.

mirable; "Cleopatra" still goes on in the old way, but only during vacant hours, and without taking up too much time. I generally take a nap upon it; the character pleases me more than the style. I own that I like the sentiments; they have something so perfect in them, that they fully come up to my idea of heroism.

Mademoiselle du Plessis honours us often with her company: yesterday at dinner she said, that they kept admirable tables in Lower Brittany, and that at her sister-in-law's wedding they consumed in one day twelve hundred dishes. We all sat like so many statues. At last I took courage, and said, "Recollect yourself, Mademoiselle; you must mean twelve; the most accurate may make a mistake sometimes." "Oh! dear Madame, not at all; there were twelve hundred or eleven hundred, I will not be positive which, because I would not willingly tell a lie, but I am sure it was one or the other." And this she repeated twenty times, and would not take a single chicken from the number. When we came to reckon, we found that there must have been at least three hundred people to lard the fowls, and that the place where the entertainment was given must have been a large field, with a number of tents erected for the purpose; and that supposing them only fifty, preparations must have been made at least a month beforehand. This table-talk would have afforded you a good deal of amusement. Have you no *puffer* like this among your ladies in Provence?

The watch you gave me, my dear child, and which was always an hour or two too fast or too slow, is now so exactly true, that it does not vary a second by our time-piece: I am vastly pleased with it, and now return you thanks for your present. The Abbé tells me, that he adores you, and that he intends to render you some service; he cannot just say what or where; but, however, he loves you as well as he loves me.

LETTER 118

From Madame DE SÉVIGNÉ *to Madame* DE GRIGNAN.

The Rocks, Sunday, July 19, 1671.

I find you are engaged in family affairs in every way; and I perceive you do the honours of your house extremely well: let me assure you, that this mode of behaviour is much more honourable and amiable than cold indifference, which is very unbecoming in one's own house. You are very far from deserving reproach on this head, my dear child, and nothing can be better than what you do: I only wish you materials; as for an inclination to make use of them, that you do not want. You must have laughed at my talking to you so much about the Coadjutor, when he was with you all the while; but I did not know of his having the gout, at the time I wrote to you. Ah! *Seigneur Corbeau,* if you had contented yourself with barely asking for *un poco di pane, un poco di vino*[1], you would not have been in the condition you are in now. We must bear with the gout when we have deserved it. Ah! my poor friend, I am really sorry for you; but you are well paid. I think you are in no great danger of dying in solitude: I am heartily glad that you find so many persons ready to amuse you. You will soon have Madame de Rochebonne[2]. The Coadjutor will do well to stay a long time with you. The offer you made him of finishing your Castle, he will doubtless accept. What has he else to do with his money? It will never appear in his year's savings. What you say of the maxim I made without thinking, is very good and very just. I am willing to believe, for my own sake, that if I had not written so fast, but taken a little more time and pains to consider it, I should have said much the same thing as you: in a word, you are perfectly right, and I am

[1] A little bread and a little wine. [Translation.]

[2] Sister of the Comte de Grignan.

resolved never to publish anything without having first consulted you. I have a letter from Brancas so very tender and affectionate, that it makes up for all his past forgetfulness; he breathes his soul in every line; and if I was to answer him in the same style, it would be a perfect *Portugues*[1]. We should praise nobody before he is dead, was excellently well said; we have examples of this every day: but after all, my dear friend, the public is seldom deceived, it praises when we do well; and as its discernment is tolerably keen, it cannot be long deceived, and it censures as freely when we do ill: in like manner, when we change from bad to good, it agrees with us; it does not pretend to answer for the future; it speaks only of what it sees. The Comtesse de Gramont, and some others, have experienced the effects of its inconstancy; but the public was not the first to change: you have no reason to find fault with it, for it will not begin with you. We are all very busy about our Chapel, it will be finished about All-Saints. I am perfectly contented with the profound solitude we live in here: the park is much more beautiful than you ever saw it, and my little trees now cast a delightful shade, which was unknown to the diminutive twigs of your time. I am disturbed at the noise and hurry we are going to have here. They say that Madame de Chaulnes[2] arrived yesterday: I must go to see her to-morrow, there is no avoiding it; but I had much rather be in a cloister, or reading Tasso: I am become such a proficient in it as would surprise you, indeed it surprises me. You commend my letters too much; I am well assured of your tenderness; I have long said that you were *true,* a commendation I am fond of; it is new and distinguished from the common ones; but sometimes it may do harm: I feel in my heart the good that opinion now does me. Ah, how few are there of the really *true*! Consider the word a little, and you will like it. In the sense I apply it, I find it in-

[1] Alluding to *Letters from a Portuguese Nun to a Cavalier,* remarkable for the softness and tenderness of the language.

[2] Elisabeth Le Féron, widow of the Marquis de Saint Mégrin, and afterwards married to Charles d'Ailli, Duc de Chaulnes.

finitely more expressive than in the common and acccepted signification. The divine Plessis is most completely *false.* I do her too much honour, even in speaking ill of her: she plays all kinds of characters, the devotee, the skillful, the timorous, the indisposed, the amiable; but above all she mimics me, but in such a manner, that it diverts me as much as a glass that turned my face into ridicule, or an echo that, like Hudibras', answered nothing but nonsense: but I wonder where I find all the nonsense I write to you. Adieu, my beloved child; how happy are the people of Provence, who can see you every day! What joy will be mine, when I can fold you in my arms! for the day will come; but I have many anxious hours to pass in the meanwhile, especially when you draw near your confinement.

There has been a place in MONSIEUR's family vacant lately, reputed to be worth twenty thousand crowns, which he has given to the *Angel* [1], to the great displeasure of all his family. Madame du Broutai, after having been two years privately married to Fromantau [2], has, at length, made it public: she now lives in the same house with him. Fromantau is a good match for her. [3]

Have I told you, that there are two young ladies at Vitré, one of whom is called Mademoiselle de *Croqueoison,* and the other Mademoiselle de *Kerborgne*? I call Mademoiselle du Plessis, Mademoiselle de *Kerlouche.* I am vastly delighted with these names.

---

[1] Madame de Grancey.

[2] He afterwards had the title of Comte de La Vauguyon, and was Knight of the King's Orders. He shot himself with a pistol the 29th of November, 1693.

[3] He was a man of low origin.

LETTER 119

From Madame DE SÉVIGNÉ *to Madame* DE GRIGNAN.

The Rocks, Wednesday, July 22, 1671.
St. Magdalen's-day, on which a father
of mine was killed some years ago.[1]

Madame de Chaulnes came here on Sunday; but can you guess in what way? No otherwise than on foot, and between eleven and twelve at night: she and her suite were taken at Vitré for a company of Bohemians. She wished to have no ceremony on her coming into the town; and her wish was complied with; for nobody looked at her, and those who saw her, took her for what I have told you. She came from Nantes by way of Guerche. Her carriages had stuck between two rocks, at about half a league from Vitré, the road being too narrow for them to pass; so that the rocks were obliged to be chiseled, which was not completed till next morning at day-break, when the equipage arrived at Vitré. I visited her on Monday; and, you may suppose, she was glad to see me. The fair *Murinette*[2] is with her. They will be quite alone at Vitré, till the arrival of M. de Chaulnes, who is making the tour of Brittany, and the States who will assemble in about ten days. You may guess of what consequence I am, in such a solitude. Madame de Chaulnes does not know what to do with herself, and has no resource but in me. You may suppose that I carry it with a high hand over Mademoiselle *de Kerborgne*: I expect her here after dinner. All my walks are in order, and my park is in full beauty. I shall ask her to stay here two or three days, that she may have as much walking as she likes. As I make some merit of having waited here purposely for her, I intend to acquit myself in a way she shall not easily forget, and yet give her

[1] Baron de Chantal was killed on the 22nd of July, 1627.

[2] Anne-Marie du Pui de Murinais, who was afterwards Marquise de Kerman.

nothing but what the country affords. But enough on this subject.

The Madame Quintin whom we used to say was like you, has become paralytic, and unable to support herself: ask her the reason: she is twenty years old. As she passed my door this morning, she stopped and asked for a glass of wine: she had some brought her, and then went on to Pertre, to consult a sort of physician who is in great esteem in this country. What think you of this frank and easy way of our Bretons? she was but just come from Vitré, and could not be very thirsty: so I suppose it was only to give herself airs, and let me know that she had got a Paris-built carriage. My dear child, shall I never have done with my Brittany news? What a vile correspondence! but what can you expect of a woman from Vitré? It is said the Court is going to Fontainebleau: the journey to Rochefort and Chambor is at an end; and it is imagined, that in disarranging the plans for autumn, they will derange also the Dauphin's fever, which seized him last autumn at St.-Germain; this year it will be cheated; it will not find him there again. You know that M. de Condom [1] has had the abbacy of Rebais given him, which was once the late Abbé de Foix's, poor man! They are in mourning here for the Duc d'Anjou, which will somewhat embarrass me, if I am to stay with the States. Our Abbé cannot quit his Chapel; that will be the strongest reason in our favour: for as to the noise and bustle in Vitré, it will not be half so agreeable to me as the solitude of my woods, and the company of my books. When I leave Paris and my friends, it is not to appear at the States: my merit, small as it is, has not yet reduced me to the necessity of hiding myself in a country town, like a company of wretched strollers. Assure M. de Grignan of my love and esteem, and receive the protestations of our Abbé for yourself.

---

[1] Jacques-Bénigne Bossuet, Preceptor of the Dauphin, afterwards Bishop of Meaux.

LETTER 120

From Madame DE SÉVIGNÉ *to Madame* DE GRIGNAN.

The Rocks, Sunday, July 26, 1671.

This is to acquaint you, that yesterday, as I was sitting all alone in my library with a *précieuse* book in my hand, I saw my door opened by a tall lady-like woman, who was ready to choke herself with laughing; behind her was a man who laughed still more heartily, and behind him again, a very well-made young woman, who laughed as heartily as the rest. Seeing them all in this humour, I fell a-laughing too, without knowing who they were, or what made them do so. Though I expected Madame de Chaulnes, who is to stay two days with me, yet I did not believe it was she. Her ladyship, however, it was, and she had brought Pomenars to see me, who, when he came to Vitré, had put it into her head to surprise me thus. The *Murinette* beauty was of the party too; and Pomenars was in such high spirits, that he would have forced a smile even from Sorrow itself. They first played at battledore and shuttlecock. Madame de Chaulnes plays at it like you do. Afterwards we had a slight collation, and then took an agreeable walk: you were remembered at all these. I told Pomenars, that you had been very much interested in his affairs; and that you had written me word, that provided he had nothing to encounter but the present affair, you should not be under any great uneasiness; but the many fresh instances of injustice they were daily loading him with, made you tremble for him. We kept up this jest a long time; till the long alley put us in mind of the dreadful fall you had in it one day; the thought of which called all the blood into my face. This subject, too, lasted us a good while, and we then talked of the Bohemian dialogue; and, to crown all, of Mademoiselle du Plessis and her follies; and how, having said something very silly to you one day, and her frightful face happening to be too near yours, you did not stand upon ceremony, but gave her such a box on the ear, as made her stagger; and how I, to soften the matter a little, said, "How roughly these girls play!" And then, turning to her mother, "Do you know, Madame, these two young creatures were so rude, that they absolutely fought this morning? Mademoiselle du Plessis irritated my daughter, and so she beat her; it was the most laughable scene in the world:" and by the turn I gave it, I so delighted Madame du Plessis, that she was quite charmed to see the two girls so merry together. This trait of good-fellowship between you and Mademoiselle du Plessis, which I threw into the scale to make the box on the ear go down, had like to have made them all die with laughing. La Murinette highly approves of what you did, and declares, that the first time she runs her nose in her face, as she is apt to do when she speaks to anyone, she will serve her just in the same manner, and give her a swinging slap on her ugly phiz. I expect them all here presently. Pomenars will keep his ground, I warrant him. Mademoiselle du Plessis will come too. They are to show me a letter from Paris, written on purpose, with an account of five or six slaps on the face, that have passed between ladies there, to give a sanction to those which are designed to be bestowed by La Murinette; and even to make her wish for one, in order to be in the fashion. In short, I never saw anything so mad-headed as Pomenars; his sprightliness increases in proportion to his criminality, and if one charge more be brought against him, he will certainly die with joy. I am loaded with compliments for you: we have celebrated you here at every turn. Madame de Chaulnes says, that she could wish you such a Madame de Sévigné in Provence, as she has met with in Brittany, which would render the government desirable: and what else could do it? I shall deliver her into the hands of her husband, as soon as he arrives, and shall then give myself no further care about amusing her. But, my dear child, how I pity you with your aunt d'Harcourt! What a constraint! What trouble and fatigue are you obliged to endure! I should suffer a thousand times more in such a situation than another person, and your presence alone could make me swallow the poison. Were I at Grignan, my dear, I declare to you, that I would stir my stumps, and put everything in order in your rooms, as I have done heretofore. After this mark of friendship, ask me for no more; for I hate vacuity of thought worse than death; and should dearly love to laugh with Vardes, *Seigneur Corbeau,* and you. Pray, get rid of that trumpet of judgment as soon as you can. It is now twenty years since I took a dislike to her, and have ever since owed her a visit.

I think your way of life very regular and very good. Our Abbé has an esteem for you, that words cannot easily express: he is all impatience for the plan of Grignan, and the conversation of M. d'Arles: but above all things, he could wish you a hundred thousand crowns to complete your Castle, or do anything else with, you might choose. All my hours are not like those I pass with Pomenars, and even he would soon become tiresome; for reflections will rise sometimes, that are very contrary to mirth. I told you, that I believed I should not stir from this place, or from Vitré. Our Abbé cannot quit his Chapel. The desert of Buron, or the dull life of Nantes, with Madame de Molac, would by no means agree with his active disposition. I shall be frequently here, and Madame de Chaulnes, to prevent my being pestered with visits, will always say she is in expectation of me. My labyrinth is very neat; it has green plots and palisades breast-high; it is a charming place: but, alas! my dear child, there is little appearance of my ever seeing you here.

> Di memoria nudrirsi, più che di speme,[1]

is my true motto.

Our sentences were thought very pretty. Can you

[1] I live upon remembrance more than hope. [Translation.]

not readily conceive, that a day, an hour, a moment, does not pass, without my thinking of you, or talking of you, if possible; and that nothing can banish you an instant from my mind? We are at length upon finishing Tasso, *e Goffredo a spiegato il gran vessillo della croce sopra'l muro.* We have had much delight in reading this poem. La Mousse is greatly pleased with me, and with you too, when he thinks what an honour you have done to his philosophy. I do not think you would have had a grain less wit, if your mother had been ever so stupid; but, however, both together do very well. We have a desire to read Guichardin; for we are resolved not to quit our Italian. La Murinette speaks it like her mother-tongue. I have received a letter from our Cardinal, who says shocking things of the fat Abbé [1] who is with him. Farewell, my lovely child: I shall finish this letter to-morrow, and shall inform you in what manner my company have amused themselves.

It is midnight, and my company have all gone to bed. We took a long walk this evening. After supper we cut little Cernet's hair, and put on the first bandage, which we shall take off again to-morrow. Pomenars has but just left my room: we have been talking his affairs over very seriously; they are questions of life and death. The Comte de Créance is resolved to have his head at all events, but Pomenars will not submit to this. Such is the state of the suit between them [2]. Madame de Chaulnes told me just now, that the Abbé Têtu, after having been for some time at Richelieu, had at last, without any ceremony, taken up his residence with Madame de Fontevrault [3], where he has been these two months. It is about a month since they saw him on their way here; his pretext is the prevalence of the small-pox at Richelieu. This proceeding will do him a great deal of good, or a great deal of

[1] The Abbé de Pontcarré.

[2] Pomenars was indicted for a rape.

[3] Sister of Madame de Montespan.

harm. I did not know that M. de Condom had resigned his Bishopric. Madame de Chaulnes assures me it is true. The *little body* has sent some songs to her sister, but we did not think them good. I am very glad you approved of mine. They could not well have been set higher than the key you gave them; which is high enough, I should have thought for me to have heard them here; that I do not hear them, shows the immense distance I am from Grignan. Alas! how afflicting is that thought, and how weary am I of being so long without seeing you! Good night, my dear child! I am going to bed very low-spirited; but I embrace you most affectionately.

My grand-daughter is truly amiable, and her nurse everything we could wish. My skill in this is miraculous; and friendship has taught me to give credit to the wonderful story of a blacksmith, whom love had converted into an excellent painter.

LETTER 121

From Madame DE SÉVIGNÉ *to Madame* DE GRIGNAN.

The Rocks, Wednesday, July 29, 1671.

It will be July as long as it shall please God; and I believe the month of August will be longer still; for it will be the time of the Assembly of the States; and, with all due respect to the good company, it is always a slavery to me, to be obliged to join them at Vitré, or else live in continual apprehension of their coming here. It is troublesome, as Madame de La Fayette says, and my mind is not all in tone; but I must make the best of it, and pass my time like the rest. Madame de Chaulnes was quite charmed with her visit; and what rendered it most agreeable to her, was my leaving her a good deal alone: this was the entertainment I promised her; and she used to walk at seven o'clock in the morning in the woods by herself. In the afternoon we had a dance of peasants before the door, that amused us extremely. There was a man and a woman amongst them, that would not have been suffered to dance in any well-governed nation, for their postures were enough to kill one with laughing. Pomenars roared, for he had lost all power of speech. I shall not have done with him yet; he does not take a single step which is not likely to be his last; and every time I bid him adieu, I do not know but that it may be for ever. They all disappeared on Monday, and I was left at my ease.

M. de Vardes will be with you, when you receive this letter. Let me know if his patience is not quite exhausted, and whether he owes his firmness to philosophy or habit: in short, let me hear something about him. I have had a letter from the Marquis de Charôt full of expressions of friendship. He mentions Madame de Brissac, and says, he has written to you. I desire you will lay all cruelty aside, and answer his letter. You know he may be managed by kindness; but not by neglect: he has all his eye-teeth about him, and would never understand the honour of being refused an answer. I hear that the Comte d'Ayen is to marry Mademoiselle de Bournonville. *Matam te Lutres is just vild about it.*

You tell me, in your letter, that I should think of some means of sending your daughter to you; I beg you will not take that office from me: I shall certainly bring her to you myself, if her nurse will resign her to me; any other way of sending her would mortify me. I shall think it the most soothing and agreeable amusement I can have this winter, to see her by my fire-side; let me entreat you not to deny me that pleasure: I shall have so many things to give me uneasiness about you, that it is but just I should enjoy this single comfort, when I am a little at ease. I shall consider this point as settled, and we will talk of her journey when I am about to prepare for mine. I have just been taking a short one in my maze, I mean my wilderness, where your charming idea was my faithful companion. I own that I take great pleasure in walking by myself; we get, it is true, into a certain labyrinth of thought, from which it is sometimes difficult to extricate ourselves; but then we have the liberty of thinking on what pleases us most. Farewell, my dear girl.

LETTER 122

From Madame DE SÉVIGNÉ *to Madame* DE GRIGNAN.

The Rocks, Sunday, August 2, 1671.

What say you to this week's news? We wanted a little mischief; but, really, I think we have now rather too much of it. The death of M. du Mans [1] has quite confounded me; I no more expected it than he did himself; and from the regular life I used to see him lead, it never once entered my head that he could die; but, however, dead he is, and of a slight fever, without having had time to think of heaven or earth. During his illness he was in a lethargy; it was a tertian fever that so suddenly carried him off. Providence sometimes gives instances of its power that are not grievous to us; but we ought to turn them to our profit. Poor Lenet too is dead, which I am really sorry for. Oh! how pleased should I have been, if the news about Madame de L...... [2] had come by itself! I am not at all sorry for her; her manner of life was so scandalous, that I have long struck her out of the list of mothers; all the young people of the Court have taken part in her disgrace; she will not see her daughter; all her people are taken from her, and all her lovers dispersed. You have now the great Chevalier with you, and the Coadjutor too; but pray tell the latter, that I desire he will not write to me, but keep his right hand to play at cards: not that I dislike his letters; but I like his friendship much better. I am acquainted with his humour, and know that it is impossible for him to write

[1] Philibert Emmanuel de Beaumanoir, Commandant of the King's Orders, died the 27th July, 1671.

[2] Madame de Lionne, the *corruptrice* of the Marquise de Cœuvres, her daughter and participator in her crime.

to his friends without making them suffer for it; and I think it will be purchasing a letter too dearly, if it is to cost me a part of his regard. We are all of opinion, that if he were obliged to write twice a week to anyone, he would soon hate that person as he hates death.

LETTER 123

From Madame DE SÉVIGNÉ *to Madame* DE GRIGNAN.

The Rocks, Wednesday, August 5, 1671.

I am very glad that M. de Coulanges has sent you some news. You will hear of the death of M. de Guise, which quite overwhelms me, when I think of the grief that poor Mademoiselle de Guise must suffer. You may well suppose, my dear child, that it is only by force of imagination, that this event afflicts me; for otherwise nothing could give me less concern. You know how I dread self-reproach: Mademoiselle de Guise has to reproach herself with the death of her nephew; she would not suffer him to be bled, and the blood consequently flew to his head, and disordered his brain: a very pleasant idea this! For my part, I think, as soon as a person falls sick in Paris, it is over with him. Never was such mortality known.

You shall now have news about the States, as a reward for your being a Breton. M. de Chaulnes made his entry on Sunday evening, with all the noise that Vitré could afford; the next morning he sent me a letter, which I answered by going to dine with him. There were two tables in the same room, at one of which M. de Chaulnes presided, and his lady at the other. There was a great deal of good cheer, whole dishes were carried away untouched, and the doors were obliged to be made higher, to admit the pyramids of fruit. Our ancestors had certainly no notion of these machines, since they simply imagined, that if a door was high enough for themselves to enter, it was sufficient. A pyramid was to make its entry; one of those, for instance, that oblige you to haloo from one end of the table to the other; but so far is this from being an inconvenience in this part of the world, that you are often very well pleased at not seeing what they conceal. This pyramid, with about twenty or thirty pieces of china on it, was so completely overturned at the door, that the noise it made silenced our violins, haut-boys, and trumpets. After dinner Messieurs de Lomaria and Coëtlogon danced some excellent jigs with two Breton ladies, and minuets in a style that far exceeded anything I have seen at Court; their Bohemian and Lower Breton steps were danced with a lightness and exactness that charmed me. I thought of you incessantly, and had so tender a recollection of your dancing, that this amusement became a grief to me. I am sure you would have been delighted with Lomaria's dancing; the music and *passe-pieds* at Court are really sickening in comparison. It is very extraordinary how they can make so many different steps, and keep such excellent time: I never saw any man dance this kind of dance like Lomaria. After this little ball, we saw all those that were to open the Assembly of the States crowding in. The next morning the first President, the Procurators, the Advocates-General of the Parliament, eight Bishops; Messieurs de Molac, La Coste, and Coëtlogon the father; M. Boucherat [1] from Paris, and fifty or sixty Bas Bretons gold-laced up to the very eyes, besides a hundred of the Commons. Madame de Rohan and her son, and M. de Lavardin, at which I was greatly astonished, were expected the same evening here. I did not see the latter; for I was resolved to return here to sleep, after having been to the Tower of Sévigné to see M. d'Harouïs, and Messieurs de Fourché and Chesières, who had just arrived. Monsieur d'Harouïs will write to you; he is quite charmed with your attentions: he received two letters from you at Nantes, for which I am even more obliged to you than he is. His house is going to be the Louvre of the States: there will be such play, such entertainments, and such freedom day and night, as will attract

[1] Afterwards Chancellor of France.

every creature to him. I had never seen the States before; it is a pretty sight enough: I do not think that there is any Province whose Assembly has so grand an air as this. It will be very full, I fancy, for there is not one of the members either at Court or in Camp, except the little Guidon [1], who, perhaps, may rejoin them ere long. I am going to pay a visit to Madame de Rohan. I should have a number of people here, if I did not go to Vitré. There was a great rejoicing to see me at the States, as I never was there before: I would not be present at the opening, as it was too early in the morning. The session will not hold long: there is nothing to do, but to ask what are the King's commands; no reply is made, and the affair is over. As for the Governor, he picks up, I know not how, near forty thousand crowns by it. A multitude of presents, of pensions, of repairs of highways and towns; fifteen or twenty large tables; a continual round of dancing and gaming; plays three times a week; and a great deal of show and splendor; these constitute the States. I have forgotten three or four hundred pipes of wine, which are drank there. But if I omitted this trifling article, others do not, I assure you; it is with them the first. These are what you may call tales to make you sleep; but they run off the end of our pen when we are in Brittany, and have nothing else to say. I have a thousand compliments to make you from M. and Madame de Chaulnes: I wait for Friday, when I am to receive your letters, with an impatience worthy of the extreme friendship I bear you.

---

[1] Meaning her son, the Marquis de Sévigné, who was guidon, or cornet, in the Dauphin's *gendarmes*.

LETTER 124

From Madame DE SÉVIGNÉ *to Madame* DE GRIGNAN.

The Rocks, Sunday, August 9, 1671.

You are not sincere in praising me so much, at the expense of your own merit. It would ill become me, in writing to you, to make your panegyric, and you will never suffer me to say anything ill of myself: I shall therefore do neither the one nor the other; but, my dear child, if you have any complaint to make against me, you cannot accuse me of overlooking your good qualities, and the foundation of every virtue. You have reason to thank God for the gifts he has bestowed on you; for myself, I have not merit enough of my own to transfer any to you: but, be that as it may, you admirably reduce theory to practice. What you say relating to the inquietude we are so naturally under with respect to futurity, and how insensibly our inclination changes, and accommodates itself to necessity, would be an excellent subject for such a book as Pascal's. Nothing can be more solid and useful than such kind of meditations. But how few young people do we find capable of making them! I know not one: you have a fund of sense and courage that makes me honour you; as for me, I have by no means so much, especially when my heart takes pains to afflict me. My words may be just enough, and I may arrange them properly: but the tenderness of my sentiments destroys me. For example, I have not been deceived in my grief at being separated from you. I imagined it would be as severe as I have found it. I cannot say the proverb has been verified with respect to myself, that "as the cold is, so is the garment;" for I have no garment against this chill to my heart. But, however, I amuse myself, and time slides away, and this particular instance does not hinder the general rule from being true. We fear things as evils, which lose their name, by the change that takes place in our thoughts and sentiments. I pray God to preserve your excellent turn of mind. You say you will love me both for yourself and your child. Ah! my dear child, do not undertake so much! Were it even possible for you to love me as well as I love you, which, however, is not possible, nor even in the course of nature; yet even then my grand-daughter would have the advantage of me in your heart, and fill it with the very same tenderness that I feel for you.

I went on Wednesday to dine with M. de Chaulnes, who has kept the States sitting twice a day, to prevent them from coming to see me. I am ashamed to tell you what honour they do me in the States; it is absolutely ridiculous. However, I have not slept there yet, and no entreaties can prevail on me to abandon my woods and my walks. I have been here these four days; it is such charming weather, that I cannot shut myself up in a little dirty town.

But, my dear child, who is to be your *accoucheur,* if you lie-in at Grignan? Will you have to send for assistance? Do not forget your last lying-in, nor yet what happened to you the first time, nor the occasion you had for a bold and skillful hand. You are sometimes at a loss to know how to testify your friendship; now is the time to give me the proof I require; and if for my sake you will be particularly careful of yourself, the balance of the obligation will be mine. Ah! my dearest child, how easily may you acquit yourself of all you owe me! Could all the riches, all the treasures on earth, give a joy or satisfaction equal to that of your affection? And, to reverse the medal, what could be so dreadful as the contrary?

The letter you wrote to Madame de Villars is very good; but I do not think the style quite so easy as that of some I have seen of yours: nobody, however, can write better than you; and Madame de Villars will be extremely pleased. When the Coadjutor's foot is better, let me beg him to answer Monsieur d'Agen, about the nun who puts his whole diocese in confusion: I shall take that letter to my own account, and give him credit for three months.

But what do you mean by saying you have pains in the hip? Is your little boy become a girl? Give yourself no concern about it; I will help you to expose her on the Rhine, in a little basket of reeds, and then she will land in some Kingdom where her beauty will become the subject of a romance. Am I not a second Don Quixote? There are some horrible things in "Cleopatra," but there are some very beautiful ones too; and true Virtue has certainly established her throne there. The finishing Tasso has given us pleasure and pain; for we do not know what to begin next; we must wait till the States are gone, before we undertake anything. Was it to you I said the other day, that I thought all the stones in Vitré were metamorphosed into gentlemen? I never before saw such crowds assembled together: but, my dear child, I want to know what passes in your neighbourhood. I am quite at home in Provence; how truly has that country become mine! Why was my destiny fixed at such a distance from you?

Madame DE SÉVIGNÉ *also writes at the same time to Monsieur* DE GRIGNAN.

You alone, my dear Comte, could have prevailed on me to give my daughter to a Provençal; this is truth, as Caderousse and Mérinville will witness for me; for if I had liked the latter as well as you, I should have found so many expedients to prevent a conclusion, and she had been his. Do not entertain the least doubt of my having the highest opinion of you; a moment's reflection will convince you I am sincere. I am not at all surprised that my daughter does not mention me to you; she served me just the same by you the last year; believe, therefore, whether she tells you so or not, that I never forget you. I think I hear her scold, and say, "Ah! this is a pretence of yours to excuse your own laziness." I shall leave you to dispute this among yourselves, and assure you that, though you are perhaps the most happily formed for general love and esteem of any man in the world, yet you never were, and never will be, more sincerely loved by anyone than by me. I wish for you every day in my mall: but you are proud; I see, that you expect me to visit you first: you may think yourself very happy that I am not an old woman [1]; but am resolved to employ the remains of life and health in taking that journey: our Abbé seems to have as strong an inclination to go there as myself; that is one good thing. Adieu, my dear Grignan, love me always; treat me with a sight of you, and you shall see my woods.

Madame DE SÉVIGNÉ *then continues her Letter to her Daughter, Madame* DE GRIGNAN.

I return to you, my dear child, to let you know, that Monsieur d'Andilly has sent me the collection he has made of the Letters of M. de St. Cyran; they are the finest things in the world; they are, in fact, so many maxims and Christian sentences; but so admirably turned, that they are as easily retained by heart as those of M. de La Rochefoucauld. When this book is published, desire Madame de La Fayette, or M. d'Hacqueville, to ask Andilly for a copy for you: he will be gratified by this mark of confidence. When you reflect, that he has never gained the smallest sum by anything he ever published, you will be convinced that it is doing him a favour to ask him for one of his books. I defy M. Nicole himself to say anything better than what you wrote about the change of the passions: there is not a word more or less than there ought to be.

LETTER 125

From Madame DE SÉVIGNÉ *to Madame* DE GRIGNAN.

Vitré, Wednesday, August 12, 1671.

At length, my dear child, I am in the midst of the States, otherwise the States would have been in the midst of *The Rocks*. Last Sunday, just as I had sealed my let-

[1] Madame de Sévigné was at this time forty-five years old.

ter, I saw four coaches and six drive into the court, with fifty armed men on horseback, several led horses, and a number of pages mounted. These were M. de Chaulnes, M. de Rohan, M. de Lavardin, Messieurs de Coëtlogon, de Lomaria, the Barons de Guais, the Bishops of Rennes and of St. Malo, the Messieurs d'Argouges, and eight or ten more whom I did not know. I forgot M. d'Harouïs, who is not worth mentioning. I received them all: a great many compliments passed on both sides; and after a walk, with which they were all very well pleased, a very good and elegant collation appeared at one end of the mall; and, to crown the whole, there was Burgundy as plentiful as water. They could not be persuaded but it was the work of enchantment. M. de Chaulnes pressed me to go to Vitré; accordingly I arrived here on Monday night. Madame de Chaulnes gave me an elegant supper, with the comedy of *Tartuffe* after it, not badly played, I assure you, for a strolling company; and then we had a ball, where the minuet and jigs had very nearly reduced me to tears; for they brought you so fresh to my remembrance, that I could scarcely resist the impulse, and was obliged to seek something to divert my thoughts. They talk to me of you here very frequently, and I do not study long for an answer; for I am generally thinking of you at the same time, so that I sometimes fancy they see my thoughts through my corsets. Yesterday I received all Brittany at my Tower of Sévigné. I was at the play again: it was *Andromache*: it cost me above half a dozen tears; enough in conscience for strolling players. At night we had a supper, and a ball. I wish you could see the elegance of M. de Lomaria, and in what style he takes off and puts on his hat: he outdoes all our courtiers, and might put them to the blush: he has an income of sixty thousand livres a year, is just come from college, is very handsome and agreeable, and would very gladly have you for a wife. I would not have you suppose that your health is not drank constantly here. The obligation indeed is not very great; but, such as it is, you owe it every day to half Brittany.

They begin with me, and then Madame de Grignan comes of course. The civilities they show me are so ridiculous, and the women of this country are such fools, that you would think there was not a person of quality in the town but myself, though it is full of fashionable people. Of your acquaintance Tonquedec, the Comte des Chapelles, Pomenars, the Abbé de Montigni, who is Bishop of St. Paul-de-Léon, and a thousand others, are here; they talk of you, and we laugh a little at our neighbour. Madame de Coëtquen is ill here of a fever: Chesières is somewhat better; there has been a deputation of the States to compliment him. We are as polite here as the polite Lavardin himself, who is perfectly adored among them; he has a good share of heavy merit, like Grave wine. My Abbé goes on with his building, and cannot be prevailed on to stay at Vitré: he comes however and dines with us. I shall stay here till Monday, and then shall retire to my solitude, where I shall pass eight or ten days, after which, I shall return to take my leave of them all; for the end of the month will see the end of the whole affair. Our present has been made this week and more: the demand was for three millions [1]: we immediately offered two millions and a half; which was accepted. Over and above this the Governor is to have fifty thousand crowns, M. de Lavardin, eighty thousand francs, and the rest of the officers in proportion; the whole for two years. You may imagine, that as much wine passes through the bodies of our Bretons, as there does water under our bridges; for it is upon this commodity the immense sums of money are procured that are distributed among the States.

Now, thank God, you are pretty well instructed in what relates to your good country. But all this while I have no letter from you, and, consequently, nothing to answer: so I must of course write what I see and hear. Pomenars is a most extraordinary creature: I do not know any man to whom I would so readily wish two heads; for he will never be able to carry his own safe off. For my

[1] Of livres.

part, I long to see the week at an end, that I may repay all the civilities I have received from the good folks here in a proper manner, and then retire to enjoy myself at *The Rocks.* Farewell, my dearest child, I always expect your letters with impatience. Your health is a subject that concerns me closely: I believe you are persuaded of the truth of this; so that, without desiring you to *do me the justice of believing,* I may put an end to my letter, and sleep securely on what you think of my friendship.

LETTER 126

From Madame DE SÉVIGNÉ *to Madame* DE GRIGNAN.

Vitré, Sunday, August 16, 1671.

What, my dear child, you had like to have been burned to death, and you would not have me be alarmed! You are resolved to lie-in at Grignan, and you would not have me be uneasy! Desire me at once to cease to love you; but be assured, that while you are so dear to my heart, that is, while I have existence, I cannot look with indifference on any evil that is likely to befall you. I begged Deville to take his rounds every night, to prevent these accidents from fire. Had not M. de Grignan fortunately arose before day-light, consider what a situation you would have been in, and what would have become of your Castle. I am persuaded you did not omit returning thanks to God for your deliverance: for my part, I have too great an interest in you to omit it on my side.

Monsieur de Lavardin makes love to a little Madame here: I think it stands him in as good stead as a fan. I told Madame de Coulanges the compliments you sent her: she received them so graciously, and returned them so heartily, that I am persuaded she would be glad to have you for her Lieutenant-General, even at the expense of Molac and Lavardin [1]. Theirs are the only offices worth

[1] Lieutenants-General to the Province of Brittany.

having; the King's Lieutenants are not worthy to hold up your train. I am here still; M. and Madame de Chaulnes do all they can to retain me. These are distinctions which make me admire the ladies of this country; and but for these, you may very well think, I should hardly stay at Vitré, where I have no business. The players have amused us, the dancers have diverted us, and our walks have supplied the place of those at *The Rocks*. But all this will not hinder me from going there to-morrow, where I shall be happy to see no more fêtes, and to be once more in quiet. I perish with hunger in the midst of all their dainties; and I proposed to Pomenars to order a leg of mutton to be dressed for us at the Tower of Sévigné by midnight, when we left Madame de Chaulnes. In short, whether it be from want or disgust, I long to be once more in my mall, from whence I shall not stir for eight or ten days. Our Abbé, La Mousse, and Marphise, are in great want of my presence; the two first indeed come and dine with us sometimes. *Madame la Gouvernante* of Provence is often talked of; for you must know it is by this title that M. de Chaulnes always calls you, when he drinks your health. They were saying at supper last night, that the other day at Paris, Harlequin carried about a great stone under his cloak, and, upon being asked what he was going to do with it, "Oh!" said he, "it is the sample of a house I have to sell." This diverted me extremely; and I vowed I would let you know it in my next letter; if you like the contrivance, my dear, you may make use of it to sell your estate. What think you of the marriage of MONSIEUR? This is a stroke of the Palatine's [1]; it is a mutual niece of hers and the Princess Le Tarente. You may judge how great will be the joy of MONSIEUR to be married by proxy, and how charmed he will be to have a wife who cannot speak a word of French.

Madame de La Fayette tells me she was going to write to you, but was hindered by a headache; she is very

[1] The Princess Elisabeth-Charlotte, Comtesse Palatine of the Rhine.

subject to it. I do not know whether one had not better be without Pascal's[1] fine understanding, than be liable to such inconveniences. You have dated your letter with admirable precision; the best of it is, that it brings me back to my twentieth year; you need not therefore make yourself uneasy about my health, since I have youth on my side; think only of your own. The agitation which the alarm of fire occasioned you pained me extremely; it was a violent agitation that brought on your labour at Livry: be careful then, my dear child, to avoid as much as possible, everything that may cause you emotion. I am already in love with this Chamarier[2] de Rochebonne: you represent him to me from a good rock (*bonne roche*). M. de Grignan, to whom I address this, will understand me to mean, that you place his virtues in a good point of view, and will agree with me. I am glad I can be sure of another house at Lyons, besides the Controller's.

As certain as one can be of anything in this world, so certain am I of my journey to Provence this next year.

My dear child, take great care of yourself in the interval; this is my only concern, and the thing in which you can the most oblige me. It is by this you can give me the strongest proofs of your regard for me. I suppose you see a great number of Provençals at Grignan; but you cannot conceive the quantity of Bretons we see here every day; it is beyond imagination. You highly delighted me in telling me you love the Coadjutor, and that he loves you. I am glad of this friendship; for I think it necessary to your welfare: preserve it, and take his advice in all your affairs. Our Abbé still adores you. La Mousse has one tooth less, and my granddaughter one more: so goes the world. My blessing upon *Flachère* for preserving you from the fire. I embrace you with a thousand times more tenderness than I can express. The noise of the back-

[1] Blaise Pascal was one of the brightest geniuses of his time, but was subject to violent pains in the head. He died in 1662, in the flower of his age.

[2] Dignitary of the Chapter of Saint-Jean de Lyon.

gammon-table at M. de Harouïs' has perfectly cured Chesières.

LETTER 127

From Madame DE SÉVIGNÉ *to Madame* DE GRIGNAN.

The Rocks, Wednesday, August 19, 1671.

You describe very humorously the disorder my perfumed paper occasioned you. Those who saw you read my letters must have thought I was dead, and could never imagine that they contained nothing but chit-chat. I am very far from correcting myself in the way you imagined. I shall always run into extremes in what is for your good, if it depends upon me. I already began to think that my paper might do you harm; but I did not intend to change it till about November. However, I begin from this day; and for the future you will have nothing to guard against but the smell.

You have a tolerable number of the Grignans with you: the Lord deliver you from the aunt[1]; I feel her troublesome even here. The Chevalier's sleeves must have had a curious effect at table; but though they draw everything along with them, I much question whether they would draw me; fond as I am of fashion, I have a great aversion to slovenliness. Vitré would be a famous place for him. I think I never saw such profusion before. There is not a table at Court that can come up to the meanest of the twelve or fifteen that are constantly kept up here: and, indeed, there is occasion for all this, for there are no less than three hundred people to be provided for, who have nowhere else to eat. I left this good town last Monday, after having made your compliments to Madame de Chaulnes, and Mademoiselle de Murinais. Nothing could be more cordially received, or more warmly returned. All Brittany was drunk on that day. We dined apart. Forty

[1] Anne d'Ornano, Comtesse d'Harcourt, aunt of M. de Grignan.

gentlemen dined in a lower room, each of whom drank forty toasts: the King's was the first, and then the glasses were broken. All this was done under pretence of extreme joy and gratitude for a hundred thousand crowns which His Majesty had remitted out of the free gift the Province had made him, as a recompense for their having so cheerfully complied with his request. So now there is only two millions two hundred thousand livres, instead of five hundred thousand. The King too has written a letter with his own hand, full of the kindest expressions to his good Province of Brittany. This letter the Governor read to the States assembled, and a copy of it was registered. Upon this they shouted *Vive le Roi,* and immediately fell to drinking; and drink they did, God knows!

Monsieur de Chaulnes did not forget the Gouvernante of Provence; and a Breton gentleman going to toast you by your name, and not well remembering it, got up, and, in a loud voice, exclaimed, "Here is to Madame de *Carignan.*" This ridiculous mistake made M. de Chaulnes laugh till the tears came into his eyes. The Bretons drank it, thinking it was right; and, for a week to come, you will be nothing but Madame de Carignan; some called you the Comtesse of Carignan: this was the state of things when I left them.

I have shown Pomenars what you say of him: he is highly delighted with it; but I assure you, he is so hardened and impudent, that once or twice in a day he makes the first President leave the room, to whom he is a mortal enemy, as well as to the Procurator-General. Madame de Coëtquen had just received the news of the death of her little girl, and fainted away: she is in great affliction, and says she shall never have so pretty a one; her husband is quite inconsolable; he had just returned from Paris, after having made matters up with Le Bordage. This was a most extraordinary affair: he has transferred all his resentment to Monsieur de Turenne [1]. I suppose you

[1] Glory, which is the last passion of the sage, was not the only

know nothing of this; but it fell unintentionally from my pen. There was a pretty ball on Sunday. We saw a girl of Lower Brittany, who, they said, bore away the palm. She was the most ridiculous creature I ever saw, and threw herself into such attitudes as made us ready to die with laughing. But there were other dancers, both men and women, who were really admirable.

If you ask me how I find *The Rocks* after all this hurry, I shall tell you, that I am delighted to be here again. I shall stay for a week or ten days at least, in spite of their endeavours to get me back. I want rest more than I can describe to you: I want to sleep; I want to eat; for I am starved at these fêtes: I want the fresh air; I want silence; for I was attacked on all sides, and my lungs were almost worn out with talking. In short, my dear, I found our Abbé, La Mousse, my dog, my mall, Pilois, and my masons, all as I left them; and they are the only things that can do me any good in my present condition. When I begin to be tired of them, I will take another trip to Vitré. There are some good among the crowd of Bretons, and some who have a tolerable share of wit, and are not unworthy of talking to me of you.

I was as much hurt as you with the *puffing up of the heart*[1]. That word *puffing* displeases me mightily; I told you the texture was much like Pascal's, and that texture is so beautiful that it always pleases me. Never was the human heart better anatomised than by these two authors. If you intend to go on giving your opinion of it, La Mousse will answer you better than I can; for I have not yet read twenty pages of it. I am in perfect despair at the loss of my packets; those dear, those charming letters, with which I am surrounded, which I read again and again, which I gaze upon, which I so much approve. Is it not a distracting thing for me to know, that you write to me twice a week, and yet to have received but one let-

passion of Turenne; for, at the age of sixty, he was in love with Madame de Coëtquen.

[1] *Enflure du cœur.* An expression used by M. Nicole in his *Moral Essays.*

ter in four weeks? If it were a relief to you, I should approve of hearing no oftener, and even desire it might be so; but you have written, and I cannot obtain your letters. If you keep a memorandum of the dates, you will find how many are missing. I know you used to do it for that fellow Grignan; and shall I embrace him after such a preference? Let me know something about Madame de Rochebonne [1], and make my kind remembrances to the Coadjutor, and the elegant Chevalier, whom I expressly forbid to get on horseback in your presence. I hear that my *little heart* [2] is very well: she is going to be put in frocks; that is good, my *little heart* in a frock!

If Madame de Simiane wishes to hear news of her first seneschal, you may tell her, that after herself, he married the wife of a man who at last resigned her to him, and who he soon after deserted for another married woman, very beautiful, whom he ran away with: he has a brother who has done the same thing in Lower Brittany: officers of justice are sent to bring him away: the fate of some people makes one laugh.

Monsieur d'Harouïs is as much surprised as yourself at Madame de Lionne's adventure. Your way of reasoning is very just: but though the husband was accustomed to his own disgrace, he was not to that of his son-in-law; and it was that which made him break out. The mother's trade was very well known. You did well in writing to Madame de Lavardin: it was what I wished: you have anticipated my desires. The Abbé's lacquey, playing just now with the amiable Jacquine, threw her down, broke her arm and dislocated her wrist: her cries are shocking; the cries of a Fury in the infernal regions on the same occasion could not exceed them. The man who attended St. Aubin has been sent for. It is surprising to me how accidents happen; and yet you would not have me be in fear

[1] Thérèse Adhémar-de-Monteil, wife of Charles-François de Châteauneuf, Comte de Rochebonne, and sister of M. de Grignan.

[2] *Mes petites entrailles.* Thus Madame de Sévigné used to call her little grand-daughter (Marie Blanche), whom she had left with her nurse in Paris.

of overturning! That is what I am most afraid of; for if anyone could assure me that I should not be hurt, I should have no objection to rolling now and then five or six miles in a chariot; the novelty would amuse me; but after what I have just seen, I shall be always in terror of a broken arm. Farewell, my dearest; you know how much I am yours, and that maternal love has less share in it than inclination.

LETTER 128

From Madame DE SÉVIGNÉ *to Madame* DE GRIGNAN.

The Rocks, Sunday, August 23, 1671.

You were with the President de Charmes' lady then when you wrote to me; her husband was the intimate friend of Monsieur Fouquet; am I right in this? In short, my dear, you were not alone; and M. de Grignan acted wisely in making you leave your room to entertain your company; he might however have spared his Capuchin's beard, though he did not appear much the worse for it in your eyes; for when he was at Livry with *his bushy tuft* [1], you thought him handsomer than Adonis. I often repeat these four verses with admiration. It is surprising what an impression the remembrance of any particular time makes upon the mind, whether good or bad. Sometimes I think of that delicious autumn: and then again, when I reflect on the latter part of it, I sweat with horror [2]: yet we ought to be thankful to Providence, who delivered you out of the danger you were in.

Your reflections upon the death of M. de Guise are admirable; they have made me plough up my mall with

[1] *Sa touffe ébouriffée.* Part of a *bout rimé,* filled up by Madame de Grignan. A *bout rimé* is poetry made on given rhymes.

[2] On account of a miscarriage that Madame de Grignan had at Livry, the 4th November, 1669.

my eyes; for it is there I meditate with most pleasure. Poor La Mousse has been afflicted with the tooth-ache; so that for a long time I have walked alone till night, and thought of—God knows what I have not thought of. Do not be under apprehensions of my growing weary of solitude: set aside the ills that arise from my own heart, and against which I have not strength to struggle; and I am not to be pitied in any respect. I am of a happy temper; I can accommodate myself to, and be pleased with, anything: and I prefer my retirement here, to all the noise and pageantry of Vitré. I have been here a week, and the tranquillity I have enjoyed has cured me of a dreadful cold. I have drank nothing but water; have talked very little; have left off suppers; and by this method, without having shortened my walks, I am quite well again. Madame de Chaulnes, Mademoiselle de Murinais, Madame Fourché, and a very fine girl from Nantes, came here last Thursday: Madame de Chaulnes told me, as she came into my room, that she could exist no longer without seeing me; that she had the weight of all Brittany upon her shoulders, and should die with fatigue. She then flung herself upon my bed; we sat round her, and she was fast asleep in a minute, from sheer fatigue, though we continued talking; at last she awoke, highly charmed with the ease and freedom we enjoy at *The Rocks*. We then took a walk: afterwards she and I sat down to rest ourselves in the centre of the wood, and while the others were diverting themselves at mall, I made her tell me how she came to marry M. de Chaulnes; for I always love to fish out something by way of amusement; but in the midst of our entertainment there came on just so treacherous a shower, like the one you may remember at Livry, that we were nearly drowned: the water ran from our clothes in streams; it came through the trees in a moment, and we were instantly wet to the skin. We ran as fast as we could, some screaming, others sliding, others falling; at last we got in, a roaring fire was made, we changed our dress from head to foot, I furnishing the whole wardrobe;

we dried our shoes, and were ready to die with laughing all the while. In this manner was the Gouvernante of Brittany treated in her own government. After this we had a slight repast, and then the poor woman left us, more vexed, I dare say, at the part she had to play when she got home, than at the drenching she had received here. She made me promise to relate this happening to you, and to come and assist her to-morrow, in entertaining the States, which will break up in about a week: I engaged to do both; of the one I now acquit myself, and of the other I shall acquit myself to-morrow, as I cannot help showing her this civility.

Madame de La Fayette will have told you, how M. de La Rochefoucauld has made his son (the Prince de Marsillac) a Duc, and in what manner the King gave him a new pension. Is not the way in which it was done worth all the rest? We used sometimes to laugh at such discourse, so common with courtiers. You have the Prince Adhémar [1] with you now; tell him that I received his last letter; and embrace him for me. You have, if I reckon right, five or six Grignans: it must be a great happiness, for you say they are all agreeable and sociable; were it otherwise, it would be the torment of your life. I hear that the measles are prevalent at Sucy, and that my aunt is going to take *my little heart* home with her: her nurse will be very sorry; but what can be done? This is a case of necessity; but it would be a much harder case to remain in Provence at your salary, when you will see your neighbour, Madame de Senneterre, set out for Paris. I should hope, my dear child, you have sufficient love for me not to play me the same trick when I come to see you next year. I could wish, that between this and that, you did more almost than is possible in your domestic management. I think of, and torment myself very much about them. I must therefore take you away to my own house, which is yours.

[1] The Chevalier de Grignan, who at this time was twenty-seven years of age.

Monsieur de Chesières is here; he found all my trees finely grown, which surprised him greatly, having seen them a little while ago *no higher than that,* as M. de Montbazon used to say of his children. I am very glad that poor Grignan's indisposition was of so short duration; I embrace him, and wish him all health and happiness, as well as his better half, whom I love more than myself; at least I feel it a thousand times more. Our Abbé is very much yours. La Mousse waits for the letter you are composing.

LETTER 129

From Madame DE SÉVIGNÉ *to Madame* DE GRIGNAN.

Vitré, Wednesday, August 26, 1671,
in Madame de CHAULNES's private room.

In the first place, I am desired to make you a thousand protestations of friendship, love, and esteem. After so happy a beginning, you will doubtless look for a very agreeable letter; but I much fear you will be disappointed; for in truth I know of nothing to write to you about. If I were to entertain you with my own thoughts, I should talk of nothing but you, and you are too near the subject to render it agreeable. I came here last Sunday rather late in the evening: Monsieur de Chaulnes, by way of jest, sent his guards after me, with a note to let me know, that I was wanted on His Majesty's service, and that Madame de Chaulnes would expect me to supper: accordingly I went, and found a great many new faces; so much the worse. Monday, Monsieur d'Harouïs gave a dinner to M. and Madame de Chaulnes, and all the principal Magistrates and Commissioners. I was there, and the Abbé came to us, under pretence of seeing what repairs I wanted to have done to my Tower of Sévigné; though he never looked at it. It was one of the finest entertainments I ever saw: but hear what a misfortune we had. As we were getting into the coach to go there, Monsieur de

Chaulnes was taken with a shivering and fainting; it was an attack of fever. Madame de Chaulnes in great affliction stayed at home with him; and Mademoiselle de Murinais and myself supplied their places. Monsieur d'Harouïs was very much disconcerted; everybody was dull, and nothing was thought of but this unlucky occurrence. In the evening the fever quitted him; but I believe he has it again, and that it is an ague. How suddenly illnesses seize us! pray take care of yourself. If you were in any other condition, I should desire you to walk; but not a word of that now. I am persuaded that the greater part of our complaints arise from want of exercise. Pomenars sends you ten thousand compliments. He says, that the other day, at Rennes, a woman, who had heard of a *media-noche* [1], and who had been paying a morning visit, said, that she was just come from a *media-noche* with the first President's lady. Does not this give you a good idea of a fool desirous of assuming airs of fashion? This is all I shall say to you from here. Perhaps I may find something to add before I make up my packet. I want to tell you of a ball we had last night, which, setting aside the grand ones we have seen, was as pretty a thing as could be. Several beauties of Lower Brittany blazed away there; and among the rest Mademoiselle de Lanion, who is a very fine girl, and dances extremely well. She had an admirer with her, whom it is said she is engaged to marry: he stood behind her. But Monsieur de Rohan, who for some time has thought her handsome, hung at her ear in so strange a manner, and she at every word was running her nose in his face to whisper him again, that the lover quitted his station. The young lady did not seem in the least affected by it. The mother gave her some winks; but it was to no purpose: in short, she seemed mad after a title, which afforded us infinite diversion. But is it possible that M. de Grignan should refuse me the pleasure of seeing you dance for a few moments only? What! must

[1] A Spanish word, signifying a midnight supper indulged in on fast days.

I never again see the dance, the graceful air, that used to find its way so directly to my heart? I see it here indeed in piecemeal; but I want to see the whole at once. I am ready to die sometimes, for want of giving vent to my tears, at a ball that reminds me of you: and sometimes I actually enjoy my tears unobserved. There are some airs and dances that almost always produce that effect on me. My little Lomaria has always a charming air; but last night I thought he was rather inebriated. We may say this where we are, without giving offence to any one.

LETTER 130

From Madame DE SÉVIGNÉ *to Madame* DE GRIGNAN.

The Rocks, Sunday, August 30, 1671.

It is now, my dear child, beyond all doubt, that I lose one of your letters every week, or at least every other week; for, if I have but one, you must be ten days without writing to me, which I am sure is not the case, for I surely ought to have received an excellent one by this day's post; I have only received the one you wrote when you were overwhelmed with your Provençals. I am very much vexed at these blunders. If you kept an account of your dates, you would easily perceive where the neglect lay. Another vexation is, that I have always to begin my letters with the same foolish subject: a fine beginning, and a very agreeable one!

But now about your health: you say your blood is not heated: I am glad of it upon one account, and sorry for it upon another, which is, that there is less relief for your condition; for, as the air occasions this, you can only remove the inconvenience by changing places with the fogs, and having that over your head which now rolls beneath your feet[1]; but I cannot well see how this is to be done. I know one remedy, however, which I hope will

[1] On account of the elevated situation of the Castle of Grignan.

be of service to you when I come to Provence. It is a great pity that your fine complexion cannot bear the air of Provence. The air of Nantes, which is impregnated slightly with the sea air, used formerly to destroy mine. But, my dear child, the air of the Isle of France is the best: that of Vitré kills every one. The night-dews in our park quite destroy me: I that used, you know, never to be affected by those at Livry. M. de Chaulnes is much better: they will all take their departure within a week: the company has been good and agreeable; but they will be heartily glad to separate. I came here on Friday, just to have a peep at my Abbé, La Mousse, and my woods. To-day I expect M. de Rennes, and three other Bishops, to dinner; I shall give them a piece of salt beef. After dinner Madame de Chaulnes will take me back in her coach to Vitré, to take leave of their worships: Monsieur de Boucherat, the Chief President, and a whole coachful of Magistracy, are to come likewise. As they will take me along with them, and I shall have no time to seal my letters, I do it this morning. The contract our Province has made with the King, was signed last Friday: but we previously gave Madame de Chaulnes two thousand louis d'or, besides several other presents: not that we are very rich here, but we have courage: we are very obliging, and between twelve and one at noon we can never refuse anything to our friends. That is the lucky minute: the perfume of your orange groves does not produce such fine effects. I do not know how your health is at present; but it is drunk here every day by upwards of a hundred gentlemen who never saw you in their lives, and in all probability never will. It is not those who have really seen you who drink your health with the greatest enthusiasm. Lavardin and Des Chapelles have filled up some *bouts rimés* I gave them; they are very pretty, and I will send them to you. You will also be pleased to hear, that M. de Bruquenvert danced a very good jig with Mademoiselle Kerikinili: these are things you ought not to be ignorant of. I desire you will not for the future attack me on the head of names: you see I am quite at home with them. Provincial splendor appears here in all its glory; but M. de Grignan's post was the other day admired and envied by everyone, for being destitute of this parade: to be alone, delights M. de Molac, who is oppressed by the presence of M. de Lavardin; M. de Lavardin by that of M. de Chaulnes, and the King's Lieutenants by the Lieutenants-General. While the rage for making presents prevailed, we had a great desire to propose to the States to pass a free gift of ten thousand crowns to M. and Madame de Grignan: M. de Chaulnes maintained that they would listen to the proposal; others, that they would actually make the present: at least, we all agreed to have it buzzed about, to make a few of the Bas-Bretons murmur, then to soften them down at table, and make them promise to propose it. But what do you say of M. de Coulanges paying you a visit? Charming fellow; how happy he is! I fancy, my dear, you will be glad to see him *skipping* about your Castle; his gaiety will communicate itself to you: he will tell you how handsome your daughter grows. What I most desire, and what alone will satisfy me, is, that you may continue well, and that for my sake you will continue careful of your health.

The philosophic and tranquil condition of your mind, in my opinion, sets you more above the fogs and thick vapours, than the Castle of Grignan does: you have in reality the clouds under your feet, and appear mounted in the middle region: and you will never hinder me from believing that the fine appellations, which you say you give to natural qualities, are not the effect of your own reason and the strength of your understanding. God grant you may continue in this just way of thinking; it will be very useful to you: but you should keep yourself in action too, that your philosophy may not turn to indolence; and that you may once more be enabled to revisit a country where the clouds will be over your head. Methinks I see you wrapt up in all the indolence which arises from supposed impossibilities: do not, however, indulge in this, farther than is absolutely necessary for your repose; and not so as to deprive you of action and courage. I sincerely pity you in being confined so much to the society of women; you know how I hate them: and yet your statues of men on pedestals are very tiresome; you will make me prefer the drolleries and amusements of our Bretons to the perfumed indolence of your Provençals. But where are the sprightly wits, the lively geniuses, the hot-headed sparks, whose imaginations take fire by being so near the sun? Surely you must have some fools, and from these you might find one at least who would amuse you: but Provence, and its Provençals too, are beyond my comprehension: ah, how much better do I understand my own Bretons! If I were to name all who send their compliments to you, a volume would scarcely suffice: M. and Madame de Chaulnes, M. de Lavardin, the Comte des Chapelles, Tonquedec, the Abbé de Montigni, the Bishop de Léon, d'Harouïs, Fourché, Chesières, etc., not to mention my Abbé, who has not yet received your last letter; and our La Mousse, who is still in expectation of the one you are composing. As for me, my dear child, not to make two businesses of one, I desire you will embrace all your amiable Grignans at once for me. I have seen sleeves like those of your Chevalier. Ah! what a charming figure they make dancing in a mess of soup, or sweeping over a salad bowl! Farewell, my lovely, and infinitely dear child: I shall say nothing of the love I have for you, for I have none at all.

LETTER 131

From Madame DE SÉVIGNÉ *to Madame* DE GRIGNAN.

Vitré, Wednesday, September 2, 1671.

Here is a letter that comes to me directly from Paris, without passing through the hands of du Bois [1]; and what

[1] The Postmaster charged with the care of Madame de Sévigné's letters, to send them the speediest way to Brittany.

is more, according to the date, I received it just five days after it was written, so that it is altogether a miraculous one. There is no need of a miracle to render your letters dear to me. The remembrance of you is not to be banished by any consideration; but itself banishes all others. Our States may sing, and dance, and drink, as long as they please, your dear idea makes its way through all, and fixes itself in my heart, as on its proper throne. There has been a little grumbling here, but it is subsiding, and I hope in two or three days it will be at an end; I wish it earnestly. I dare not go any more to *The Rocks*; the way there is now too well known: Sunday there were no less than five coaches-and-six. I long to return to my beloved solitude, which has been very much admired; Combourg [1] is not to be compared to it. But you must not think our houses in Brittany are like Grignan; there is a wide difference between them. As to Monsieur de Lomaria, without mincing the matter, he has all the air of a Mercury, in his dancing, his bow, his manner of pulling off and putting on his hat, his figure, his face; in short, the fellow is quite captivating. The *Murinette* beauty would have him with all her heart; but he has not the same inclination for her. The Comte des Chapelles is charmed with what you say of him in your letter. Pomenars sends you word, that he is now bolder than ever, for he is sure he will never be hanged, as he has escaped so long. The Abbé comes and dines with us sometimes, and La Mousse with him, who does not seem at all embarrassed: I have set him upon such a good footing with M. and Madame de Chaulnes, M. Boucherat, and the Bishop of Léon, that he is received by them all just like myself. He talks about the particles called atoms with the Bishop, who is as violent a Cartesian as himself, and yet, in the same breath, they maintain the faculty of thinking in brutes [2]; these are my gentleman's notions,

[1] Combourg is an old Château with great towers, and is on the road from Dol in Brittany to Rennes.

[2] It is well known what long disputes the question, whether brutes have souls, excited, and that Descartes maintained that they are mere machines. It is well known too, that hypocrites did not fail to involve

and he argues very learnedly upon them: he is as far gone in this philosophy as a man can well be, and the Prince has likewise given in to his opinion. Their discussions entertain me highly. I hear that our dear little one is very pretty; she will amuse me very much at home this winter. Farewell, my dearest child! I embrace you; but what will be the joy of my heart, when I hear once more the sound of your voice? I flatter myself that day will come, as well as so many others that are not wished for.

LETTER 132

From Madame DE SÉVIGNÉ *to Madame* DE GRIGNAN.

Vitré, Sunday, September 6, 1671.

Alas! my dear child, what can be the reason of so many fires in your neighbourhood, that put you in continual alarm? To tell you the truth, I fear it will be of serious consequence to you; remember what happened to you once, from the fright of seeing the Chevalier on horseback. I hope, at least, it will be a caution to you to see that your people take great care that no accident of fire happens in your own house. I conjure Deville, by all the affection he bears you, to be more circumspect than ever. So you think a cold is of no consequence to you in your present condition! you may take my word for it, that it is, and that you may not perhaps get rid of it till you lie-in. Above all things, be prudent and careful of yourself in the seventh month of your pregnancy: girls are lazy, and do not often come till their full time; boys are on the alert, and sometimes step into the world a month or two sooner. Remember what I say to you; Madame du Pui-du-Fou herself could not have given you better advice. After this matronly lesson, I shall make you a

religion in this philosophical problem. To allow a soul to brutes was nothing more or less than atheism: yet the very same persons accused Descartes of being an atheist; no doubt, upon equally good foundations.

thousand compliments from de Chesières. You have recollected very opportunely M. de Grignan's verse; you will have seen by a former letter, that I am far from being unmindful of the time. You have a whole tribe of the Grignans with you; but they are all such agreeable people, that I am rejoiced you have their company. I am surprised to hear that you have M. de Chate [1] with you. It is certain that I spent three days with him at Savigni, and thought him a very good kind of a man; I thought I saw some faint resemblance in him to a certain person, which did not make me like him the less. If he tells you what happened to me at Savigni, it will be, that I lost leather whilst stag-hunting with Madame de Sully, now Madame de Verneuil. You think you tell me nothing, when you say you love those who talk of me to you; it is so very natural a proof of your affection, that I thank you for it, and embrace you with all my heart. There are also certain marks of aversion which carry death with them: I am too well read on this subject; but I must own that I have paid dearly for my experience. What do you think of Marsillac being created a Duc? I greatly approve of what his father has done; it was the only way to make him enjoy the dignity without extreme grief; how would the honour have been embittered, if the loss of such a father had been the price of it! I think too, the very name of M. de La Rochefoucauld, added to its merit, carries with it a dignity far superior to the title he has bestowed. La Marans would have gone to Livry the other day with Madame de La Fayette, but they sent her back without any further ceremony. She told them the Prince had been at her house for a whole day; but nobody attended to what she said. What a mortification must that have been to a foolish boasting woman! When I come

[1] This was the Clermont de Chate, whose letters written in the army, and intercepted, first made the King acquainted with the circumstance of his intrigue with the Princess de Conti, and even that he sacrificed her to the ugly but artful Demoiselle Choin, who had so far captivated the Dauphin, that he was on the point of marrying her.

towards the conclusion of my letter, I will tell you something about the States, and my happy return to *The Rocks*.

"The best company must part," said M. de Chaulnes, on dismissing the States. The Assembly broke up about midnight. I was present with Madame de Chaulnes and other ladies. It was a very fine, very grand, and very magnificent gathering. M. de Chaulnes spoke to everybody with great dignity, and expressed himself extremely well. After dinner we all go which way we please. I am rejoiced at the idea of getting back to *my Rocks*. I have had an opportunity of obliging several persons; have made a Deputy and a Pensionary: have spoken for several unhappy wretches, but not a word for myself; for I cannot ask without a reason. I must tell you of a droll mistake of mine: you know how apt I am to make blunders. I was at M. de Chaulnes' the other day, and before dinner I saw a man standing at the farther end of the room, whom I took for the *maître d'hôtel*; upon which I went up to him, and said, "My good sir, do let us have dinner; it is almost one o'clock, and I am almost like to die with hunger." "Madame," says he, looking very gravely at me, "I should think myself extremely happy to offer you a dinner at my house: my name is Pécaudière; I reside only two leagues from Landerneau." My dear child, this was a gentleman of Lower Brittany all the while; you will guess how foolish I felt on finding it out. I cannot help laughing while I write it. M. de Chaulnes sends you a composition which I believe to be one of Pélisson's: some say it is Despréaux's. Let me know what you think of it: in my opinion it is a finished piece: read it with attention, and you will find it full of wit. I am charged with a thousand remembrances and compliments for you. Our States have granted one hundred thousand crowns in presents; two thousand pistoles to M. de Lavardin, the same sum to M. de Molac, to M. Boucherat, to the first President, to the King's Lieutenants, etc., two thousand crowns to the Comte des Chapelles, the same to young Coëtlogon, and, in short, have been munificence itself. Here is a Province for you!

Madame de La Fayette is at Livry, from where she writes me the most entertaining letters imaginable, notwithstanding all her ailments: M. de La Rochefoucauld has written to me too: they both tell me they wish I were with them; but it is I who truly wish to see you there, this hope is the support of my life. I have calculated that you will finish the translation of Petrarch in about fifty years, allowing you to do a sonnet a month. It is a work highly worthy of you, and will not be a crude performance. Adieu, my dearest child: I am going back to *my Rocks,* so overjoyed to leave this place, that I am almost ashamed of being so gladsome in your absence. I am always tempted to burn my letters when I read them over, and see what trifling stuff I write to you: tell me truly, do they not exhaust your patience? I could very well shorten them without diminishing the least particle of my affection.

LETTER 133

From Madame DE SÉVIGNÉ *to Madame* DE GRIGNAN.

The Rocks, Wednesday, September 9, 1671.

At length I am quite settled, quite calm, and quite content, in my solitude. I have occasionally the remains of the States here. M. de Lavardin [1] stays behind at Vitré to make his entry into Rennes. He has been chief Governor since the departure of M. de Chaulnes, by whose presence he is no longer oppressed; so that trumpets, kettledrums, and guards, are all drawn out. He came in this style to pay me a visit, with a retinue of twenty gentlemen: the whole together looked like a little army. Among them were the Lomarias, the Coëtlogons, the Abbés de

[1] Lieutenant-General of the government of Upper and Lower Brittany.

Feuquières, and several who have no less an opinion of themselves than the rest. We walked; had a slight collation; and the Comte des Chapelles, whom I brought with me from Vitré, assisted me in doing the honours of the house. He is still here, and looks as if he had a great inclination to let you know himself how much we talk of you, and how everything recalls you to our remembrance. We experience more than ever, that the heart is the seat of memory; for when it does not come from that quarter, we have no more heart than so many hares. We have found a little place in the wood, where, among several other pretty things which you had written, we saw this, "Gods, how I love tigerism[1]!" This is the profession of wits! But we wish to know whether this virtue of yours does not lie dormant for want of practice; for we do not well see on whom you can exercise your taste, and have therefore some hope that you will soon loose it.

Monsieur DES CHAPELLES *writes to Madame* DE GRIGNAN *in her Mother's Letter.*

It would be something extraordinary, Madame, if you should find less occupation for this virtue where you are, than when you wrote this fine sentiment. I remember I was then pale and dying, and you were charming and happy; consequently you could have no reason to amuse yourself with this exercise. I would rather remind you of another device which I found near the former, and was written nearly at the same time: *Meglio morir in presenza, che viver in assenza*[2]. This pleases me so much, that I believe I shall realise the maxim, and not quit *The Rocks* a second time without dying with regret. But, methinks, if one must die, it would have been better to have died at first; for, lovely and charming as you are, no

[1] *Dieux, que j'aime la tigrerie!* This is a word of Madame de Grignan's making, and signifies malice or cruelty.

[2] It is better to die in the presence of those we love, than to live absent from them. [Translation.]

one has yet died in honour of you; and if I had had the wit to have done it then, both our names might have been rendered illustrious. But you know, Madame, what is not done at one time, may be done at another; and I am of opinion, that provided we can divest our Marquise of the part she pretends to have in it, it would be more extraordinary to die upon this latter occasion; for then it might truly be said, that the memory is in the heart, or the heart is in the memory. Take your choice: though I greatly fear you experience neither the one nor the other for me, since you will not take the pains of giving me an answer. I am more afflicted, however, than offended; for I should have taken infinite pleasure in once more beholding a handwriting for which I have still so great a taste, though it was never yet employed in showing the least mark of friendship or regard for me. But what am I doing? Reproaches made to a *tigress* are like pearls before swine. M. de Lavardin has just honoured *The Rocks* with his presence, accompanied with many of the nobility: he was received with the greatest politeness imaginable, and an excellent and elegant collation was prepared for him in the wood; after which we saw him surrounded by his guards. So ends the history, and so ends my letter: may it have been agreeable to you! I cannot get rid of the dull and melancholy humour I have been thrown into by the remembrance of having so often seen you in this very place.

Madame DE SÉVIGNÉ *concludes her Letter to her Daughter.*

I have taken the pen from him, for he would never have done: he was so lost in the affecting remembrance of having seen you here, that M. de Lavardin found us both melancholy. This gave us a culpable appearance, and made us look as if we were tired of our company; and so indeed we were, for we had business in Provence when they came in; or, more properly speaking, our business was here; for it was the remembrance of having seen you here, that made us regret we could see you no longer. For my part, I cannot reconcile myself to have my daughter taken away from me by force, and carried to such a distance; and I believe I should sink under the idea, were it not for the regard I have for M. de Grignan, and all the Grignans, and, I may add, my persuasion of their tenderness for you.

LETTER 134

From Madame DE SÉVIGNÉ *to Madame* DE GRIGNAN.

The Rocks, Sunday, September 13, 1671.

The fright, which has obliged you to keep your bed, has alarmed me more, my dear child, than you. I am persuaded that nothing can be more injurious to you than these agitations: they were the sole cause of your misfortune at Livry [1]; and if it was the same Chevalier upon the same horse, that occasioned them, he should receive his death from no other hand than mine. Indeed you ought to have sent me word what occasioned this fright. Consider, I must now live a whole week without knowing what you ought to have informed me of. Our Coadjutor has written me some wonderful things; but I am not at present in a humour to answer them. My right hand is more affected by the pain of my mind, than by the gout in my left hand, notwithstanding the clear and demonstrative manner in which he explains to me the relation there is between them. I was almost tempted, after all his reasoning, to make him the same reply as the doctor in Molière's *Médecin malgré lui* does to a person, who was talking much in the same strain: "That is the precise reason of your daughter's being dumb." I saw this comedy very well played by a company of strollers the other day at Vitré: everyone was ready to die with laughing. Your

[1] A miscarriage which is mentioned in Letter 128, of 23rd August, 1671, in this volume.

remark on *La Murinette* is extremely just: she is of an amiable disposition, and her blunt dry manner is tempered with such excellent sentiments, that it is impossible it should displease. I am going to send your letters to d'Harouïs and the Comte des Chapelles, to Nantes; the latter of these lives only in the hopes of it; as to d'Harouïs [1], you must know he had engaged to the States to pay a hundred thousand francs more than he had in his hands, but did not think it a thing worth speaking of. One of his friends found it out, and every creature was in arms till he had justice done him: he is adored by every-one, and not without reason. One morning our States gave presents to the amount of one hundred thousand crowns; upon which a gentleman of Lower Brittany humorously said to me, that he fancied they were going to die soon, by making their wills, and disposing of their effects in this manner. I wish to God they were as liberal in proportion in Provence. I like our Bretons much; they smell a little of wine indeed, but your orange-flower gentry have not half such honest hearts. I must here except one, two, three, four, five, six, of your Grignans, whom I love, esteem, and honour, each according to his particular rank and dignity. You have fruits there which I devour in imagination; I hope to eat some of them next year, if I live so long. What happiness, my dearest child! cruel as Time has been to me in many respects, I cannot but love him, when I think on the blessings he is every day heaping on me. Preserve your health, your beauty, and your affection, that my joy may be complete. How delighted M. d'Andilly must be to see M. de Pomponne become Minister and Secretary of State [2]! Indeed the King merits great applause for having made so excellent a choice; he was in Sweden when His Majesty thought of him, and

[1] He was Treasurer of the States of Brittany.

[2] M. de Pomponne was Ambassador in Sweden at the time he was made Secretary of State for Foreign Affairs. He lost his place in 1679, but the esteem of the public, and even of the King, still followed him. He gave offence by sometimes preferring society to business. His greatest crime was his hatred of Louvois and the Jesuits.

gave him the post which was M. de Lionne's, and at the same time made him a present of a sum sufficient to defray the expenses attending the entrance into his new office. What great things will he not do in this place, and what a satisfaction will it not be to all his friends! You know how much I am interested in him; and I do not know whether I may not be tempted to write an ode on the occasion in praise of His Majesty. Would not a word or two of congratulation to the father and son come extremely well from you, who are so much beloved by the family? But, my dear, you must take care of yourself, lest this fright should have done any injury. I think you are now in your seventh month. I tremble for you, and the more as it is a boy; at least, so you have promised me it shall be; do not now by your negligence let it turn into a girl. I own to you, that I shall open your packet on Friday with great impatience, and great emotion; but my emotion is seldom attended with any great consequence; a glass of water sets all to rights again. You seem to have a taste for Nicole. I do not know where to look for another book of morality to fortify your heart; and so must refer you to our friends the ancients. I am told that M. de Condom has lately published one [1], wherein he assures us, that provided we have a firm belief in the Holy Mysteries, it is sufficient; and condemns all the sophistries about the Lord's supper, which, he says, are the fruitful source of heresies. Nothing they say can be better written. This is just the thing you want.

La Mousse is already preparing his answer to the fine piece you are composing. Surely you are laughing at me when you talk of my liberal presents: is it to make me ashamed of myself? Alas, my dear, what trash in comparison to what I would bestow! I am delighted with M. de Pomponne when I reflect, that I may perhaps be able to serve you through him: but you want nothing but M. de Grignan and yourself. However, we could not have wished anyone to have held the position who is more truly

[1] An Exposition of the Catholic Faith.

our friend. M. de Coulanges, who is going to see you, will tell you in what a handsome manner the King conferred the favour.

LETTER 135

From Madame DE SÉVIGNÉ *to Madame* DE GRIGNAN.

The Rocks, Wednesday, September 16, 1671.

I am wicked to-day, my child. I am just in the same humour as when you used to say, *You are wicked.* I am very dull and spiritless: I have not heard from you: "Great friendships are never tranquil:" *a Maxim.* It rains; we are quite alone: in short, I wish you a pleasanter day than I am likely to have. What greatly perplexes the Abbé, La Mousse, and the rest of my party, is, that there is no remedy for the evil. I want it to be Friday, that I may have a letter from you, and it is but Wednesday. This puzzles them: they do not know what to do for me in this case; for if, in the excess of their friendship, they were to assure me it was Friday, that would be still worse; for if I had not a letter from you then, I should be lost to all reason. I am obliged to have patience; though patience, you know, is a virtue that I am not much in the habit of practising; but I shall be calm before three days have passed. I am very anxious to know how you are after your alarm. These alarms are my aversion; for though I am not with child myself, they make me become so, that is, they put me in a condition that entirely destroys my health. However, my uneasiness does not at present reach so far; for I am persuaded you have been prudent enough to keep your bed, and that will have set all matters right again. Do not tell me, that you will not let me know anything about your health; that would make me desperate, and having no longer any confidence in what you say, I should be always in the way I am in at present. We are, it must be owned, at a fine distance from each other, and if either of us had anything upon the mind that required immediate relief, we should have plenty of time to hang ourselves in.

I thought it necessary yesterday to take a small dose of morality, and I found myself a great deal the better for it; and still more so for a little criticism on the *Bérénice* of Racine, which I thought very diverting and ingenious. It is by the author [1] of the *Sylphs, Gnomes, and Salamanders.* There are a few words which are not quite so good as they should be, and even unbecoming a man who knows the world; these grate the ear; but, as they occur only here and there, they ought not to prejudice us against the whole, which I assure you upon examination I found a very well written *critique.* As I fancied this trifle would have diverted you, I heartily wish for you by my side in the room, provided you could return again to your magnificent Castle as soon as you had read it: and yet I own I should have felt some pain in letting you go so soon: I know too well what the last parting cost me; it would partake of the humour I have just been complaining of: I cannot think of it even now without shuddering: but you are safe from this inconvenience. I hope this letter will find you cheerful; if so, I beg you will burn it directly; for it would be very extraordinary if it should be agreeable to you, considering the horrid humour I write it in. It is very lucky for the Coadjutor that I do not answer his letter to-day.

I have a very great inclination to ask you twenty-five or thirty questions by way of finishing this performance worthily. Have you many grapes? you tell me only of figs. Is the weather very hot? you do not say a word about it. Have you such charming cattle as we have at Paris? Has your aunt d'Harcourt been with you long? You see that, having lost so many of your letters, I am quite ignorant how matters stand, and have entirely lost the thread of your discourse. Ah! how I long to beat somebody! and

[1] The Abbé de Villars, author of *The Comte de Gabalis,* a very rare and remarkable occult work.

how much I should be obliged to any Breton, who would come and say something very silly, to put me in a passion! You told me the other day, that you were glad I had returned to my solitude, that I might think of you. Very pretty that! as if I did not think sufficiently of you in every other place. Farewell, my dear: this is the best part of my letter. I finish, because I think I talk foolishly: and I must preserve my credit.

LETTER 136

From Madame DE SÉVIGNÉ *to Madame* DE GRIGNAN.

The Rocks, Sunday, September 20, 1671.

It was not without reason, my dear child, that you were concerned at the illness of the poor Chevalier de Buous: it was of an extraordinary nature. I took a fancy to him at Paris, and am therefore the more inclined to believe the fine things you say of him. But what I think the most extraordinary, is his extreme fear of death. His situation, as you describe it to me, furnishes an admirable subject for reflection. It is certain, that at that awful period we shall have much to repent: this will occasion us uneasiness and despair: we shall then wish ourselves in possession of the time which we now wish to pass so rapidly away; and would willingly give up everything, for a single day that we now lose with indifference. Such are my meditations in the mall you are so well acquainted with. The Christian system of morality is an excellent remedy against all evils; but I would have it truly Christian, otherwise it is empty and unprofitable. La Mousse thinks I sometimes reason pretty well on this subject, but then a breath of air, or the dancing of a sun-beam, dissipates the reflections of the night. We sometimes talk of the opinion of Origen, and compare it with our own; and you would have no easy task in persuading us into the belief of an eternity of punishments, unless submission to you should induce us to yield.

I am glad you are pleased with the *Examination* [1]; though I am not so well skilled in these matters as yourself, I contrived to understand it, and thought it an excellent piece. La Mousse is very proud of having made such an excellent scholar of you [2].

I am sorry you are going to leave Grignan: you had good company there, a fine house, a charming prospect, and wholesome air: whereas you will now be crammed up in a little close town [3], where there may be many disorders, and a very bad air, and poor Coulanges besides will miss you; I really pity him: I think it is not his fortune to see you at Grignan, but perhaps you will take him to the States with you; but that will be very different, and you will certainly find this journey disagreeable in your present condition, and at this season of the year. When you are there, you will see what sincerity there is in M. de Marseilles' protestations; for my part, I think him very deceitful, and very illiberal. The assurances of friendship I have sent him on my side, are nearly in the same style; he promises you his service conditionally; and I assure him of my friendship conditionally too, telling him, that I make not the least doubt of your always finding fresh subject of obligation to him.

M. de Lavardin came here on his way from Rennes last Thursday night, and gave me a full account of his magnificent reception there: he took the oaths to the Parliament, and made a very handsome speech on the occasion. I carried him back to Vitré the next morning, to resume his own carriage, and make the best of his way to Paris.

The Bishop of Léon has been at the point of death at Vitré, with a delirium, which rendered him very little dif-

[1] Examination of Aristotle's Philosophy against Reason. See the *Menagiana,* vol. iv. page 271, the Paris edition of 1715.

[2] In the philosophy of Descartes.

[3] Lambesc, a small town in Provence, the seat of the Assembly of the States of the Province.

ferent from Marphise [1]; he is now out of danger. I shall stay here till the end of November, then I shall go and fetch my *little heart,* and carry her home with me; and in the spring, to Provence, if God spares our lives. The Abbé wishes it, that he may accompany me and bring you back with us; you will then have been long enough in Provence. We should never, however, build too much upon anything, for we hourly meet with disappointments in great things as well as in those of less importance. But what is to be done? We should have this moral always in the hand, like a smelling-bottle to the nose, to keep us from fainting. I declare to you, my dear child, that my heart makes me suffer extremely: my mind and disposition treat me much better.

It is, to be sure, admirable in you to talk of drawing portraits of me, at the beauty of which even you yourself are surprised! Do you know that you reduce me to the lowest standard of mediocrity when you estimate me by your exaggerated notions? This may, perhaps, savour a little of fishing for a compliment; but it is true nevertheless, so no more of that. I laughed heartily at your story of *Carpentras* [2], whom you always lock up when you have anything to do, persuading him that he wants his *siesta* [3]. The description of your ladies, with their tinsel dresses, is excellent: but what horrid faces! I never met with such in my life. How pleasing and lovely does yours appear, in your plain and simple dress! Ah! would I could behold it, and cover it with my kisses. For heaven's sake, my child, take care of yourself, and above all things avoid frights. I cannot approve this journey of yours, just at this time. I beseech heaven to restore the poor Chevalier de Buous. My service to the good-for-nothings. You could not have given me a more insignificant idea of the place I hold in M. de Grignan's heart, than in telling

[1] Madame de Sévigné's little dog, which, according to Descartes, whose philosophy the Bishop followed, was no more than a machine.

[2] The Bishop of Carpentras, a very troublesome man.

[3] An afternoon's nap, a prevailing custom in Provence as in all hot countries.

me, that I possess all that remains unoccupied by you. I must be of a very easy disposition to be satisfied with this. Do you know, the King has received M. d'Andilly as you or I should have done? Bravo! Let us now leave M. de Pomponne to establish himself in his glorious place.

LETTER 137

From Madame DE SÉVIGNÉ *to Madame* DE GRIGNAN.

The Rocks, Wednesday, September 23, 1671.

We have again, my dear child, the most horrid weather you can imagine. It has been one continuous storm for these four days past. All our walks are under water; there is no such thing as stirring out. Our masons and carpenters keep close within doors: in short, I detest this country, and am every moment wishing for your sunshine, while you, perhaps, wish as much for my rain. We are both right.

The poor Abbé of Montigni, Bishop of Léon, is at Vitré; he sets out, I believe, to-day for a more pleasant country than this: in a word, after having been five or six times bandied between life and death, an increase of fever has at length decided in favour of the latter: he is under no concern about it, for he is perfectly delirious; but it is a great shock to his brother the Advocate-General[1]. We often weep together, for I constantly visit him, and am indeed his only comfort: it is on such occasions as these that we should exert ourselves. I am at present reading in my room, without daring to show my face out of doors: my heart, however, is at ease, in the belief that you are well, and that makes me proof against tempests; for we have nothing else here: were it not for the repose in which my heart indulges, I should not very patiently submit to the affronts I have received from this month of September: at this time of the year, and in the midst of all one's

[1] In the Parliament of Rennes.

workmen, it is downright treachery. Oh! I could make a fine noise! *Quos ego.*

I still go on with Nicole, who delights me; I have not yet met with any lessons against rain; but expect to find some on every page, for nothing is wanting; and that conformity to the will of God, which he so admirably inculcates, would be sufficient to make me easy on this head, did I not stand in need of a specific. In short, I think it an excellent book: no one has as yet come up to these authors, for I give Pascal credit for half the fine things in it. We are so fond of hearing ourselves spoken of, that, be it good or ill, it is still pleasing. I have even forgiven him his *puffing up* of the heart, in consideration of the rest; and I maintain that there cannot be a more expressive word to describe the pride and vanity of the human heart, which is nothing but wind: find a better if you can, and in the meanwhile I will finish my perusal of the book. We are likewise reading the History of France, from the reign of King Jean: I wish to be as well acquainted with the history of my own country as I am with that of Rome, where I have neither relations nor friends: here we find names familiar to us; and while we can get books, we are in no danger of hanging ourselves. You may easily suppose that, as long as I hold in this humour, I cannot fail of being very agreeable to La Mousse. For our devotions, we have the collection of Letters of M. de Saint-Cyran; M. d'Andilly will send them to you, and you will find them admirable. Is not this, my dear child, in the language of a true recluse?

I am told that Madame de Verneuil is very ill. The King talked a whole hour with the worthy d'Andilly in as free, as gracious, and as pleasant a manner as possible: he took pains to show himself to the good old man, and obtain his just admiration: he expressed great pleasure in having made choice of M. de Pomponne; adding, that he expected his arrival with impatience, and should take the care of his fortune upon himself, as he knew he was not very rich. He told d'Andilly, that it was downright vanity in him to mention in the preface to his *Josephus*, that he was eighty years of age; it was a perfect sin: in short, they were very gay, and witty. His Majesty said besides, that he must not expect he would suffer him to remain shut up in his desert, for he should very frequently send for him to Court where he should be glad to distinguish him as a person who had in so many respects rendered himself illustrious. When the good old man assured him of his fidelity and attachment, the King replied, that he had not the least doubt of it, for he who served his God well, could not fail of serving his King well also. In short, it was a most extraordinary interview. His Majesty took care to have his dinner sent from his own table; and ordered one of his own coaches to take him an airing. He talked of him the whole day with the greatest admiration. As for d'Andilly, he was so transported, that he cried out every moment, "I must humble myself!" finding how much he stood in need of it. You may guess the pleasure this has given me, and the interest I take in it. I wish my letters may afford you as much pleasure as yours give me.

LETTER 138

From Madame DE SÉVIGNÉ *to Madame* DE GRIGNAN.

The Rocks, Sunday, September 27, 1671.

Well, my dear child, be it so; we will say no more of the loss of our letters; it is, indeed, a disagreeable and tiresome subject; I can now easily dispense with it, as I have, thank God, for this month past, received them as regularly as I could desire; and you may write a little more freely to me than to the man who has pilfered them, and with whom you always think you are conversing when you write to me: however, you were determined to let him see that you love me; you do not conceal your affection, and seem to speak of it as a thing you wish all the world to know. What you say to me on that subject fills my heart; yes, I own that I believe you, that this belief is the greatest joy and comfort of my life, and the ultimate aim of my ambition: it is accompanied with some bitterness, it is true; but that is an inevitable consequence; and when we suffer from tenderness and affection, we are more disposed to be patient. I always make this chapter as short as I can; but I assure you I should never make an end if I did not take great pains to do it.

I am charmed to find you have so amiable a sister-in-law, who serves as a companion and comfort to you. It is what I am continually wishing for you, for no one in the world has more need of an agreeable companion than yourself; otherwise you harass your mind till you make yourself ill: you do not amuse yourself with trifles; but if left alone your meditations are of the deepest and most melancholy cast. It is impossible to be more delighted than I am with the praise you bestow on this new friend: I suppose it is Madame de Rochebonne, who takes very much after the Coadjutor, in his wit, humour, and pleasantry. If you will make her my compliments beforehand, I shall be obliged to you.

M. de Pomponne is now in an enviable position. You express yourself very agreeably upon the subject. I am going to write to the good old father[1]. I have already told you all I know about this affair. He has written to me twice since his favourable reception by the King, and I have answered both his letters. He tells me there is nothing he esteems so much as my friendship, and that he is gratified to find and to see that my approbation has had the start by twenty years of all that will shortly be given to his son, years of which many have been difficult to bear. In short, it is a miraculous and pleasing change. Another surprising change has happened to the Comte de Guiche, who has returned from banishment: but I am taking d'Hacqueville's business out of his hands; he has

[1] Monsieur d'Andilly, who was the father of Monsieur de Pomponne.

been for a fortnight by the Maréchal de Gramont's [1] bedside, and has, without doubt, told you everything, and of the King's visit to him five or six days ago. I fancy it will not be long before Vardes receives the same favour as the Comte. I think their misfortunes are pretty much alike [2]; but I must learn from you what is thought of this affair in your country. I enclose a letter to your Bishop, read it; you will judge better than I, if it is to the purpose: I think it not bad; but I am not the proper judge. You know I write off-hand, so that my letters are very careless; but it is my style, and, perhaps, may have as much effect as a more studied one. If I were within reach of consulting you, you know what deference I should pay to your opinion, and how often I have improved by it; but we are at the two extremities of France, so that there is no resource left but to see if my letter will do or not, and accordingly to deliver it or burn it as you think fit. I am of your opinion as to the dates, and I think it shows a fickleness to be changing every day; if the twenty-sixth or the sixteenth will do, why change it? There is even something in it disobliging to those who informed us of it. A man of honour and integrity tells us a thing plainly and truly as it is, and we believe him for a day; the next day another person tells us a different story, and we believe him: we are always on the side of those who speak last; this is the way to create as many enemies as there are days in the year. Do not therefore act in this manner; but keep to the twenty-sixth, or to the sixteenth, when you find it right, and do not follow my example, and that of a bad world, to follow the times, and change with them: keep your ground, and be assured that I am so far from desiring to subject you to my calendar, that I will very readily conform to yours: I leave the Coadjutor, or Madame de Rochebonne, to judge if I am not in

[1] The father of the Comte de Guiche.

[2] The Comte de Guiche and the Marquis de Vardes were both banished about the same time; but the latter was not recalled till the year 1682.

the right. I want much to know whether you have seen poor Coulanges; it is a hard thing for him to have been at the pains of going so far, to get a sight of you, and then perhaps to miss seeing you after all. The poor Bishop of Léon has continued in agonies ever since I wrote you word that he was dying; he is, if possible, worse, and will soon know better than you, whether matter can reason or not. The death of this poor little Bishop will be a great loss to the world. He had, as our friends say, a brilliant turn for philosophy; so have you: your letters are my life. I shall not tell you half, nor the fourth part, of the affection I have for you.

LETTER 139

From Madame DE SÉVIGNÉ *to Madame* DE GRIGNAN.

The Rocks, Wednesday, September 30, 1671.

I believe the *Léonic* opinion is now the most ascertained. He understands the subject completely, can tell whether matter reasons or not, what kind of intelligence God has given to the brute creation, with other subjects that occupied his thoughts. You may perceive by this that I suppose him in heaven, *O che spero*[1]! he died on Monday morning: I was then at Vitré and saw him, but I wish I had not seen him: his brother seems inconsolable: I invited him to my woods, that he might weep at liberty; but he told me he was too deeply afflicted to seek consolation. The poor Bishop was only five and thirty years of age: he was well provided for, and had an admirable taste for science; this was in fact the cause of his death, as it was of Pascal's; he wore himself out with study. You are not much interested in this detail; but it is the news of the place, and you must therefore bear with it: death, in my opinion, is the concern of everyone, and its consequences strike home to our bosoms.

[1] Oh, how I wish it! [Translation.]

I read M. Nicole with a degree of pleasure that lifts me above the earth: I am particularly charmed with his third treatise, "On the Means of Preserving Peace and Harmony among Mankind:" read it, I beseech you, and with attention; you will see how clearly he develops the intricacies of the human heart, in which every sect is alike included, philosophers, Jansenists, Molinists, in short, all mankind: this may truly be called searching to the bottom of the heart with a lantern: he makes known to us sensations that we feel daily, but which we have neither the wit to comprehend, nor the sincerity to acknowledge: in a word, I never read anything like it, except Pascal. Were it not for the amusement of our books, we should be moped to death for want of occupation. It rains incessantly. I need say no more to make you conceive how dull our condition is. But you who enjoy a sunshine which is so much the object of my envy, how do I pity you to be torn from Grignan, while the weather is delightful, in the middle of autumn, and from an agreeable society, and all this to be shut up in a little dirty town! I cannot bear the idea. Could not M. de Grignan have put off the Assembly a little longer? is he not master in this respect? and poor Coulanges, what will become of him? Our recluse mode of life has so turned our brains, that we make matters of consequence of everything: receiving and answering letters takes up some portion of our time indeed; but we have always enough left upon our hands. You make our Abbé proud by the kind things you say of him in your letters. I am satisfied with him on your account. As for La Mousse, he catechises Sundays and holidays; he is resolved to go to heaven. I tell him it is only out of curiosity, to see whether the sun is a heap of dust, continually in motion, or a globe of fire. The other day he assembled all the children of the village about him, and was catechising them; but after several questions, they had so confounded things, that when he asked them who the Blessed Virgin was, they all with one accord answered, "the Creator of heaven and earth:" his faith was not shaken by the children; but finding the men and women, and even the old people, all in the same story, he began to doubt and at length joined in the opinion: in short, he did not know what he was about; and if I had not luckily come to his aid, he would never have got out of the scrape. This new opinion would certainly have been productive of more mischief than that of the motion of atoms. Farewell, my dear child, you see we tickle ourselves in order to laugh: to so low an ebb are we reduced.

LETTER 140

From Madame DE SÉVIGNÉ *to Madame* DE GRIGNAN.

The Rocks, Sunday, October 4, 1671.

So you have at last arrived at your Assembly. I told you in my last how wrong I thought it of M. de Grignan, to contrive its meeting just at this time, to deprive you of the pleasures of the country, and the good society you had there. You have left poor Coulanges too; he wrote to me from Lyons; he is full of complaints at his disappointment, and thinks of nothing but returning to Paris; that is, to Autry, which he would never have quitted, but for the hope of seeing you: all the comfort he has now left, is in talking of you to the *chamarier* [1] de Rochebonne, who is never silent on your perfections. If I did not think it ridiculous to send you all the letters I receive, I would have enclosed his, together with one from the Comte des Chapelles: but you have the answer to it, which will be sufficient, with two others I send you, one from M. Le Camus, and the other from M. de Harouïs. I think, in order to give you time to read all these, I ought, in common civility, to put an end to my own: but I wish first to know, if you did not laugh at my blunder at Vitré, in desiring the gentleman of Lower Brittany to get dinner ready as soon as possible: did it not put you

[1] An office or dignity in the Chapter of St. Jean de Lyon.

in mind of a similar one at Merci, when I desired a clerk to one of the King's secretaries to set my sleeves right for me? What you observe about the sun and the moon, with regard to M. de Chaulnes and M. de Lavardin, is very good; for yourself, you are always above the horizon. It is true, my child, you are never at rest, you are always in motion, and I tremble sometimes when I think of your condition, and how much your spirits exceed your strength. I agree with you, that when you would wish to be still, it will no longer be in your power, and that you will have no resource for your late fatigues. This idea occupies me incessantly and painfully; for, in short, it is not the first step but the last, it is breach upon breach, abyss upon abyss. The Abbé and I often talk upon the subject, though we know little about it: but we can judge how far it may extend: this is worthy your attention, for it is not a trifling loss that is at stake. We may walk a great way even when we are tired, as the saying is; but when our legs are broken, we cannot walk at all. I hope you will reflect upon this, and consult the Coadjutor, who is very capable of giving you proper advice; for he is a man of excellent understanding, of fine sense, and possesses a greatness of soul worthy the name he bears; and all these are requisite to decide properly in an affair of this nature. Our Abbé is glad you do not despise his counsel; he only desires life and health to advise with you in person. This letter may not, perhaps, be a very agreeable one; but, my dear child, we must sometimes give vent to things of importance that hang upon the heart: besides, you know, as I once said to you in a song, "Mirth is not for every hour." Far from it; however, take care and do not give in to lowness of spirits; think of nothing but your health, if you have any regard for mine, and be assured that as soon as I remove at Easter, I shall think only of coming to see you, and doing all that lies in my power to render your return with me feasible. What says Adhémar to the return of the Comte de Guiche?

LETTER 141

From Madame DE SÉVIGNÉ *to Madame* DE GRIGNAN.

The Rocks, Wednesday, October 7, 1671.

You know I am always a little opinionated with respect to my reading; so that it is for the interest of those I converse with, that I should read none but the best books. I can think of nothing at present but M. Nicole's *Moral Reflections.* His treatise "On the Means of Preserving Peace among Men," delights me. I never met with anything so truly practical, yet so full of fire and imagination. If you have not yet read it, I beg you will. If you have read it, read it again with additional attention; for my part, I think all mankind are included in it. I am persuaded it was made for me, and hope to profit by it; at least I shall endeavour to do so. You know I could never bear to hear the old say, "I am too old to mend:" I could much sooner pardon the young for saying, "I am too young." Youth is in itself so amiable, that were the soul as perfect as the body, we could not forbear adoring it; but when youth is past, it is then we ought to think of improvements, and endeavour to supply the loss of personal charms by the graces and perfections of the mind. I have long made this the subject of meditation, and am determined to work every day at my mind, my soul, my heart, and my sentiments. I am full of this at present, and therefore fill my letter with it, having besides nothing of greater consequence to tell you.

I suppose you are at Lambesc; but I cannot see you clearly from here: there is a mist about my imagination, that conceals you from my sight. I had formed an idea of Grignan, I saw your rooms, used to walk upon your terrace, and went to mass at your beautiful Chapel; but now I am quite at a loss as I no more know where I am: I wait, with very great impatience, for intelligence from your new quarters. I will write no more to-day, though I have a great deal of time upon my hands; for I have nothing but trifles to tell you, which would be an affront to the Lady-Lieutenant of a Province, who is holding the States, and, consequently, has weighty affairs upon her hands; it may do well enough when you are in your little Palace of Apollo. Our Abbé and our La Mousse are very much yours; and I, my dear child, need I tell you what I am, or what you are to me? The Comte de Guiche is at Court so singular in his air and manner, that he is quite the hero of a romance, and scarcely resembles the rest of mankind; at least so they tell me.

LETTER 142

From Madame DE SÉVIGNÉ *to Madame* DE GRIGNAN.

The Rocks, Sunday, October 11, 1671.

You were sorry to leave Grignan; well you might be: I have been almost as grieved about it as you are, and felt your removal twenty leagues further off, as I should feel a change of climate. Nothing can comfort me but the safety you will be in at Aix in regard to your health. You will lie-in about the close of the present year. My days are all spent in thinking on those I passed with you last year. Certainly no one can have made more of the time than you have done; but if, after this lying-in, M. de Grignan does not allow you rest, as he would to a piece of good ground, I shall be so far from believing in his affection for you, that I shall imagine, on the contrary, he wishes to get rid of you. How is it possible you can bear up against such repeated fatigues? Your youth and beauty will both be destroyed. In short, I expect this proof of his tenderness and complaisance for you. I will not have you with child when I come: I shall want you to walk about with me in the fields, as you promised, and to eat some of those delicious grapes with me without being under apprehensions of the colic. We think of nothing else but our journey; and if our Abbé can be of any service to you, he will have gained the summit of his ambition. You wish us to be with you: there wanted not that to make us fly to you: we shall leave *The Rocks* the latter end of next month: that seems to me the first step towards you. I feel real joy in the thought, and that joy will be increased, when I hear you have arrived at Aix in good health. I cannot think it prudent of you to have taken this journey to Lambesc in your seventh month. But what folly in these people to call themselves *Monsieur and Madame de Grignan, and the Chevalier de Grignan* [1], and to think of paying their respects to you! Who are these Grignans? Why are you not the one and only unique of your kind?

Your scorpions terrify me; for I suppose their bite to be deadly. As you have buildings constructed to guard you against the heat, so you are not surely without oil of scorpions to serve as a counter-poison. I know Provence only by its pomegranates, its orange-trees, and its jessamine; for thus it is described to us: for our own country, chestnuts are the greatest ornaments we boast. The other day I was surrounded by four or five large baskets full of them; some I boiled, some I roasted, and with others filled my pockets: they are served up at table, and they are trodden under foot: this is Brittany in all its glory.

Monsieur d'Usèz is at his Abbey near Angers. He has sent an express, to let me know that he intends to pay me a visit: I do not believe a word of it. He says you are adorable, and are accordingly adored by all the Grignans; that I most firmly believe: you are as much so here; no offense to anyone. My uncle thinks of you just as I could wish him to do: God preserve him to us. La Mousse highly approved your letting your letter rest for a while: there is no forming a judgment of productions of this kind at first sight; he would therefore advise you

[1] They were of an ancient house settled at Salon in Provence, and bore the name of *Grignan.*

to show it to some of your friends, who will judge better of it than we can do, and in the meanwhile he remains wholly yours. What shall I say to our Grignans? You are very wicked to make them acquainted with my follies: it is impossible to hide them from you, who know them so well; but for others, with whom I have my honour and reputation to maintain, ... Adieu, my dear child, I commend my life to your care: you know the only way to preserve it.

LETTER 143

From Madame DE SÉVIGNÉ *to Madame* DE GRIGNAN.

The Rocks, Wednesday, October 14, 1671.

I am going to let you into a little secret: do not say a word of it to anyone, I beseech you, if you have not been told of it already. Our poor d'Hacqueville [1] has so worried himself in the service of his friends, that he has fallen sick: some people will have it that it is the small-pox; for he went every day to see M. de Chevreuse, who lies ill of the disorder; but this I do not believe. The truth of the matter is this: he has had a letter sent him in an unknown hand, in which he is desired to give his attendance for an hour at a consultation which was to be held the next morning at Cardinal de Retz's: every hour of the day is then mentioned in the manner in which he generally used to employ them: he is desired to be at M. the Maréchal de Gramont's by five o'clock, to see a clyster administered; then to take his chariot and convey M. Brayer to the little Monaco's; then to send and inquire after the several sick persons, whose names are in a list enclosed; and the writer begs of all things he will not omit being at Mademoiselle de Clisson's in the evening, as she is extremely ill, being mother-sick. His correspondence with Provence, and with

[1] Remarkable for his great officiousness and readiness to serve his friends.

all the countries of Europe, is mentioned; and the whole concludes with, *Dormez, dormez, vous ne sauriez mieux faire*: [*Sleep, sleep, you cannot do better*]. In short, he has shown this letter about with such vexation, that I am apprehensive of its increasing his fever. Do not bring my name in question upon any account; you will probably hear the circumstance from other quarters.

The Abbé Têtu has gone back to Touraine, not being able to stay any longer in Paris; and, for the sake of a little change, has taken the Richelieus with him in this second journey. You would certainly be proud, if you could believe it was upon your account Paris had become insupportable to him; but you would be the only one who thought so. There is a difference in the De Gramont family between the two brothers [1]: our friend d'Hacqueville is deeply mixed up in it. Louvigny has not money enough to purchase his post [2]: I do not know whether you have heard these particulars from any other person. I was yesterday in a little walk on the left of the mall, which was very shady; I thought it so beautiful, that I immediately had this written upon one of the trees: *E di mezzo l'orrore, esce il diletto* [3]. If M. de Coulanges is still with you, embrace him for me, and assure him that I am much pleased with him. And the poor Grignans, are they to have nothing? And you, my dear child, what! not one kind word for you?

LETTER 144

From Madame DE SÉVIGNÉ *to Madame* DE GRIGNAN.

The Rocks, Sunday, October 18, 1671.

I cannot help laughing at your idea of sending your first letter to me to some other person, that it might not

[1] The Comte de Guiche and the Comte de Louvigny, afterwards Duc de Gramont.

[2] Of Colonel in the French Guards.

[3] And from the midst of horror springs delight. [Translation.]

be lost. It puts me in mind of a Breton lady, who desired she might have the pleadings that gained me a law-suit, as the infallible means of gaining hers.

You are at Lambesc then, my child, but with your size increased to your chin. I am frightened at your Provence fashion: so they think nothing of it, it seems, when there is only one child at a birth; a girl would not dare complain of so trifling a circumstance, and the married women of that country have generally two or three at a time. I do not like your being so immense; it must, at least, be very troublesome to you.

Attend, Monsieur le Comte, it is to you I am now speaking; you shall meet with nothing but abuse from me for all your civilities: you delight so much in your own works, that instead of having pity on my poor child, you do nothing but laugh at her; this plainly shows that you do not know what it is to bear children: but hear me, I have something else to say to you, which is this: that if, after this boy, you do not give her a little rest, I shall not think you have the least regard either for her or for me, and I will not come to Provence: your swallows may twitter as long as they please; I shall not heed them: and more than that, I have to tell you, that I shall take your wife from you. Do you think I gave her to you to be killed; to have her health, youth, and beauty, all destroyed at once? This is no jest: I shall ask the favour of you on my knees, in proper time and place: in the meantime you may admire my assurance, in threatening you with not coming to Provence. You see by this, that your friendship and civilities are not lost upon me. Both the Abbé and myself are persuaded you will be glad to see us. We shall bring you La Mousse, who sends you his thanks for your kind remembrance; and provided I do not find this woman everlastingly with child, you shall see if we are not persons of our word: meanwhile be careful of her; and mind that she does not lie-in at Lambesc. My dear Comte, farewell.

Now, my beautiful, I return to you, and assure you that I greatly pity you. Pray take care not to lie-in at

Lambesc. When you are past your eighth month, you have not an hour certain. You have M. de Coulanges with you now. How happy is he in beholding you! He did well to take courage, and you to press him to it: embrace him for me, and all your Grignans likewise; for there is no refraining from loving them. My aunt tells me, that your little girl pinches just as you used to do: she is a great rogue: I long to see her. Alas! I shall stand in great need of your black man to take me a journey through the air; that by land is horrible to think of. I am absolutely afraid of being surrounded in this place by water. Indeed, after seeing you set out for Provence through unfathomable depths, I may think nothing impossible.

But, to return to your story; I made a jest of La Mousse's, but I do not do so of yours; for indeed it is very well told, and so well, that it made me shudder in reading it; my heart fluttered; indeed it is the most extraordinary thing that can be. But this *Auger* I have certainly seen, and shall take an opportunity of talking to him, and the person who tells this so naturally can certainly be no other than a sylph. After the promise you have made me, I do not doubt but there will be great disputes as to who shall bring you here. The reward is worthy of being disputed; and if I do not see you arrive quickly, I shall fancy a war has broken out amongst your champions. It will be a war very justly founded; and, if sylphs could die, they could not die on a more noble occasion. In short, my dear, I give you many thanks for your agreeable manner of relating this original story: it is the first of the kind that I would answer for the truth of.

There is something very droll in the pretended miracles of your hermit; but if he believes the truth of them himself, I am much mistaken. M. de Grignan is very right to give him a lecture now and then, or his vanity might lead him from the midst of his desert into the midst of purgatory. A fine jaunt truly! If he is bound no further, he need not be at so much pains, there are a great many roads thither. I shall be in great fear for his salvation, till I am assured by you that it is secure. I can give credit to you; for I know that you are not to be imposed upon by appearances. God is all-powerful; no one doubts it: but we in no wise merit that he should make his power known to us.

I am very glad M. de Grignan made so good a speech; this must be pleasant to him; others are out of the question. M. de Chaulnes spoke very well too; a little heavily, but that was not amiss in a Governor. M. de Lavardin has a happy way of expressing himself. I have told Corbinelli that his packet must certainly have been lost with the letters I so deeply regret. Adieu, my dear child: I love you so passionately, that I hide a great part of my love, not to oppress you with it. I thank you for your cares, your affection, and your letters: my life hangs on these.

LETTER 145

From Madame DE SÉVIGNÉ *to Madame* DE GRIGNAN.

The Rocks, Wednesday, October 21, 1671.

How I feel the weight of your burden, my dear child! Do not imagine you are the only one who is in danger of being choked: if I were with you, the interest I have in your health would make me very skillful in what relates to you. The advice I have given Deville's wife will make Madame Moreau[1] fancy that I must have had children: indeed I have learned a great deal within these three years. I must own that, at first, modesty, and the natural *prudishness* of a long widowhood, had left me in profound ignorance; but, when it is necessary, I become the *matron* in an instant.

Coulanges is with you still; he must have contributed greatly to raise your spirits; but when you receive this

[1] She was to be Madame de Grignan's midwife at the approaching confinement.

letter, you will have lost him. I shall love him as long as I live for his courage in going so far as Lambesc to see you. I want sadly to hear something about that country. I am wearied to death with the continual repetition of the same thing over and over again from Paris, especially the marriage of MONSIEUR; it drives me almost mad; and, what is worse than all, those who never wrote to me before, begin now, unfortunately, to rouse themselves, that I might not be ignorant of this news. I have just written to the Abbé de Pontcarré, to entreat him not to fill my head with any more of this, nor of the Palatine, who is gone to fetch home the Princess; nor of the Maréchal du Plessis, who is going to Metz to marry her; nor of MONSIEUR's going to Châlons to consummate his nuptials; nor of the King's going to see them at Villers-Cotterets: in a word, I tell him that I will not hear a syllable more about the business till they have slept together again and again: that I long to be at Paris, to be out of the way of hearing news; that if I had anyway of revenging myself on the Bretons for what my friends make me suffer, I should have a degree of patience, but for six months together they send the same piece of news, in different shapes; that, for my part, I have still some little remains of fashion about me, which may, perhaps, render me nice and quickly tired of such things. And this is true; for I immediately fly from letters that I think have any news in them, to those of business. I took great pleasure yesterday in reading a letter from the good man Lamaison, who I was very sure would not mention a word of this marriage to me, and who still salutes my Lady Comtesse with all humility, in the same manner as if she were close at my elbow. Alas! I do not want to be asked to weep just now; a turn or two in the mall will do it presently.

Apropos, my woods are infested with wolves: I have two or three guards following me every night with their muskets on their shoulders; *Beaulieu* is their captain: we have for these two days honoured the moon with our presence between eleven and twelve at night. The night before last, we saw a black man coming towards us: I thought on *Auger,* and was ready to refuse him the garter; but, upon his coming nearer, it proved to be La Mousse. Going a little further, we spied a large white body extended upon the ground: we made up to this too; and behold, it was a tree that I had cut down the week before! These are extraordinary adventures! I wish you may not be frightened at them in your present condition; if you are, take a glass of water, my dear. If we had a few sylphs at our command now, one might produce a story which would divert you. I must take a journey to Provence, if it were only to speak to that *Auger.* The history both occupied and amused me greatly: I have sent a copy of it to my aunt, thinking you had not courage enough to write it twice over, and in so correct a manner. God knows how differently I taste this kind of thing to what I do the Renaudots[1] who employ their pens at my expense. Farewell, my sweet love; I see you and think of you incessantly. A thousand kind things to all the Grignans, in proportion to the degree of love you think they bear me: I entirely trust to you in this.

LETTER 146

From Madame DE SÉVIGNÉ *to Madame* DE GRIGNAN.

The Rocks, Sunday, October 25, 1671.

I am again returned to my lamentations of Jeremiah. I have had but one packet this week, and I have reason to believe the other lost. You can never have been seven days without writing to me. Some demon certainly steals your letters, and diverts himself with them. It is *Auger's* sylph: be it as it may, I am inconsolable about it. Here is a letter for your Bishop. You were quite right to open his: it is crammed with love; I take him at his word, and

[1] Meaning the news-mongers: the invention of newspapers was the work of the two Renaudots.

shall reckon more upon it, I fancy, than he would have me; but it is serving him right: what business has he to make such protestations? I think my answer is not bad: the conclusion is poor, and common; I had almost given in to the *justice to believe*: but it is quite indifferent to me. I am told, the King has given a regiment to the Chevalier de Grignan: I suppose it is Adhémar's; if it is worth having, I am extremely glad. But what shall we say of Coulanges? Is not he the cleverest fellow in the world? I have read his letter; and, as you imagined, was ready to die with laughing all the while: it was all excellent; but then his division into chapters! Good God! how I long to see and embrace him, and talk about you to him! He is charmed with everything you do, and not without reason. One cannot sufficiently admire you. I could not do you those honours myself; but I am as sensible of them as any other person, and perfectly agree with my good friends, without doing like the lady of M. President Jeannin: do you remember that story? In short, my child, what more can you obtain? Your honours even exceed M. de Pomponne's. In the midst of my mirth, I have felt an oppression of the heart, which ought not to exist, and which I am too apt to cherish. Every road leads to Rome, that is, everything goes straight to my heart. Monsieur de Coulanges writes very agreeably, and made us laugh very heartily as you foresaw, and I dare say at the very same passages. I propose examining all the chapters with him this winter, especially that of the head-dress; it seems to be much of the same kind as that of Aristotle on hats. But what shall we say of chocolate? Are you under no apprehension of heating your blood with it? May not all its boasted effects conceal some latent fire at the bottom? Make me easy upon this subject, my dear; for in your present condition I fear everything. You know I was very fond of chocolate; but I thought it heated me; and, besides, I was told it was a bad thing; but from your account of it, and the wonders which you say it has wrought in you, I know not what to think. That part of Coulanges's letter is very droll; but indeed it is all so. Farewell, my dearest and best-beloved; I shall take great pleasure in reading the chapter on your love for me: I promise you I am steadfast in this opinion; but to make it more sure, be steadfast yourself in giving me always such proofs of it as you now do. Our little friend's letters are far from being agreeable; he is too prolix; I wish he would carry his civilities elsewhere.

LETTER 147

From Madame DE SÉVIGNÉ *to Madame* DE GRIGNAN.

The Rocks, Wednesday, October 28, 1671.

Scorpions, my dear! they are certainly worthy of a chapter in M. de Coulanges' book. The surprise of your bowels at the ice and chocolate is a matter I am resolved to sift to the bottom with him, or rather with you, and ask you seriously if your bowels were not offended with it; and if they did not give you fine colics, to teach you how to give them such *antipéristases* [1]; there is a grand word for you. I had a mind to be friends again with chocolate, and so took some the day before yesterday, by way of digesting my dinner, that I might make the better supper; and yesterday took some again by way of nourishment, to enable me to fast till supper time: it had every way the desired effect; and what I think very extraordinary is, that it acted according to my wishes. I do not know what you may have been doing this morning; but I have been half-way up my legs in dew, laying lines for some walks that I am making round my park, which will be very beautiful when finished. If my son is fond of woods and of walks, he will have reason to bless my memory. I fancy this brother of yours is in Paris: he chooses to wait for me

[1] A term in philosophy borrowed from the Greek, and signifying the action of any two opposite qualities which mutually increase the vigour and activity of each other.

there, rather than come back here; and I think he is in the right. But what think you of my husband the Abbé d'Effiat? I am very unfortunate in my husbands; he is on the point of marrying a young nymph of fifteen[1], daughter of Monsieur and Madame de La Bazinière; a complete piece of affectation and coquetry. The marriage is to take place in Touraine; he has given up forty thousand livres per annum in benefices for...... God grant he may be happy with her; but it is much doubted by everyone, and most people think he had better have kept to me.

Monsieur d'Harouïs writes to me as follows: "Let Madame de *Carignan*[2] know that I adore her. She is with her little States; they are not such folks as we are, who give one hundred thousand crowns at a time; but I hope they will, at least, give her as much as we did to Madame de Chaulnes by way of welcome." He may wish, and I may wish too; but your folks are too dry and close-fisted: the sun sucks up all their moisture, which is the only source of goodness and affection. I am still grieving for the packet I lost last week. Provence is become my native country, from thence spring all my joys and all my sorrows. I always wait with impatience for Friday: it is the day I receive letters from you. St. Pavin[3] some time ago made an epigram upon Friday, the day he used to see me at the Abbé's: he addressed himself to the gods, and finished with the two following lines:

[1] Marie-Anne Bertrand de La Bazinière was married to the Abbé d'Effiat, as the report then went, but was married afterwards to the Comte de Nancré.

[2] This is of course Madame de Grignan, see Letter 127, of the 19th August, 1671, in this volume.

[3] This was a jovial Abbé, of whom Despréaux thus speaks, *St. Pavin devot*, etc. He passed, like Desbarreaux and Theophilus, for an atheist; but he was not the less credulous. He was converted by means of a vision. The very night Theophilus, his master and his friend, died, he heard his name pronounced by him in a frightful voice. His valet having assured him he heard the same voice, he was convinced. He renounced the impious opinions he had professed, or rather the irreligious and voluptuous life he led.

Multipliez les Vendredis,
Je vous quitte tout le reste [1].

A l'applicazione, Signora. M. d'Angers [2] writes me wonders concerning you; he has been frequently with M. d'Usèz [3], who cannot speak sufficiently in your praise: you are much obliged to him for the great regard he expresses for you; he seems brimful of affection, which dilates itself into a thousand praises, that make you much admired. My Abbé too loves you perfectly well; La Mousse honours you, and I leave you to yourself. Cruel step-mother! a word to the dear Grignans.

LETTER 148

From Madame DE SÉVIGNÉ *to Madame* DE GRIGNAN.

The Rocks, Sunday, November 1, 1671.

If the first letter of Coulanges', which was lost, was like the other three, I could absolutely cry for vexation; for no one can write better: you make a little dialogue between you that is worth all that can be said in the common way, each throws in his part so pleasantly. With regard to you, my dear child, I understand you perfectly, when you consent that de Coulanges should set out tomorrow, rather than stay with you all his life-time. You dread that kind of eternity, as I dread going in a litter with any one: there is only one person in the world with whom I would consent to go; I shall not tell you who. I am very glad to be acquainted with *Jacquemart and Marguerite* [4]. I fancy myself with you all, and think I see you and Coulanges. I hope to alter your dress when

[1] Let every day be Friday,
I care not for the rest. [Translation.]

[2] Henri Arnauld, Bishop of Angers.

[3] Jacques Adhémar de Monteil, Bishop of Usèz.

[4] The two figures are so called that strike the hours on the bells of the clock in the steeple at Lambesc.

I get to Grignan, and to make you quite smart: but no more pregnancies, my dear Grignan, I affectionately conjure you; have some pity on your charming wife, and let her lie, like good fallow ground, for a while; promise me but this, and I will love you from the bottom of my heart. I can easily guess, my dear child, what your apprehensions were in the fear of losing your first President; your imagination goes too fast, for there is no danger; mine too plays me the same tricks every moment: I fancy all that is dear or good to me is on the point of being torn from me for ever, and my heart is filled with such bitter pangs, that if they were as lasting as they are violent, I should sink under them. On these occasions, we should call to our assistance an entire resignation to the dispensations and will of God. Does not M. Nicole expatiate admirably on that subject? I am quite in raptures over him: I never met with his equal. It is true, the indifference he requires of us about worldly esteem or censure, demands more than human perfection. I am less capable than anyone of entering into his opinion here, at least in practice; yet it is still a pleasure to meditate with him on the subject, and to reflect properly on the vanity of being affected with pleasure or concern for such a bubble; perhaps, from being convinced of the truth of his arguments, we may in time make use of them on some certain occasion. In short, it is a real treasure to have so good a mirror in which to view the weakness and impotence of our own hearts, however we may act. M. d'Andilly is no less charmed than ourselves with this excellent work.

M. de Coulanges has won your money, you say; but surely you had laughing enough for it. Nothing can equal what he wrote to his wife. I do not think I shall part with him this winter, I shall be so happy to converse with a man who has seen and admired you so lately: as for Adhémar, since he is a wicked creature, I will turn him out of doors: to be sure, he has a regiment, and may enter by force. I am told that this regiment is an agreeable distinction; but is it not ruinous likewise? What I like best in it, is the King's remembering Adhémar in his absence; would to God he may remember his elder brother too, since he can go as far as Sweden in search of faithful servants [1].

I love the Coadjutor for loving me so long: Chevalier Adhémar, approach, so that I may embrace you: I am strangely attached to these Grignans: it will be long before M. Nicole's book will produce such fine effects in me as it has done in M. de Grignan. I have ties on all sides; but there is one particular one that I feel in my very marrow; and what can M. Nicole do there? Good God! how truly I can admire him! But how far am I from that happy indifference he wishes to inspire! Farewell, my dearest child! Do you not pity me for what I must feel now I know you are in the last stage of your pregnancy? Take care of yourself, if you have any love for me. I am grieved to see all your Parisian faces quit you one after another: you have your husband with you indeed, and his is a Parisian face. My child, you must not suffer yourself to be totally forgotten in that country: I must take you back with me: you must agree to it.

The Abbé d'Effiat's marriage has not taken place yet; he has required time to consider of it: in my opinion the affair is at an end.

LETTER 149

From Madame DE SÉVIGNÉ *to Madame* DE GRIGNAN.

The Rocks, Wednesday, November 4, 1671.

Ah! my daughter, what a strange scene passed this day two years at Livry [2]! How was my heart pierced with anguish at that period! but I ought not to dwell on such

[1] See the note relating to M. de Pomponne, Letter 134, of the 13th September, 1671, in this volume.

[2] This relates to a miscarriage of Madame de Grignan's at Livry, the 4th of November, 1669. See Letter 128, of the 23rd August, 1671, in this volume.

melancholy recollections. Let us talk a little of M. Nicole, it is a long time since we have said a word about him. There is a great deal of justice in your observation respecting the indifference he requires us to show to the opinion of the world; I think with you, that philosophy will hardly be found sufficient of itself, without the assistance of grace. He lays so great a stress on preserving peace and good fellowship with our neighbour, and recommends so many things to us in order to attain these, that it is next to an impossibility, after this, to be indifferent to what the world thinks of us. Guess what I am doing; I am beginning this treatise again: methinks I could wish to make a soup of it so that I could swallow it all down into myself. I am delighted with what he says on the subject of pride and self-love, which enter into all disputes, under the feigned name of the love of truth: in short, this treatise will apply to more than one in the world; but I cannot help thinking, that he had me principally in view when he wrote it. He says, eloquence, and a flow of words, give a *lustre* to the thoughts; I greatly admire that expression; I thought it beautiful and new. The word *lustre* is extremely apposite there, do you not think so? We must read this book together at Grignan. Were I to nurse you in your lying-in, it would be a fine opportunity: but what can I do for you at this distance? I pass my time in having masses said for you every day, and in a multitude of disagreeable thoughts, which can be of no service to you; but which, however, it is impossible to avoid. I have at present ten or twelve workmen in the air, raising the timbers of our Chapel; they run backwards and forwards upon the outside of it like so many rats; they hold by nothing, and are every instant in danger of breaking their necks, and make my back ache with endeavouring to help them below. One cannot but admire the wonderful effects of Providence in the desire of gain, and be thankful, that such people are created, who are willing to do for a few pennies what others would not do for a hundred thousand crowns. "O thrice-happy they who plant cabbages! when they have one foot on the ground, the other is not far off." I have this from a very good author [1]. We have planters too with us, who are forming new avenues; I hold the young trees myself while they set them in the ground, unless it rains so that there is no being abroad: but the weather almost drives me to despair, and makes me wish for a sylph to transport me to Paris. Madame de La Fayette says, that since you tell the story of *Auger* in so serious a manner, she is persuaded nothing can be more true; and that you are by no means jesting with me: she thought at first that it had been a joke of Coulanges'; and it looks very like it. If you write to him upon the subject, pray let it be in that style.

You see M. de Louvigny has not been able to purchase the post [2] which was his father's: but M. de La Feuillade [3] is well provided for. I did not think he would ever have been so much in fortune's way. My aunt has had a fit of the ague, which has greatly alarmed me. Your daughter is cutting teeth, and pinches as you used to do, which is odd enough. What shall I tell you next? Consider, child, I am in a desert. La Troche, whom I expected here, is very ill; so that we are quite alone: we read a great deal, and spend the evenings and mornings as usual.

LETTER 150

From Madame DE SÉVIGNÉ *to Madame* DE GRIGNAN.

The Rocks, Wednesday, November 11, 1671.

Would to heaven, my daughter, that to be continually thinking of you, with the utmost anxiety and tenderness,

[1] Panurge, in *Rabelais*.

[2] Of Colonel of the French Guards, enjoyed by Maréchal de Gramont, with the reversion to his son, the Comte de Guiche, who had then obtained leave of the King to resign.

[3] François d'Aubusson, Duc de La Feuillade, who was afterwards Maréchal of France, succeeded Maréchal de Gramont, as Colonel of the French Guards, and was installed by the King the 4th of January, 1672.

could be of any real service to you! one would think, it might not be altogether useless to you; and yet of what service can I be to you, at the distance of two hundred leagues? I do not doubt that every necessary precaution is taken where you are; that the best plan has been chosen between going to Aix and returning to Grignan; that a midwife has been sent for in proper time, to accustom you a little to the sight of her, and save you the chagrin and impatience that one naturally feels at seeing a new face: as to a nurse, your own women must take care of you on this occasion; they will remember Madame Moreau's way of managing; and as to yourself, my dear, you must be sure to keep yourself as quiet as possible, and not hazard a fever for the sake of talking, as you did at Paris. What more shall I say to you? and what can I say to you that is not in the same style? It is natural, when the head is occupied with these things, to make them the subject of discourse; it is as natural for you to be tired of them: for my part, I never dislike things in their proper place; I ought not therefore to write to you, I think, till I know you are brought to bed: and that would be very strange too; it is better, my child, that you should accustom yourself to thoughts which are so just and natural upon proper occasions. Perhaps you may be brought to bed when this reaches you; but what will that signify, if it finds you in good health? I wait for Friday with the greatest impatience: see how continually I forestall time, which I was never fond of doing, and never did before, being of opinion, that time flies fast enough, without being hurried on. Madame de La Fayette informs me, she intends to write to you soon; I suppose she will not forget to tell you, that La Marans came into the Queen's apartment the other night, while they were acting a Spanish play: she looked like one lost and bewildered, and began with an egregious blunder, by taking the upper-hand of Madame Dufresnoi, which made her laughed at by everybody, as a very ignorant and ill-bred creature.

Pomenars passed through our village the other day

on his way to Laval, where he saw a great crowd assembled; and upon asking what was the matter, was told they were hanging a gentleman in effigy, who had stolen the daughter of the Comte de Créance; this happened to be himself: he got as near as he could to the scaffold, and finding the painter had made a frightful resemblance of him, he complained of it bitterly; and afterwards supped and slept at the house of the very judge who had passed sentence on him. The next morning he came here, and was ready to die with laughter, in telling us what had passed; however, he thought it best to decamp the morning after, as soon as it was light.

As to devices, my dear child, my poor brain is in a very bad condition for thinking of any, much less for inventing them; however, as there are twelve hours in the day, and above fifty in the night, my memory has furnished me with a rocket raised to a great height in the air, with these words: *Che peri, pur che m'innalzi*: I wish with all my heart it had been mine; I think it exactly made for Adhémar, *Let it perish, so it be exalted.* I am afraid I have seen this somewhere in the late tournaments, though I cannot exactly say where or when; for I think it too pretty to be my own. I remember also having seen in some book, a rocket on the subject of a lover who had been bold enough to declare himself to his mistress, with these words, *da l'ardore l'ardire* [1], which is pretty, but does not apply in this instance. I am not quite sure whether the first I have mentioned is in strict conformity to the rules of devices; for I do not perfectly understand them; all I know is, that it pleased me, and whether it was in a tournament, or on a seal, is a matter of no great importance; it is scarcely possible to invent new ones for every occasion. You have heard me a thousand times repeat that part of a line in Tasso, *l'alte non temo* [2]: I used to repeat this so often, that the Comte des Chapelles had a seal engraved with an eagle flying towards the sun,

[1] My boldness arises from my ardour. [Translation.]

[2] I rise without fear. [Translation.]

and *l'alte non temo* for the motto: a very happy device. Perhaps, my dear, this is all to no purpose. I care for nothing provided you are in health.

LETTER 151

From Madame DE SÉVIGNÉ *to Madame* DE GRIGNAN.

The Rocks, Sunday, November 15, 1671.

The question, whether you had not thrown away my last letters, was only an air; for though they do not merit the honour you do them, yet, I believe, after keeping those I used to write to you, when you were playing with a doll, that you would keep these: a box of a moderate size would not now be able to hold them; you must have a large chest on purpose.

There certainly never was anything more humorous than what you say about Adhémar's name; and it is a fact, that there is no part of his letters blotted or scratched out, but his signature. I am a good deal puzzled about a name for his regiment: I have sent you my thoughts upon the subject before: you know I prefer the name of Adhémar, and would maintain it at the hazard of my life [1]; but I am afraid we are on the weakest side in this affair. I like the device [2] extremely, *Che peri, pur che m'innalzi.* This is the true language of a little Sultan, a little Alexander, a proud, ambitious, rash, impetuous little Maréchal of France. I want sadly to know what you think of it, and where I have stolen it [3]: for I am sure I

[1] The regiment mentioned here, is one of the regiments of horse called the *Gentlemen's Regiments,* which take the name of the Colonel: this was called the *Regiment of Grignan,* and went by that name till the death of the Marquis de Grignan in 1704.

[2] The body of this device was a sky-rocket.

[3] Father Bouhours, in his *Discourse on Devices,* mentions that of the Comte d'Illiers, the body of which was the same as the foregoing, and the motto *Poco duri pur che m'innalzi.*

did not make it. As to M. de Grignan, I firmly believe him; I am sure that he loves a *thrush* better than you; and so in return I love an *owl* better than him. Let him examine his own heart; as he loves you, in the same degree shall I love him: there is but one way in which he can convince me of his love for you. But, my dear child, do you not sometimes wonder at the blunders and mistakes that arise from being separated so long, and placed at such a distance from each other? I am in pain for you when, perhaps, you are in good health; and when you are ill, a letter from you makes me perfectly easy at the time I receive it: but this satisfaction cannot last long; for after all you must be brought to bed: and I shall be miserable, and not without reason, till I hear of your safe delivery. You are resolved, it seems, to lie-in at Lambesc: have you engaged your surgeon? Deville's wife writes me word that you are acquainted with him; that is a great deal: but I fear, as he bleeds you, that he is young, and young people have not had much experience in this way. I know not what I say: but, above all things, take care of yourself: experience ought to have made you wise: for my own part, I am astonished at my extensive knowledge in this respect.

Did I tell you that I have planted one of the prettiest spots imaginable? In the middle of this spot I plant myself, where nobody will keep me company for fear of perishing with cold. La Mousse takes a few turns to get himself warm, and the Abbé runs backwards and forwards on business; but I am fixed there, wrapped up in my long cloak, and thinking of Provence; for that thought never quits me. I wish much to hear of your being safely delivered, before I set out from here; for you must know I look upon the fatigue of the journey, and the great anxiety of mind I shall necessarily endure, as two things impossible to be supported at once.

Let me know what name Adhémar has made choice of: I think he seems undecided about it. M. de Grignan stands up for *Grignan,* and with a great deal of justice.

Rouville [1] is for the other. I think we must reduce it at last to *Le petit glorieux* [2].

You ask me if we have any green leaves with us: indeed we have a great many; they are mixed with yellow and brown, which you know makes an admirable mixture for a gown.

Madame de Senneterre, and Madame de Leuville are two brisk widows: one has plenty of money, and the other of beauty. You do not mention your Assembly; I think it endures longer than ours: at least let me hear something about your own health. What you call trifles and nonsense, are what I most delight in. Alas! if these are unpleasant to you, you should never read my letters, but burn them. Farewell, my dear and lovely child; I commend my life to your care.

LETTER 152

From Madame DE SÉVIGNÉ *to Madame* DE GRIGNAN.

The Rocks, Wednesday, November 18, 1671.

Good heavens! my dear child, in what a situation may this letter find you! It will be the twenty-eighth before you receive it; and, by that time, I hope and trust you will be safely delivered. I am obliged to repeat these words frequently to keep up my spirits; for my heart is sometimes so painfully oppressed, that I know not what to do; but this is nothing more than natural on such an occasion as the present. I wait with impatience for my Friday's letters; and entreat those who have hitherto diverted themselves with keeping yours back, to suspend their game till you have lain-in. They seem of late to

[1] François, Comte de Rouville, remarkable for the great authority he had gained by always telling the truth.

[2] M. de Guilleragues saying once, that all the Grignans were proud (*glorieux*), and being asked whether he thought Adhémar so, replied, *He is proudish* (*glorieuset*), and ever afterwards he went by the name of *Le petit glorieux,* or the *Little proud one.*

have been busy with mine: I am quite in despair; for you know, that though I do not set great value upon my letters, yet I would choose that those to whom I write them should receive them; and as I neither write for other people, nor to have them lost, I regret all that do not reach you. What a fancy, to meddle with my letters! Surely we are too nearly related for our correspondence to furnish matter for curiosity; in short, it is unbearable; let us say no more about it. D'Hacqueville writes me word that he left Madame de Montausier at the point of death: I suppose she is dead by this time. If I am obliged to write to M. de Montausier and Madame de Crussol[1], I shall be more at a loss than poor Adhémar was, when he had to write to the King and the Ministry. I cannot write now; since I have found that my letters do not come to your hands, mine have been fettered. I think sometimes, that while I am perplexing my head here with a thousand fancies, they may be firing guns, and rejoicing, for your safe delivery: this, however, I am not sure of; but must, as yet, languish in expectation. It freezes hard, and I am all day wandering in the woods. It will be fine weather, I suppose, till we set out, and then we shall have a deluge of rain. Such are the reflections in which I employ my time, and when one has nothing else to say, it is as well to finish.

LETTER 153

From Madame DE SÉVIGNÉ *to Madame* DE GRIGNAN.

The Rocks, Sunday, November 22, 1671.

Madame de Louvigny[2] is brought to bed of a son: you see, my dear child, you must certainly have one too; you expect it so firmly, that, as you say, *la Signora qui mit*

[1] Madame de Montausier's daughter.

[2] Marie-Charlotte de Castelnau, wife of Antoine-Charles, Comte de Louvigny, afterwards Duc de Gramont.

au monde une fille, was not more taken in than you would be, if such an accident were to happen. I pray incessantly for the happy termination of an event upon which my life depends more than yours. I do not think I shall be able to leave this place till my mind is at rest upon the subject. There is no carrying such a cruel disquiet with one on the road, where there will be no chance of having a letter from you: it is you therefore, my dear child, who detains me.

I am extremely concerned at the dangerous state of health of your first President[1]: his death will be a very great loss to you; besides the misfortune of having so young, so elegant, and so handsome a man, torn from you in this manner: if he recovers, it will be next to a miracle: I am sure I never thought I should take much interest in a first President of Provence; but Provence is become my country since you have inhabited it.

Madame de Richelieu has at last stepped into Madame de Montausier's place; what joy to some! what vexation to others! Such is the way of the world! You are greatly beloved by all that family: for my part, I am very little interested in these changes; and keep up my connections at Court with no other view than that of being serviceable to you in your absence. I have had a letter from M. de Pomponne full of the most sincere and affectionate expressions of friendship: he is highly satisfied with his Royal Master; and will, I am certain, fully answer the good opinion everyone has formed of him.

I have no doubt of the history of *Auger* being true, nor ever had; it was only a notion of Madame de La Fayette's, from a knowledge of Coulanges' odd way. She believes it now as firmly as myself. Winter reigns here in all its horrors. I am either walking about my gardens, or sitting by the chimney-corner: there is no taking any diversion: if we are not by the fire-side, we must be running about to catch heat. I shall pass two more Fridays at *The Rocks,* by which time I hope to hear of your safe

[1] Henri de Forbin d'Oppède.

delivery. M. de Grignan is in justice obliged to take as much care of me now, as I did of him on a similar occasion [1].

LETTER 154

From Madame DE SÉVIGNÉ *to Madame* DE GRIGNAN.

The Rocks, Wednesday, November 25, 1671.

My letters from Paris inform me of the death of your first President: I cannot express what concern it has given me. He was a very worthy man, as well as a very handsome one; but what rendered him of still greater consequence to me, was the friendship that subsisted between you, and the advantages you might have derived from such a connection. When I have exhausted this subject, I return to myself again, and find my heart overwhelmed with anxiety for your health, and the thoughts of your approaching confinement. I do not know how it happened that I had not the wit to advise you to do as you have done, considering that I was equally fearful of your encountering the small-pox at Aix, and of returning all the way back to Grignan: you had no alternative therefore, but to remain where you were, which is certainly the wisest step you could have taken. I suppose you have been bled; I suppose too, that you have taken all the precautions that are necessary: in short, I suppose and hope all will go right. Madame de Louvigny has set you a very good example; but I shall suffer much in waiting for the happy tidings; I could wish to receive them here. I expect your Friday's packet with my usual impatience. I suppose you will say a good deal on the death of the poor President: I am apprehensive it may have shocked you, and have been of ill consequence in your present condition. My own condition will not let me say any more to you now; though it is not for want of leisure, I assure you; on the

[1] See Letter 48 of the 19th November, 1670, in this volume.

contrary, it is that alone which makes me yield to the train of anxious thoughts that haunt me respecting Provence; and as I have nothing but melancholy things to say to you, which I know you are in no need of at present, I shall take my leave of you, with the assurance that I am most affectionately yours.

LETTER 155

From Madame DE SÉVIGNÉ *to Madame* DE GRIGNAN.

The Rocks, Sunday, November 29, 1671.

It is impossible, wholly impossible, my dearest child, for me to express the joy I received on opening the blessed packet that contained the news of your safe delivery. When I saw a letter in it from M. de Grignan, I did not doubt for a moment that you were brought to bed; but then it was so strange a circumstance not to see the usual dear handwriting on the superscription! However, there was one from you dated the fifteenth; but, though I saw it, I passed it by unnoticed, that from M. de Grignan having strangely confused my poor intellect. At last I ventured to open it with trembling hands and a beating heart, and found everything that my most ardent wishes could desire. How do you imagine one acts in such an excess of joy? Ask the Coadjutor; you cannot be a judge yourself, having never experienced it. Shall I tell you then, how one acts? Why the heart sinks, and tears flow apace without our being able to prevent them. This was precisely my case: I wept, my dear child, but with infinite pleasure: tears like these are accompanied with sensations not to be equalled by the most lively joy. As you are a philosopher you will be able to account for these effects; I can only feel them. I am now going to have as many masses said by way of thanksgiving to God for this inestimable blessing, as I did before to request it of him. Were my present feelings to continue for any length of time, life would be too agreeable; we must therefore enjoy happiness while it is in our power; sorrow and vexation will return but too soon. How charming it was to have a boy after all, and to have him named after Provence[1]! It was everything that could be wished. My dear, I give you a thousand and a thousand thanks for the few lines you wrote me: they completed the measure of my felicity. The Abbé is as transported as myself, and our La Mousse is in raptures. Adieu, my angel; I have many letters to write besides this.

LETTER 156

From Madame DE SÉVIGNÉ *to Madame* DE GRIGNAN.

The Rocks, Wednesday, December 2, 1671.

After my first transports of joy had a little subsided, I began to perceive, my dear child, that I should still be anxious for letters from Provence next Friday to complete my satisfaction. Lying-in women are liable to so many accidents, and your tongue is so well hung, as M. de Grignan says, that till nine days at least are happily over with you, I shall not leave this place with any degree of comfort or pleasure: so I shall wait for my letters, and then set out: those of the following Friday, I shall receive at Malicorne. I am surprised at no longer feeling the load at my heart, which used to oppress me day and night, while I was in doubt about your safety. I am now so completely happy, that I cannot cease returning thanks to God, for my peace of mind, which I did not expect so soon. I have received letters of compliment without end and without number from Paris, and here the young Lord's health has been drank for miles round. I have distributed money for drink, and feasted my own people like Kings. But nothing gave me greater pleasure than a compliment

[1] The Procurators of Provence were his godfathers, and gave him the name of Louis-Provence.

I received from Pilois [1], who came this morning with his spade upon his back, and said, "My lady, I am come to let you know that I am heartily glad to hear that my lady Comtesse has got a fine boy." Now this is to me worth all the fine speeches in the world. M. de Montmoron [2] came hither post: among other things we were talking of devices: he assures me he does not remember to have seen anywhere the one I proposed for Adhémar: he knew the one, with these words, *Da l'ardore l'ardire* [3]; but that is not the thing: the other, he says, is much more complete, *Che peri, pur che m'innalzi.* And whether it is my own, or borrowed, he thinks it excellent. But what do you say to M. de Lauzun? You know what a noise he made this time twelvemonth. Should we have believed it, if any one had told us, that in less than a year he would be a prisoner? *Vanity of vanities, all is vanity*! They say the new MADAME is quite dazzled with her grandeur. You shall hear what kind of personage she is: when her physician was presented to her, she said, she had no business for one; that she had never been bled nor taken physic in her life; and that it was her custom, if she was ill, to take a walk of five or six miles, and that cured her at once. But let her go, and joy go with her. You see I write to you, as I would to one who has lain-in for a month. But now for M. de Grignan: he cannot be ignorant of what you must have suffered; and, if he really loves you, must it not give him the greatest concern, to be the cause of your being thus circumstanced every year? After such good reasons as these, I have no more to say to him on the subject, further than to assure him, that I will not come to Provence if you are with child again. I wish he may take this as a warning: for my part, it would absolutely drive me to despair; but, however, I will keep my word: it will not be for the first time. Farewell, divine Comtesse; I kiss the dear infant, for whom I have a great

[1] Madame de Sévigné's gardener.

[2] He was of the Sévigné family.

[3] This was a device of the Maréchal de Bassompierre.

affection; but not so much as for the lady his mother: it will be a long while before he attains to that. I have a great desire to hear some news of your Assembly, the christening, etc. A little patience, and I shall know all; but this is a virtue I am not much practised in.

LETTER 157

From Madame DE SÉVIGNÉ *to Madame* DE GRIGNAN.

The Rocks, Sunday, December 6, 1671.

The last letters were as necessary to my happiness, as those I received the week before. The joy of your being safely delivered was so exquisite, that being unable to bear its excess, I began to torment myself with apprehensions of the accidents which might follow. I then longed for a second packet, and now I have it, it is just what I could have wished. You have had the colic, you have had the milk-fever, but are now got over all. The Coadjutor tells me, that the boy was three hours without making water, and that you were in the most dreadful fright imaginable. Upon my word! You make a fine figure with your motherly love! What a joke! Do you really love the child? But he is fair, and it is that that charms you! You love fair people; very civil indeed! M. de Grignan may well be jealous: you leave him, he says, for the first comer; the last comer he should have said: in short, this boy will make a great many jealous. The good Coadjutor writes me a string of particulars worthy the pen of M. Chais, or Madame Robinette[1]. I fancy you and he fall out a little now and then: is it not so? I hope my presence is not necessary to make you friends: I should wish to find that matter thoroughly settled to my hands. But hark ye, good Mr. Secretary[2],

[1] The one Madame de Grignan's surgeon at Lambesc, the other her midwife at Paris.

[2] M. d'Adhémar.

come this way a little if you please: and so you laugh at my device! You pretend to say it is to be met with in every book of that kind! It may be so; but a person who understands these things better than you, tells me he has never met with it. To tell you the truth, I never thought it was my own, and agree with you, that somebody else made it to my hands: but, be it as it may, you will at least own, that I could have no other view in the application than merely to give you pleasure. To return to you, my poor Comte, I am really sorry for you, I see plainly you are a mere cipher in comparison with this fair young gentleman. However, the balance will now be equal in your family, which unluckily was wanting before. But I really ask your pardon for the comparison of the *owl*[1]: I own it was a little shocking; but I was at that time quite incensed at you for openly proposing a *thrush* to my daughter: if you are sorry for your fault, I will be sorry for mine. I have a great desire to know something of your Assembly; it would be vexatious to have it break up without coming to some conclusion. The Monsieur de Marseilles overwhelms me with civilities; he has given me an account of his dispute with the Coadjutor, and of my daughter's health. They have heard of this dispute in Paris, and have sent me word of it, as if I held no sort of correspondence myself with Provence. Lord bless them! It is my own country. Farewell, my dear Comte, and you, brave Adhémar, and you my ever-dear, my ever-amiable woman in the straw. I think I must say to you, as Barillon said to me the other day: "Those who love you better than I do, love you too well." At such a distance, we scarcely say or do anything properly; we cry when we should laugh, and laugh when we should cry: we are frightened at young surgeons of sixty-four. In short, my child, these are the blunders of distance; to which let me add my total ignorance of Provence. Now you have an advantage on your side, which prevents you from being laughed at in turn, and that is your knowledge of

[1] See Letter 151, of the 15th November, 1671, in this volume.

the place where I am: all these things together will certainly oblige me to get nearer to you, and afterwards to go quite to Provence, in order to inform myself more fully upon the spot. As I am now easy on your account, I shall set out in about three days; so that I shall receive no more letters till I get to Malicorne. I cannot thank you sufficiently for the few lines you add in the letters I have from the Grignans.

Madame de Richelieu is now well settled: if Madame Scarron had a hand in this, she is worthy of envy; for she must taste the most solid joy that this world can afford. I am told Vardes is coming back.

LETTER 158

From Madame DE SÉVIGNÉ *to Madame* DE GRIGNAN.

The Rocks, Wednesday, December 9, 1671.

I am just going to start, my dear, but leave my solitude with some regret, as I shall not find you in Paris. I much question whether I should have returned there this winter, but for my Provence journey, which makes it in my way, it being impracticable to go all the way there from here, or to go to Paris as one does to Orléans. Well then, you may suppose me started: I shall sleep at Madame de Loresse's, who is a relation of yours, to avoid the stones of Laval. I shall be there to-morrow: and Friday next I shall send to Laval for my letters, which will be brought me to Mêlé, where I intend to pass the night; after that I shall think of nothing but Paris. If during this journey you should chance to be longer than usual without hearing from me, do not be uneasy about it. I am neither with child nor lately brought to bed, nor am I afraid of a coach. I have no Avignon bridge to pass: the weather is extremely fine; and I shall have nothing to interfere with me; as I am no longer under any concern about you, do not you be unhappy about me. I am loaded with compliments on the birth of my little grandson; of whom I should be glad to hear next Friday, and still more so of you. Poor M. de Lauzun is at Pignerol; for which M. d'Harouïs is in great affliction; but he tells me, that the news of your safe delivery, and of the birth and christening of your little boy, shot a gleam of joy to his heart, through all the sorrow in which it was whelmed: and I in return assured him, that his affliction had thrown a cloud over my joy. Adieu, my beloved child, we must part. I am overwhelmed with regret at leaving these woods. I will not tell you how great a part you have in my indifference for Paris. You know but too well already, how dear you are to me.

LETTER 159

From Madame DE SÉVIGNÉ *to Madame* DE GRIGNAN.

Malicorne, Sunday, December 13, 1671.

At length, my dear child, I am so far on my journey. It is the finest weather imaginable, so that I am very well able, as MADAME says, to take a walk of five or six miles; as for La Mousse, he runs about like a wild thing: he is a little uncomfortable for want of sleep at night; for he has not been accustomed to inconvenience. I set out on Wednesday, as I told you I should; I got to Loresse, where they insisted upon my having two of their horses, which at last I yielded to. We have now four in each coach, and fly like the wind. Friday I got to Laval, and stopped directly at the Postoffice, where I met with that honest, obliging, good man, all mire and dirt to his very neck, who had just arrived, and gave me your letters; I thought I should have kissed him: you will judge, from my talking in this manner, that I am no longer angry with the Post; and in truth, the fault was not theirs; it is certainly, as you said, some enemy of Dubois's [1], who hearing him talk of our correspondence, and plume himself

[1] The Postmaster at Paris.

upon the employment we had given him, had, out of diversion, stole our letters from him. I did not discover it at first, thinking you wrote to me only once a week; but when I found that you wrote twice, I cannot easily express the vexation and grief I felt at the loss of the letters. But I return to the pleasure I had in receiving the packet, with two of your letters enclosed, from the dirty hands of the postillion: I saw him open his little mail before me; and at the same time, *frast, frast,* I opened mine, and found you were well. You write to me in Adhémar's letter; and then I have another from yourself, dated from your fireside a fortnight after your lying-in. Nothing can exceed the joy this certainty of your health gave me. Let me beg you not to make too free with it, nor write me long letters; recruit yourself, and be very careful not to subject yourself to fatigue. Alas! my dear child, you were very ill. To have seen you suffer so tedious a labour would have killed me. They were forced to bleed you at last, it seems, and even began to be in some fears about you. When I think of the danger you were in, I shudder involuntarily; I am seized with a trembling all over: in short, it makes such an impression on my imagination, that I cannot compose myself to sleep afterwards. I have imparted what you told me to Madame de La Fayette and to d'Hacqueville; I thought as you do, and that La Marans might now be easy, or rather uneasy, as she had no longer a subject for her very obliging and modest conjectures: I cannot but laugh at your thinking of her. But the post waits for me, as if I were Lady Gouvernante of Maine; and I take a pleasure in making him wait, to show my consequence. But I must say a word about my little boy; ah! how pretty he is; his large eyes are good signs of your having played your husband fair; but I beg his nose may not long remain between hope and fear. It is a strange kind of uncertainty that! Never had a little nose so much to fear and so much to hope; there are many noses, for him to make choice of; but since he has got large eyes, let him endeavour now to please you, or else he will only have your mouth, as it is small; but that is not enough. My child! you dote on him; but resign him to Providence, that he may be preserved to you. What is the reason of his being so very weak? It was that surely that prevented him from helping himself in the birth; for I have heard people who have had children say, that this weakness in the child is the occasion of the difficulty in the mother. However be very careful of the dear little creature; but at the same time resign him to Providence, if you hope to receive him from thence: this is a very Christian and *grandmotherly* repetition; Madame Pernelle [1] would say the same. Adieu, my dear Comtesse: my friend the postillion is out of all patience; I must not abuse his civility: I shall receive no more letters from you till I get to Paris: I shall be charmed to embrace my poor little girl; you do not think of her now, and therefore I am determined to love her out of pure generosity.

LETTER 160

From Madame DE SÉVIGNÉ *to Madame* DE GRIGNAN.

Paris, Friday, December 18, 1671.

I have this moment arrived, my dear daughter; and am at my aunt's, surrounded, embraced, and questioned a thousand times, by all my family and hers; but I leave them all, resolved to pay my compliments to you as well as to other people. M. de Coulanges is waiting to take me home with him, where he insists I shall take up my abode, because one of Madame de Bonneuil's sons has the small-pox; she very obligingly intended to keep it a secret; but the mystery was discovered, and they carried my little one to M. de Coulanges'. I expect her here every minute, and shall then return with her; but my aunt is resolved to witness our first interview. It would have been a vexatious circumstance for me to have exposed the poor child,

[1] A ridiculous character in the Comedy of *Tartuffe*.

and to have been banished myself from the society of my friends for a month or six weeks, because Madame Bonneuil's child had the small-pox. Suppose me now at M. de Coulanges', whom I adore, because he is always talking to me of you: but can you guess what happens between us? Why I cry, and my heart is so strangely oppressed, that I make a sign with my hand for him to be silent, and silent he is. He tells me, that when he saw you, you shut your eyes, and said, you were in my room; yes,....... truly, you were sure you were at Paris, for there was M. de Coulanges. He acted this very drolly, and it gives me great pleasure to find you have still a little of the madcap about you: I was frightened to death lest you should be always the Governor's lady. My God! what a deal of conversation shall I have with M. de Coulanges! I entreat you to be careful of yourself, that is, be as much yourself as possible, and do not let me find you altered. I would have you likewise be attentive to your beauty: get fat; recruit yourself; and remember all the good resolutions you have made: and if M. de Grignan has any regard for you, he will give you time to recover yourself, otherwise it is all over with you, I can tell you; you will be always as thin as Madame de Saint-Hérem. I am glad I thought of putting this in your head, nothing can frighten you more than such a resemblance; take care then to avoid it. As for your little boy, the condition he was in does not reconcile me to chocolate: I am sure he has been burnt up; it is happy for him that he has got a little moisture since, and is recovered: he has been snatched out of the fire; I heartily rejoice with you at the circumstance.

Monsieur DE COULANGES *writes to Madame* DE GRIGNAN *in her Mother's Letter.*

I shut my eyes, and on opening them again I behold the lovely mother, who is so much your delight and mine; by this I know I am in Paris; I am going to entertain her with all your perfections. Do you know that I am more bewitched with you than ever, and fear that I shall take the Chevalier de Breteuil's place? I know this would not please M. de Grignan, and it is the only thing that gives me concern in so great an undertaking. But seriously speaking, fair Comtesse, you are Nature's master-piece, and thus I represent you whenever I have occasion to mention you. I was yesterday at M. de La Rochefoucauld's, where I met M. de Longueville; we talked of nothing but Provence, and the bright planet that shines there. Adieu, my charming Comtesse; I am looking at the man in the tapestry, who is opening his breast: believe me, if you could see mine at this instant, you would see my heart as you see his; a heart which is wholly yours, and languishes for you; but do not tell this to M. de Grignan. Your daughter is a little brown beauty; she is very pretty; here she is, kissing me, and prattling to me; but she never cries. I love her, that is certain; but not so well as I do you. There is no such thing as talking to your lovely mother about you; large round drops roll from her eyes. Good heavens! what a mother!

LETTER 161

From Madame DE SÉVIGNÉ *to Madame* DE GRIGNAN.

Paris, Wednesday, December 23, 1671.

I write to you now somewhat beforehand, because I want to have a little chat with you. Just as I had sent away my packet, the day I arrived here, Dubois brought me the letter of yours which I supposed lost; you may guess with what pleasure I received it: I could not answer it then, for Madame de La Fayette, Madame de Saint-Géran, and Madame de Villars, all came to welcome me to Paris. You seem to be in all the astonishment that might be expected from such a misfortune as M. de Lauzun's: your reflections on that subject are very just and natural; every person of understanding has made the same; but now it begins to be no more thought of. This is an excellent country for forgetting the unhappy. The state of despair in which he began his journey was such, that it was resolved not to quit him for a moment. When those who were with him would have had him alight in a dangerous part of the road, where they were apprehensive of the coach being overset, he made answer: "Accidents of this kind are not made for me." He declares himself innocent of anything relating to the King, and says his only crime is having too powerful enemies. The King has said nothing about the matter, a silence that shows sufficiently the nature of his crime. He imagined he was to have been left at Pierre-Encise, and accordingly, when he got to Lyons, he began by paying his compliments to M. d'Artagnan; but when he was informed they were carrying him to Pignerol, he sighed, and said, "I am lost." He was greatly pitied in all the towns through which he passed; and certainly his disgrace is great.

The day after he left Paris, the King sent for M. de Marsillac, and told him, that he gave him "the government of Berry, which was lately Lauzun's." "Sire," replied Marsillac, "let Your Majesty, who is so well acquainted with the rules of honour, be pleased to reflect that I was no friend to M. de Lauzun; have the goodness to put yourself but for a moment in my place, and then judge whether I ought to accept the favour you are pleased to offer me."—"You are too scrupulous," said the King; "I know as much of that affair as anyone, and see no reason you have to make any difficulty on that account."—"Since Your Majesty is pleased to approve it," replied Marsillac, "I have no more to say, but throw myself at your feet in grateful acknowledgement."—"But," said the King, "I gave you a pension of twelve thousand francs, till something better could be done for you." "It is true, Sire; I now return it to you again."—"And I," replied the King, "give it you a second time, and shall now do your gallant sentiments all the honour they deserve."

Upon which he turned to his ministers, and acquainted them with the scruples of M. de Marsillac, adding, "I admire the difference between these two men; Lauzun did not think it worth his while so much as to thank me for the government of Berry, nor even to take the least care about it; and here is one who expresses the most lively gratitude." The whole of this is strictly true; I had it from M. de La Rochefoucauld. I thought this little detail would not be displeasing to you; if I was mistaken, let me know, in your next. This poor man is very ill with the gout, much worse than he was last year: he talks very frequently of you, and I believe loves you as if you were his own child. The Prince de Marsillac has been to see me. Everybody talks to me of my dear child. I have at length taken courage, and been talking these twelve hours with M. de Coulanges: I cannot leave the man! it was great good fortune that brought me to reside with him. I do not know whether you have heard that Villarceaux, in speaking to the King about a post for his son, artfully took the opportunity of telling him, that some people had taken it in their heads to tell his niece [1], that His Majesty had some designs upon her; that, if it was so, he begged His Majesty would make use of him, as an affair of that kind would be better in his hands than in any other; and that he did not doubt of success: the King burst into a laugh, and told him, "Villarceaux, you and I are too old to think of attacking young ladies of fifteen;" and, like a generous and gallant man, made a jest of the old fellow, and spread the story about among the ladies. The *angels* are greatly enraged at their uncle for it, and have resolved never to see him again; and he, on his part is a little ashamed of the figure he made on the occasion. I write without disguise; for His Majesty appears so much to advantage in all he does, that there is no occasion for mystery.

[1] Louise-Elisabeth Rouxel, known afterwards by the name of Madame de Grancey, when she was one of the dressers to Marie-Louise of Orléans, Queen of Spain: she was younger sister of Marie-Louise Rouxel, Comtesse de Marci. They were called *the Angels*.

It is reported, that there were a great number of very beautiful things found in M. de Lauzun's rooms; pictures without end; naked figures, one without a head, and others with the eyes put out; this was the lady *your neighbour* [1]; locks of hair, some large, some small, ticketed to avoid confusion, and a thousand pretty things of this kind: but I would not answer for the truth of all this; you know what a loose is given to invention on such occasions.

I have seen M. de Mêmes, who has at length lost his dear wife. When he saw me, he began sighing and weeping, and I could not refrain from tears myself. Everybody visits the family, and I would have you make him the compliment of condolence; you ought to do it for the remembrance of Livry, which you are still so fond of.

Is it possible, that my letters should be so entertaining as you say they are? I do not think them so when they come out of my hands; I fancy they get it in passing through yours. It is very lucky for you that you do like them; for you are so loaded with them, that you would be heartily to be pitied, were it otherwise. M. de Coulanges wants sadly to know which of your ladies it is that has a taste for them; we reckon it a favourable sign for her, for my style is so loose, that it requires a good share of natural understanding and knowledge of the world, to be able to bear with it.

The Abbé Têtu has time enough upon his hands now, as he has no longer the Richelieu Mansion; so we profit by it. You would think, to look at Madame de Soubise, that she will have double twins at least. The King sets out the sixth of next month for Châlons; he is to make several other little tours, and some reviews by the way: his journey will last about twelve days; but the officers and troops will proceed further. I have a notion of another expedition being on foot like that of the Franche-Comté. You know the King is *the hero of every season* [2]. The

[1] Madame de Monaco, a Gramont by birth, whom Lauzun loved to distraction.

[2] A thought in a madrigal of Mademoiselle de Scuderi's.

poor courtiers are quite broke; they have not a penny left. Brancas asked me yesterday, very seriously, to lend him money upon a pledge; he gave me his word, that he would never mention it to anyone, and had rather, he said, be concerned with me than with another. La Trousse begged of me to let him into the secret of Pomenars' method of getting a genteel livelihood: in short, they are all put to their shifts. Farewell, dearest Comtesse, there is reason in everything; this letter is swelled into a perfect volume. I embrace the laborious Grignan, *Seigneur Corbeau,* the presumptuous Adhémar, and the fortunate *Louis-Provence,* on whom the fairies and astrologers have breathed good fortune. *E con questo mi raccommundo*: and with this I take my leave.

LETTER 162

From Madame DE SÉVIGNÉ *to Madame* DE GRIGNAN.

Paris, Friday, Christmas-Day, 1671.

The day after I received yours, M. Le Camus came to pay me a visit. I spent the time in inquiring of him what his sentiments were with regard to the care, zeal, and assiduity, which M. de Grignan had shown in his endeavours to bring the King's affairs in Provence to a successful issue. M. de Lavardin came in afterwards, and gave me his word, that he should take care to set it in its true light, in a proper place, before the day was over. I could not have met with two persons more suited to my purpose: they are bass and tenor. In the evening I went to M. d'Usèz, who still keeps his room, and we talked a good deal of your affairs. We had both heard the same news, and that an order was intended to be sent for dissolving the Assembly, and to take another opportunity of showing them what it was to be refractory.

Indeed, my dear, my heart is heavy, very heavy, in not having you here with me. I should be much more happy, if I knew anyone whom I loved as well as I do you, for then I should have the means of comforting myself in your absence; but I have not been able to meet with your equal in my affections as yet, nor indeed anything that comes near you. A thousand unlooked-for things offer themselves to awaken a more than common remembrance of you, and for the time I am completely overset. I am anxious to know where you propose going after your Assembly is dissolved. The small-pox rages at Aix and Arles, Grignan is very cold, Salon very lonely; pray then, come and take an apartment with me; indeed you will be very welcome. Adieu; you shall get rid of me for the present; this shall not be volume the second. I have no more news in my budget: if you have any questions to ask me, I will endeavour to answer them. I was last night at the Minimes; I am going now to hear Bourdaloue: it is said he begins to be very personal, and that the other day he made three pointed allusions to the retirement of Tréville[1]; he omitted his name indeed, but everyone knows whom he meant: they say, however, he outdoes everything, and that no one ever before preached as he does. A thousand compliments to all the Grignans.

LETTER 163

From Madame DE SÉVIGNÉ *to Madame* DE GRIGNAN.

Paris, Christmas-Day, at 11 o'clock at night, 1671.

I have written to you this morning already; but I have just received from M. d'Usèz the letter you sent by Rip-

[1] Bourdaloue often abused the pulpit in this way. He was told that Boileau had introduced his name in a song: he replied, "Tell him, if he satirises me, I will sermonise him." He had served Molière thus on account of his *Tartuffe,* which is as good a sermon as any of Bourdaloue's.

M. de Tréville was a man of wit, a soldier, and a courtier, whose grief for the death of Madame Henriette led him suddenly from the world to a life of retirement and devotion. Other accounts of this personage will be found elsewhere.

pert. You give a very good account of affairs in Provence. I wish to God the King may be contented with what the Provençals have agreed to do; your description of their heads, and the manner in which it is necessary to treat them, is admirable; and the coming-to of the good Bishop, is quite natural. We have had Madame Scarron here to supper; she says, that of the vast number of letters that Madame de Richelieu has received, not one comes up to M. de Grignan's; she says, she kept it a long time in her pocket, and showed it to several people; that nothing could be better written, nor could any one express himself more elegantly, nobly, and affectionately, than he did with regard to the late Madame de Montausier[1]: in a word, she seemed charmed with it; I vowed I would acquaint you with this. I shall communicate your letter to d'Hacqueville and to M. Le Camus. I think of nothing but Provence, and begin to look upon myself now in your neighbourhood. I expected your brother: they send him part of the way on account of the length of the journey. I have been to sermon; my heart was not affected, but that was perhaps my fault. Adieu, my dearest child.

LETTER 164

From Madame DE SÉVIGNÉ *to Madame* DE GRIGNAN.

Paris, Wednesday, December 30, 1671.

One sure sign of the little disposition I have to hate you, is, that I would with my own will write to you a dozen times a day: does not this proof, my dear, appear to you much like that of M. de Coulanges, when he made you the offer of passing the remainder of his days with you? Indeed, if that were to be the case, you would have enough to do; for I am as prolix in writing to you, as I

[1] Madame de Richelieu succeeded Madame de Montausier, as one of the Ladies of Honour to the Queen.

am laconic when I write to others. I have inquired much of Rippert about your health. I am not pleased with you: you deserve to be scolded: you behaved in your lying-in as if you had been the wife of some Swiss captain: you do not take broths enough: you had not been confined three days, before you began to chatter and talk; you got up before the tenth day; and after all this you are surprised that you are thin! I was in hopes that you would have taken a little more care of yourself, and endeavoured to recruit and grow fat. Where did you get this whim of mimicking Madame de Crussol? I am always striving to reform you, by setting examples before your eyes: this way of going on has not affected her, but it will affect you, believe me: in short, you cannot offend or vex me more highly, than in spoiling your pretty face: you know how fond I am of it; ought you not then to take some care of it for my sake?

You are much in the right to say, that Provence is my fixed residence since it is become yours. Paris quite stifles me: I long to be on the road to Grignan. But, my dear child, how lonely you will be, if you return to your Castle! Why, you will be like Psyche upon the mountains. I can have no content where you are not: this is a truth, the force of which I experience more and more every hour. You seem wanting to me everywhere, and whatever recalls you to my remembrance goes to my heart. The King's journey is as yet uncertain; but the troops still continue their march. Poor La Trousse is going, and Sévigné is already upon his way: they are to go to Cologne. They are quite wild about this expedition. Farewell, my angel; I am perfectly well at M. de Coulanges', and shall take care to keep as far from the air of the small-pox as possible. I have no great relish for returning to that immense rambling house, where, instead of you, I shall meet only with Madame de Bonneuil. Coulanges is my dear delight; we are forever talking of you. I shall give M. de La Rochefoucauld your letter: I am persuaded he will like it much. I hate the direction of your letter when it is, *To Madame la Marquise de Sévigné*; call me *Pierrot*. Your others are amiable, and excite a desire to read the rest.

LETTER 165

From Madame DE SÉVIGNÉ *to Madame* DE GRIGNAN.

Paris, the First Day of the New Year, 1672.

I was last night at M. d'Usèz's. We came to a resolution to send you a courier. He promised to let me know the success of his audience with M. Le Tellier, and whether he would have me bring Madame de Coulanges[1] thither with me; but as it is now past ten at night, and I have not yet heard anything from him, I shall write to you by myself. M. d'Usèz will take care to inform you of what he has done. There should be some endeavours used to soften the rigour of the orders, by representing, that it would be entirely depriving M. de Grignan of the power of serving His Majesty, if he should by this means be rendered disagreeable to the Province; and if, after all, it will be necessary to send the orders, it is the opinion of the wisest people here, that it would be prudent to suspend the execution of them till an answer can be had from the King, to whom M. de Grignan has written as from a person on the spot, who is convinced that it would be best for his service to grant a pardon for this time at least. If you knew how some people blame M. de Grignan for the little regard he shows to his own country, in endeavouring to exact so strict an obedience, you would see how difficult it is to please everybody, and it would have been still worse if he had done otherwise. Those who find such charms in his post, do not know the difficulties which attend it. The King's intended journey is now broken off; but the troops continue their march to Metz. Sévigné is there by this time; La Trousse is going; and both of them

[1] Madame de Coulanges was niece of the wife of M. Le Tellier, Minister of State, and afterwards Chancellor of France.

fuller of loyalty than ready-money. The Archbishop of Rheims [1] is here; who first sends you his good wishes, and then acquaints you, that M. d'Usèz has not been able to see his father to-day: he assures me also, that the King is very well pleased with your husband; that he accepts of the present the Province has made him; but, as his orders have not been punctually observed, he has sent *lettres de cachet* to banish the Consuls. I can say no more to you by letter. All that remains now is, to be entirely devoted to His Majesty's service; but, at the same time, to endeavour to manage a little the minds of the Provençals, which will be found the best means of having the King punctually obeyed in that country.

M. de La Rochefoucauld sends you word, and I join with him, that if you are not pleased with the letter you wrote him, it is for want of knowing better: I think he is quite in the right; for it is full of life and spirit. You have an answer to it enclosed. Adieu, my dear Comtesse, I think of you night and day. Furnish me with some opportunity of serving you: it will be a pleasing occupation for my affection.

LETTER 166

From Madame DE SÉVIGNÉ *to Madame* DE GRIGNAN.

Paris, Tuesday, January 5, 1672.

Yesterday the King gave audience to the Ambassador from Holland, at which he would have the Prince, Maréchal de Turenne, the Duc de Bouillon, and M. de Créqui present, that they might hear all that passed. The Ambassador presented his letter to the King, which was not read, though the Ambassador proposed it; as the King said he already knew the contents, having a copy of it in his pocket. The Ambassador expatiated largely on the justifications mentioned in the letter, and on the strict

[1] Charles-Maurice Le Tellier.

manner in which the States had examined their conduct to find out in what they could possibly have given offence to His Majesty; that they were not conscious of ever having been wanting in the respect that was due to him; and yet, to their great surprise, they had heard that the extensive preparations His Majesty was making were destined against them [1]; that they were ready to satisfy His Majesty in everything he should be pleased to require from them, and humbly implored him to remember the good-will his royal predecessors had ever shown them, to whom they owed their present flourishing condition. The King, with inimitable grace and dignity, replied, that he was not now to learn the endeavours that had been used to stir up his enemies against him; that he thought it but prudent to prevent a surprise, and that he found it necessary for his own defence to make himself thus prepared and powerful by sea and land; that after giving a few more necessary orders, he should, in the beginning of spring, take such steps as he might judge most advantageous for his own glory, and the good of his kingdom; and then gave the Ambassador to understand, by a motion of his head, that he would permit no reply. The letter corresponded exactly with the Ambassador's speech, except that it concluded with assuring His Majesty, that they (the States) would do whatever he should be pleased to order them, provided it did not oblige them to break with their allies.

The same day M. de La Feuillade was received at the head of the regiment of Guards, and had the customary oaths administered to him by a Maréchal of France. The King, who was present, spoke himself to the regiment, and told them that he had given them M. de La Feuillade for their *mestre-de-camp*; and then, with his own hand, presented him with the pike [2], which is commonly done by

[1] The war against the United Provinces, for which Louis XIV. had leagued with England and several German Princes, was on the point of breaking out. The English began it in March by attacking the Dutch fleet, and, in their old way, made war first, and declared it afterwards.

[2] It was a custom then to receive the pike on such occasions.

a Commissioner appointed by the King; but His Majesty was resolved that no mark of distinction or favour should be wanting on the occasion.

You know Langlée; he is as insolent and impertinent as possible: he was at play the other day with the Comte de Gramont, who, upon his taking too great liberties, said, "M. de Langlée, keep these familiarities till you play with the King."

Maréchal de Bellefonds has requested leave of the King to dispose of his post [1]. No one will do it so well as he. Everybody believes, and I especially, that it is to pay his debts, and retire from the world, to think of his salvation.

The Procurator-General of the Court of Aids [2] is made first President there: this is a great advancement for him. Do not fail to write to him on the occasion, one or other of you; and whichever it is, let the other add a line or two in the letter. The President Nicolaï is restored to his post [3]. This is what may be called news.

LETTER 167

From Madame DE SÉVIGNÉ *to Madame* DE GRIGNAN.

Paris, Wednesday, January 6, 1672.

So then, my dear child, you wish me not to weep at seeing you separated so many miles from me! but you cannot prevent this disposition of Providence from being very hard and painful to me: it will be a long time before I shall be able to accustom myself to it; but I will stop short, and not involve you in a long train of sentiments, which this would naturally lead me into. I will not set you a bad example, nor stagger your fortitude with a narrative of my weakness: preserve your reason in its full force; enjoy the greatness of soul you are possessed of;

[1] Of Chief Master of the household of the King.

[2] Nicolas Le Camus.

[3] Of first President of the Chamber of Accounts.

while I, on my side, shall seek consolation and assistance from the tenderness and affection of mine. I was yesterday at St.-Germain: the Queen made the first advances to me, and I made my court, as usual, at your expense. We had all the affair of your lying-in over; and then talked about my journey to Provence, not forgetting the late one to Brittany; and how lucky Madame de Chaulnes had been in meeting me there. I should have told you, that the lady went to St.-Germain with me. As for MONSIEUR, he drew me aside to a window, to talk to me about you, and ordered me very seriously to make his compliments to you, and let you know how glad he was to hear of your being safely brought to bed: he said so many obliging things on the subject, and in so peculiar a manner, that it must have been my own fault, if I did not understand, that he was desirous of attaching himself to your service; for they say he is grown weary of worshipping *the angel.* I found MADAME much better than I expected. I could not see M. de Montausier, he was closeted with MONSEIGNEUR. I should never have done repeating all the compliments that were made both to you and me; but they are all lost in the air. I was quite happy to get home. But whom do you think I found there? The Presidents Reauville and Galiffet; and whom should they be talking of but Madame de Grignan!

Your little girl is coming here: you say she serves to put me sometimes in mind of you; I know what answer you expect, that there is no occasion for that. I am going out in the coach. "Whither?" say you: to Madame de Valavoire's. "What to do there?" "To talk of Provence." "Observe that good woman," said Coulanges the other day, "she is for ever in company with her daughter."

I have received yours of the thirtieth of last month. Indeed, my dear, you displease me greatly in talking of your charming letters in the manner you do. What pleasure can you take in finding fault with your manner and style, and comparing yourself to the Princess d'Harcourt? I cannot conceive where you got this false and injurious humility: it is wounding my heart, offending justice, and doing injury to truth. What depravity of manners! For heaven's sake leave off this practice, and see things as they really are: you will then have nothing to do but to guard against vanity, an affair that may be settled between your confessor and you. I am distracted at the thoughts of your being so thin. What is become of the time when you would eat only the head of a snipe, or the wing of a lark, in a day, for fear of growing too fat? If you should be with child again, be assured it is all over with you; you will be lost beyond hope.

We were talking of you yesterday at Madame de Coulanges', when Madame Scarron reminded us with how much wit and spirit you supported a bad cause once in the same place, and on the very carpet we were then standing upon. There were Madame de La Fayette, Madame Scarron [1], Segrais, Caderousse, the Abbé Têtu, Guilleragues, and Brancas. You and your merit are never forgotten; your friends preserve the most lively remembrance of both; but, when I come to reflect where you are, though I know you are a little Queen, yet how can I forbear sighing? We sigh too at the life we lead at St.-Germain and here; so that we are for ever sighing. You know, I suppose, that Lauzun, as he was going into the place of his confinement, repeated, *In Sæcula sæculorum*: I fancy there are some here who would gladly answer, *Amen*; and others again be as ready to cry out, *No*. Indeed, when he was jealous of your *neighbour* [2], he used her very ill; and how did he serve many others?

Your little girl is very pretty: the sound of her voice goes to my very heart: she has a thousand little engaging ways, which amuse me, and make me love her; but I never can conceive it possible for her to equal you in my affections.

---

[1] Françoise d'Aubigné, afterwards Marquise de Maintenon.
[2] See Letter 161, of the 23rd December, 1671, in this volume.

LETTER 168

From Madame DE SÉVIGNÉ *to Madame* DE GRIGNAN.

Paris, Wednesday, January 13, 1672.

For heaven's sake, my dear child, what do you mean? What pleasure can you take in thus abusing your person and understanding, vilifying your conduct, and saying, that one must have great good nature to think of you sometimes? Though I am certain you cannot believe all you say, yet it hurts me to hear it: you really make me angry with you; and though, perhaps, I ought not to answer seriously things that are only said in jest, yet I cannot help scolding you before I go any farther. You are excellent again, when you say you are afraid of wits. Alas! if you knew how insignificant they are when you are by, and how encumbered they are with their own dear persons, you would not value them at all. Do you remember how you used to be deceived in them sometimes? Do not let distance magnify objects too much; but it is one of its common effects.

We sup every evening at Madame Scarron's; she has a most engaging wit, and an understanding surprisingly just and clear. It is a pleasure to hear her sometimes reason upon the horrid confusion and distractions of a country with which she is very well acquainted. The vexations that d'Heudicourt undergoes in a place that appears so dazzling and glorious; the continual rage of Lauzun; the gloomy chagrin and cares of the Court ladies, from which the most envied are not always exempt; are things which she describes in the most agreeable and entertaining manner. Such conversations as these lead us insensibly from one moral reflection to another, sometimes of a religious, sometimes of a political kind. You are frequently one of our subjects: she admires your wit and manners; and, whenever you return here, you are sure of being highly in favour.

But let me give you an instance of the King's goodness and generosity, to show you what a pleasure it is to serve so amiable a master. He sent for Maréchal de Bellefonds, into his private room the other day, and thus accosted him: "Monsieur le Maréchal, I insist upon knowing your reasons for quitting my service. Is it through a principle of devotion? Is it from an inclination to retire? Or is it on account of your debts? If it be the latter, I myself will take charge of them, and inform myself of the state of your affairs." The Maréchal was sensibly affected with this goodness: "Sire," said he, "it is my debts; I am overwhelmed with them, and cannot bear to see some of my friends, who assisted me with their fortunes, likely to suffer on my account, without having it in my power to satisfy them." "Well then," said the King, "they shall have security for what is owing to them: I now give you a hundred thousand francs on your house at Versailles, and a grant of four hundred thousand more, as a security in case of your death. The hundred thousand francs will enable you to pay off the arrears, and so now you remain in my service." That heart must be insensible indeed, that could refuse the most implicit obedience to such a master, who enters with so much goodness and condescension into the interests of his servants. Accordingly the Maréchal made no further resistance: he is now reinstated in his place, and loaded with favours. This is all strictly true.

Not a single night passes at St.-Germain without balls, plays, or masquerades. The King shows an assiduity to divert this MADAME, that he never did for the other. Racine has brought out a new piece called *Bajazet,* which they say carries everything before it: indeed it does not go *in empirando,* as the others did. Monsieur de Tallard says, that it as much exceeds the best piece of Corneille's, as Corneille's does one of Boyer's; this now is what you may call praising by the lump: there is nothing like telling truth:

however, our eyes and ears will inform us more fully; for

Du bruit de Bajazet mon ame importunée [1]

obliges me to go immediately to the play; we shall see what it is.

I have been to Livry; ah, my dear child, how well did I keep my word with you, and how many tender thoughts of you filled my breast! It was delightful weather, though very cold; but the sun shone finely, and every tree was hung with pearls and crystals, that formed a pleasing diversity of colours. I walked a great deal; the next day I dined at Pomponne: it would not be an easy matter to recount all that passed during a stay of five hours: however, I was not at all tired with my visit. Monsieur de Pomponne will be here in three or four days: I should be very much vexed, if I was obliged to apply to him about your Provence affairs; I am persuaded he will not hear me: you see I give myself airs of knowledge. But really nothing comes up to M. d'Usèz; I never saw a man of better understanding, nor one more capable of giving sound advice: I wait to see him, that I may inform you of what he has done at St.-Germain.

You desire me to write you long letters; I think you have now sufficient reason to be contented: I am sometimes frightened at the length of them myself; and were it not for your agreeable flattery, I should never think of venturing them out of my hands. Madame de Brissac is excellently provided for, for the winter, in M. de Longueville and the Comte de Guiche; but nothing is meant but what is fair and honourable, only she takes a pleasure in being adored. La Marans is never seen now, either at Madame de La Fayette's or at M. de La Rochefoucauld's: we cannot find out what she is doing; we are apt to judge a little rashly now and then: she took it into her head this summer, that she should be ravished, as if she wished it; but I am of opinion, that she is in no great danger. Good heavens, what a mad creature it is, and how long have I

[1] Madame de Sévigné parodies a line of Despréaux's.

looked on her in the same light, as you do now! But now let me tell you, my dear, it is not my fault that I do not see Madame de Valavoire[1]. I am sure there is no occasion to bid me go and see her, it is enough that she has seen you, for me to run after her; but then she is running after somebody else: for I might for ever desire her to wait at home for me; I cannot get her to do me that favour. Your jest applies admirably to M. Le Grand, and a very good one it is. Poor Châtillon is every day teasing us with the most wretched ones imaginable.

[1] A lady of quality in Provence, who had just then come to Paris.

THE END OF THE FIRST VOLUME.